Praise for *Big Snake*

'Offbeat and likeable . . . The jungle forays of Redmond O'Hanlon seem to gleam with logistical brilliance by comparison' *Sunday Times*

'Moving and comic; both a poetic quest and a real adventure, *Big Snake* paints a hitherto unseen portrait of the Malay and Indonesian archipelagos and will leave you checking under your bed for your own hidden monster snake. A terrific read' *Irish News*

'Gripping herpetological detail . . .' Sara Wheeler, *Daily Telegraph*

'This tale about the search for the world's longest python in the jungles of Malaysia and Borneo is in the British tradition of mad amateurs setting off on hare-brained adventure . . . A fantastic book' *Daily Mail*

Praise for *Angry White Pyjamas*

'Brilliant . . . everyone should read it' Tony Parsons

'Here is a cult book all right' Frank Keating

'A book of unexpected brilliance . . . subtle, funny, stimulating and original' Patrick French

Big Snake

The Hunt for the World's Longest Python

ROBERT TWIGGER

PHŒNIX

A PHOENIX PAPERBACK

First published in Great Britain by Victor Gollancz in 1999
This paperback edition published in 1999 by Phoenix
an imprint of Orion Books Ltd,
Orion House, 5 Upper St Martin's Lane,
London WC2H 9EA

A CIP catalogue record for this book
is available from the British Library.

ISBN: 0 75380 857 9

Printed and bound in Great Britain by
Clays Ltd, St Ives plc

C. J. Ionides, snake hunter, on people who don't like snakes: 'Misguided people. Unfortunately a lot of them are people I like.'

Contents

For my grandfather
and Mr B.

ONE

Know Your Onions

> In marriage as in literature, the whole art consists
> in the grace of transitions.   *Balzac*

In a studio flat in south London I spoke over a hissing
international line to Cairo. The voice coming back to me
was precise, accented and elderly. It was the first time I had
spoken to a retired Egyptian general and I was asking him if
I could marry his daughter. Come to think of it, this was the
first time I'd asked anyone for their daughter's hand in
marriage. He graciously acceded and then the line went dead.
I turned to Samia, whom I still thought of as my girlfriend.
'Well, it's done now,' I said.

'Yes,' she said, in a voice both unsure and reflective, a
voice strikingly like mine. Usually Samia was firm-minded,
sensible-sounding, a reassuring presence in the echoing, self-
doubting world I inhabited. She knew what she wanted and
went out and got it. I thought I knew, but halfway into
getting it I often changed my mind. I was a vacillator, a
procrastinator, a Hamlet without a sword or a scene for
sticking someone. The vague plan I'd formulated was that I
would become more like Samia, not the other way round.
Maybe we'd got ourselves into something we couldn't control. Marriage was for other people, not me. Marriage was
for people like my parents and their friends. What was
happening?

We cracked open a bottle of Piper-Heidsieck champagne

to celebrate. I fumbled the cork and it shot at high velocity into the soft plaster of the ceiling, making a dent, the first physical manifestation of our marriage to be. The bubbles quickly went, and the champagne had that slightly vomity taste it has when you don't really want to celebrate. I looked at Samia. She looked at me. We both tittered nervously and sipped our vomity champers.

How I'd got here, asking for permission down a crackling telephone, was perfectly logical. I had fallen in love with Samia. Samia was from a traditional family in the Middle East. If I wanted to live with her and not hide every time a relative appeared in London, then I would have to marry her. Inescapable logic, which suddenly, sipping the champagne, I wanted to escape. It was as if the action itself was one huge gulp too much. Now I had indigestion.

By some divinatory process a date was set for the marriage in Egypt. It was five months away. Plenty of time to order Bedouin tents, dwarf tumblers, belly dancers and Upper Egyptian dervish whirlers to the lamb-roasting extravaganza I planned to hold by torchlight in the Sinai Desert. Then Samia told me many of her relatives had difficulty getting out of a car, let alone mounting a camel for an arduous cross-desert journey. The party was relocated to the beach next to a five-star hotel.

Before I ever gave a microsecond of attention to the idea of marriage, I was living in Japan, relentlessly single and proud of it. There I met a man called Hi-Tide Harris, 'International Blues Guitarist', his business card said. On a late night bus home to my suburb of Tokyo, he talked wisely on many subjects, but then he got on to marriage. 'The thing about my wife – she makes me feel like I ain't wild no more!'

*

'No man ever went willingly to the altar,' said my grandfather, Colonel H. Twigger, soldier, boxer, photographer, engineer and, most latterly, beekeeper. He did not know about my forthcoming marriage. He was, as usual, speaking about himself, how he had married, quite against the conventions of colonial India, a divorced lady with a two-year-old son. 'I fell in love with your grandmother,' he said, his pale-blue eyes boring into me, looking for some sign of weakness, I always felt. And after a pause, 'Your grandfather was a naughty boy.'

Now Colonel H. was ninety, it was quite all right to have been a naughty boy. He'd been naughty in other ways too, some I'd guessed or been told about, others you'd never know. He used to speak about a chap he'd known in the army who used to frequent pubs wearing 'a baggy suit'. The man was an expert boxer and the suit always drew criticism. Wearing a baggy suit in the twenties was like wearing a bow tie in a skinhead pub today. But the comments about the suit could be escalated into a fight, which was what the man wanted. He wanted to test himself, and being a jolly good boxer, and having surprise on his side, he always won. The chap was, of course, the young Colonel H.

The snake began to move in my brain. I had dreams about crossing jungles, wading through swamps, discovering lost cities. My waking thoughts were increasingly invaded by fantasies of escape. Every time I saw backpackers in Victoria Station I felt both envy and disgust. Envy for their freedom, disgust at myself for wanting to be like a teenage Sherpa with a railpass and a stash of rolling tobacco. For God's sake! I was going grey, getting married, driving my own car and hating myself for having, in some obscure way, given in. I could ditch the car, the girl, the comfortable flat we'd found. I ran that through my head and all that was left was an empty

11

bubble, a void. I needed to move *towards* something. I needed money (who doesn't?), but more than that, I needed a goal.

It was Chris, my former flatmate and mentor, who solved my problem. He discovered that there was a prize of fifty thousand dollars being offered by the Wildlife Conservation Society of New York for any snake caught alive in excess of thirty feet long. He found the information while surfing on the Internet, alternating visits to Bianca's Smut Shack with serious browsing for prizes we could perhaps win. Another $50,000 award was being offered for a book-length poem on a religious subject by someone born in Wisconsin, Wyoming or Nebraska. Perhaps these places are particularly short of poets, but I doubt it. In fact I bet they're just crawling out of the sagebrush, pen in hand, all cut up inside because they didn't win the big prize. For a few seconds I contemplated the feasibility of creating a new Wisconsonian identity. That part appealed to me. Writing the poem presented more problems.

But then and there I knew I would have to go after the snake. Telling Samia required tact and skill. I put off telling anyone while I did more research.

I rang up John Behler, the curator at the Wildlife Conservation Society, just to double-check the prize. I thought he'd want to dissuade a rank amateur like me from going on the giant snake trail, but he was helpful and friendly and very encouraging. 'Anything more than twenty-five feet and we're interested. But it has to be thirty to get the Roosevelt prize.' He gave me a tip: 'Anacondas are heavy but they ain't long. We're always getting anaconda calls, but mostly they're around seventeen, eighteen feet.'

The reward had been first offered in 1912, instigated by President Theodore Roosevelt, and had never been claimed. It had been a thousand dollars then, but with inflation it had risen.

12

This wasn't the world's first snake prize. In 1818 a reward of five thousand dollars had been offered for a fifty-foot sea serpent reported off the Boston coast. In those less enlightened times it was a 'dead or alive' reward. After the coastline had been thoroughly searched for the monster, the prize was withdrawn when all agreed that a nine-foot tunny fish had been the origin of the serpentine reporting.

Guinness supplied me with the latest long snake data: the longest snake ever captured was a reticulated python thirty-two feet nine inches long. It was shot in Celebes in 1912. The WCS would settle for one shorter than that, but alive. The longest snake ever held by a zoo (discounting reports of the 120-foot snake captured by Regulus during the Punic Wars) was a reticulated python twenty-eight and a half feet long kept by the Pittsburgh zoo in the 1950s.

There seemed to be only one other person attempting to win the prize, a professional snake hunter who also ran a leather business in Illinois. His name was Paul Raddatz. He was pleasant, but cagey: 'This is my job so I can't tell you where the longest snakes are living. I'm sorry.' Raddatz had tried to claim the prize in 1992, alerting the WCS with news that he had a thirty-foot reticulated python in a cave in Kalimantan, the Indonesian part of Borneo. When the snake was finally winkled out of its cave, it only measured twenty-one feet. It was named Samantha and sold to the Bronx zoo, where you can see it to this day.

Since moving back to live in London I had been plagued by odd dreams. Some of them involved the electrical maintenance box outside my flat. By day it was the meeting place of a gang of youngsters who routinely 'dissed' me as I went by. Sometimes I smiled benignly at them; mostly I ignored them. Silently I hoped the electrical apparatus was making them all sterile. By night the box entered my dreams as a kind of magician's hat full of surprises. Sometimes the doors on the front would open and I would enter what I knew to be a dark netherworld of monsters and mayhem.

I wondered whether these dreams were connected to the normal worries of a man about to settle down into married life. The lounging kids symbolized a carefree freedom I was about to lose, the magic box represented opportunities for escape . . . But Samia wasn't the kind of woman who wanted to tie me down. She had her own career as a producer for Arab television and encouraged me to seek journalistic assignments of an adventurous kind. I told her about the dream and she said it meant I was afraid of having children.

When I was a child I once dreamed about ghosts, and when I woke up I saw the devil. His face, with unmistakable beard and horns, was outlined in the extensive damp stain on the ceiling. I reached under the bed for my Bilofix sword, but drew my hand back at the last moment, knowing that something was lurking there, ready to strike. The bed was cold and damp, even if I kept my toes curled in and away from the icy zone at the edge. The fire in the bedroom hearth was long dead and the faint light in the room was the blue reflected night off the deep snow outside. I was five years old and it was Christmas night at my grandfather's house.

I understood that ghosts existed, I knew the word 'ghost', but I filled in the details for myself. For some reason I thought of them as giant elk that appeared out of the mist on an endless plain in front of thick forest that stretched in a line for miles. What frightened me most was a recurring dream of a skull, which came almost every night for several years until I was seven, when I willed it to come closer and closer, unafraid at last that it might devour me. Instead it just disappeared and I never had that dream again.

My grandfather, Colonel H. Twigger, lived deep in the Oxfordshire countryside in a huge, dark house that faced north and received little sunlight, surrounded by old yew trees whose branches brushed against the windows when the wind was blowing. The place was cool in summer and freezing in winter, even with the small Victorian fireplaces in every room, including the bathroom, which was a thirty-foot corridor with a bath with metal feet at the far end.

Christmas at the Colonel's had a funereal feel. We would listen to the Queen's speech at 3 p.m., all standing – except my mother, who refused – and then open our presents in the gloomy half-light of the drawing room. I say 'listen', despite the speech being relayed via the ancient black-and-white television set, because the tube had long since blown and there were no pictures. The Colonel decided it was better that way.

After the presents – Bilofix for me, a kind of wooden constructor kit like Meccano – my father would read from the Bible or *The Jungle Book*: Kipling and the Gospels were the only literature Colonel H. tolerated at Christmastime. My favourite stories did not feature Mowgli, who was a bit too much like Jesus for my liking. I preferred Rikki-tikki-tavi, the fearless mongoose who killed a cobra.

There were different disadvantages to a summer visit to the Colonel's. Early summer was worst, when we were encouraged to go into the orchard to get a 'good stinging' from the bees my grandfather kept there. Colonel H. believed this would stimulate an immunity to further bee stings. No summer visit was complete without someone getting stung, though sensibly my mother always refused to go into the orchard. Perhaps I could have refused as well but I didn't want to appear cowardly in front of the Colonel. My job was to make daring sorties close to the hives to place wasp traps made from jam jars filled with sugar water and covered with tin foil. Wasps were the sworn enemies of bees, said the Colonel, and the job had to be done. Wasps were like terrorists armed with machine guns, whereas bees had only one sting, like a Lee Enfield rifle down to its last shot, which they nobly died administering. This meant no bee sting could be counted a casual act of violence. A vague sense of guilt for killing a bee was encouraged by the Colonel, who offered no sympathy for being stung.

Colonel H. was of medium height with a barrel chest and a bald bullet head. He had pale-blue, humourless eyes and a military moustache. Like Winston Churchill, he had a penchant for building walls; in the Colonel's case they were dry-stone walls in exact imitation of the Cotswold walls of the area. The Colonel liked to keep busy, even in retirement. He had forty beehives and sold Twigger's Honey throughout the Cotswolds. He didn't get on with people of his own class; instead he preferred the company of rapscallions and gnarled country types, people who could drink heavily and didn't mind his extraordinary opinions: Jimmy 'the weasel', Sammy, who could sing bees into a swarm, Bert, an ex-farrier who liked his beer, and old John, a self-taught artist who specialized in painting watercolours of English apples and was later arrested for fencing stolen fireplaces.

In the Second World War the Colonel had spent many months in the jungles of the Naga Hills in northeast India, raising an army of Naga headhunters to thwart the Japanese advance. Everyone said he had been happiest then, alone with his army, building transshipment points and advance camps using whatever materials came to hand: bamboo for water pipes, limestone outcrops dynamited to make lime for concrete, huts erected using rattan and palm thatch. For that short period during the war the Colonel had been king, absolute law among a people he admired for their warlike demeanour.

Things were never quite the same for him after Indian independence. Ayub Khan, head of the newly formed Pakistani army, asked the Colonel to be his chief adviser. But he wanted the Colonel to take Pakistani citizenship. Some deep

16

conventionality in the Colonel balked at this prospect and he left the subcontinent in something of a huff. The Malayan Emergency was a welcome diversion, but in the end the British ran out of places that could accommodate such outsize personalities as Colonel H. He retired to Oxfordshire, where the local pub became his command headquarters and the landlord was under orders never to shut the bar while the Colonel still had drinks on the table. He made do with his rustic army of rude mechanicals and never left England again.

I had been back in England for several months before I decided to visit Colonel H. The old mansion had been sold and he now lived in a distressed gentlefolk's retirement home. I thought he would hate it, but my father told me the Colonel had entered a new, benign phase, brought on by the drugs they gave him.

The Colonel told me his version. 'They dope my tea,' he said cheerfully. 'Problem is, always running to the little boys' room.' With that he got up and shuffled into his en suite bathroom equipped with stainless-steel grip rails. The television was on full blast. 'Marvellous tool for education, that,' said the Colonel, 'if used in the right way.'

I stared dutifully at the screen. It was an afternoon chat show. Things had certainly changed since the days of the tubeless TV. I guessed the Colonel had also given up his insomniac's habit of listening to the police late at night using an illegal scanner he'd bought through *Exchange and Mart*.

'It's not too bad here,' he told me. 'Just steer clear of the other inmates. Dreadful old women! They complain about me banging around in the morning when I get up.'

'What time's that?'

'Oh, about half past four.'

A helper came in with a cup of tea. For some reason she used Colonel H.'s Christian name. It was the first time I had ever heard it spoken, and I don't think the Colonel had heard it for a long time either. He stiffened and took the tea as if

17

she didn't exist. 'Mr' was tolerated, but 'Colonel' or 'Sir' was expected. 'Distance, always keep your distance. Doesn't do to get too pally with the natives,' the Colonel always advised.

When the Colonel first went into the home, he gave most of his artefacts – the Naga spears trimmed with human hair, and headhunting *daos*, or machetes – to my uncle for safe-keeping. Something I managed to keep for myself was an ornate kris, a short sword, from my grandfather's time in Malaya. It suggested new possibilities, other jungles. I told the Colonel I just wanted to experience life in a jungle, without adding 'just as you did'.

'Any jungle will do if that's the case,' he said. 'Better have something to do while you're there, though.'

In a way I still craved the approval of the old man, wanting to show him that I wasn't the little boy who was frightened of 'a good stinging'. Before his drug-induced benign phase, he had been known to take cruel pleasure in tormenting those who sought his approval. The Colonel hated toadies. I knew the rules. You had to go away and do it on your own.

The more you study mythology the harder it is to avoid snakes. Even the word 'python' is of mythic origin. Python was a giant snake slain by Apollo on the slopes of Parnassus. Python's lair was at Delphi, and it was here that the oracle was established under his patronage. The priestess who delivered oracles was called Pythia. Hercules strangled two serpents as an infant before killing the hundred-headed water snake Hydra. Krishna, too, showed early promise, killing several snakes before he was nine. Susa-no-o, a Japanese mythical hero, fought a multiheaded serpent, and Perseus slew more than his share before taking the snake-haired head of Medusa. In Scandinavia Sigurd fought Fafnir, and Thor did endless battle with the cosmic supersnake Midgard. With a suitably watery slant, Maui of Polynesia killed a monster

18

eel in battle. Probably I'd left it a little late to demonstrate my heroic potential.

There were no snakes in the part of England where I grew up. The first I saw was a grass snake trapped by a fellow Cub Scout in a portable loo at the summer camp. It made an acrid, eggy pong, the result of being handled by thirty excited Cub Scouts in rapid succession. Later I heard it died in captivity. And though I reached out to touch its skin, I definitely had not wanted to hold it.

Snakes. I'd always thought anyone interested in snakes was peculiar. Keeping snakes was, in my books, on a par with subscribing to *Soldier of Fortune* magazine, being addicted to Bassett's Liquorice Allsorts, playing real tennis or keeping a shrine to Elvis – weird stuff done by weird people. But another part of me wanted to be pleasantly surprised. Now that I'd become interested in snakes, I was no longer judgemental. I wanted to like other snake fanciers and I wanted them to like me.

I made an appointment to visit Howlett's zoo, the one owned by John Aspinall, the famous gambler and friend of Lord Lucan. As I walked through the gate, I noticed a modern statue of Wodin, made of bronze. Wodin was the god of fury, though in later life he exchanged an eye in return for the wisdom to see things as they truly are. Aspinall's Wodin was obviously an early portrait as he still had both eyes.

At the reptile house I met Ernie Thetford, the head curator. He was very downbeat, not at all like a figure from Norse mythology. He had a precise Scottish accent and wore an ancient Barbour jacket with bulging side pockets, full of twine and torch batteries, I thought. He unlocked the door to the vivarium and introduced me to Chain and Sabre, two fifteen-foot Burmese pythons. I smelled for the first time the smell of big pythons, a wet hay smell, a bit musty, with a hint of rotting meat. With a certain diffidence

19

he explained their names. 'Big pythons are a bit like Alsatians, that's the way I look at them. They get to know you and come and meet you when you open the door. They have the temperament of Alsatians, even the colouring is a bit similar.' He picked up Chain and played him expertly through his hands.

'Can I hold him?' I asked. This was the first time I had ever held a snake but I didn't tell Ernie this. What most surprised me was how loose the flesh seemed. Then Chain tightened his grip and I could feel it was all muscle.

A small crowd had gathered at the side door and were peering in. 'What's that man doing?' asked a small boy.

'He's a vet,' said his father.

Emboldened by this, I tried to copy the way Ernie gripped behind Chain's head. There was a sudden hissing and I let go.

'He's hungry,' said Ernie.

We talked and Ernie allowed Chain to slither out of the door and around our feet. Then his head began to rear up. 'People are funny about snakes,' said Ernie. 'They think they can see into their soul or something. But it's just because snakes don't have eyelids and can't blink.'

I looked down and saw Chain's long tongue flicking in and out uncomfortably close to my flies.

'Jacobsen's organ,' said Ernie.

'I beg your pardon?'

'People think the tongue is somehow dangerous, but it's simply there to relay chemical traces to the Jacobsen's organ. It's much more than a sense of smell or taste. As far as they know it's a very precise chemical receptor.'

I liked the way Ernie referred to scientific opinion as 'they' and not 'we'. Ernie was his own man.

I wanted to see how much a fifteen-foot python weighed so I picked up Chain, rather too gingerly for Ernie's taste. 'They can sense . . . hesitation,' he said. He was too polite to say 'fear', but I knew that was what he meant. Chain had the upper hand and knew it. He started to coil around my arm, and then by an almost weightless transfer of bulk he was curling around my chest.

'Is the snake going to eat the vet?' asked the boy.

'Er, Ernie?' I said.

He regarded me with a wry look. 'He won't eat you,' he said.

Pythons kill by slow and methodical constriction. Every time you breathe out, they tighten their grip. No bones are broken, you're not crushed alive, but in the hour or so it takes to die, every last pocket of air in your lungs is squeezed out. I had read that it was an agonizing death, similar to a protracted and fatal asthma attack. I breathed out and Chain tightened his grip.

'Ernie,' I gasped, 'I think I've had enough.'

With an enviable swiftness and complete confidence, Ernie lifted Chain off me.

'Have you ever been attacked?' I asked.

'Once I was cleaning up and Sabre was on the shelf above me. He must have thought my bobbing head was food because he struck and bit me right on top. There was a lot of blood, always is from a head injury. I was lucky that another keeper was there to help pull him off.'

I looked at Ernie's slightly bald pate for scars, but his hair was long enough for concealment.

'Because their teeth face backwards it's hard to get them to disgorge without harming the snake.'

I admired Ernie's compassion, putting Sabre's welfare ahead of his own head. Chain was sneaking out through the door again and I tried to bend him back the way he'd come. It was impossible.

'It's funny that,' said Ernie. 'Because it looks like a giant worm, you think you can fool it. But they're hard to trick. If it wants to come out you can't redirect it and hope it won't

21

notice. You have to pull it right back into the cage. Because snakes aren't social creatures people think they're not intelligent, but they are.'

We drove in Ernie's beaten-up Renault van to a special series of sheds that housed baby and very young pythons. In the van Ernie talked more freely. He told me, 'I find zoos very depressing places to be. "Behavioural enrichment" is the buzz word now, but that's just ignoring the fact that zoos are basically crap. Behavioural enrichment just means putting some toys into the animal's space. Great, toys! That'll make it better that I'm trapped in a two-foot-square box!'

Ernie told me about the keeper who had been killed the previous month by a Siberian tiger. 'He just wasn't alert enough. The other keeper, Nick, is good with tigers, but I think this guy was in for the wrong reasons. I mean, it's got to be a macho thing, someone who wants to go in with a tiger. You're in trouble if it's you that's drawing you in and not the fascination of the thing.'

'Is it the same with snakes?'

'Plenty of snake experts been killed by snakes,' said Ernie.

We entered the sheds. One shed had over thirty pythons less than three feet away. They hissed and struck from inside their open-fronted boxes.

'This may not look like much, but actually this is a lot of space for a python,' said Ernie. 'The sad thing is, snakes will actually put up with a very shitty small environment. I've seen snakes in boxes you wouldn't keep a battery chicken in, but they still feed and they still breed, and really don't seem to mind.'

'Like humans in a way?'

'Maybe.'

Ernie handed me a welder's glove and a small Perspex shield, his own invention for viewing a snake safely while feeding it. 'The young snakes strike more often,' he said.

I inched forwards, glad of the glove, but still nervous. To

boost my courage I recalled that when I was child I had been unafraid of a particularly aggressive cockerel on my grandfather's farm (my other grandfather, not Colonel H.). All the other kids had run away, but I just stood my ground and in the end, after several foiled attacks, it lost interest. But there's something inherently unscary about chickens. You rarely hear, even on local news, 'Man pecked by free-range killer turkey' or 'Child in savage fowl onslaught'. The snake hissed and struck and though I didn't want to, I pulled my hand back. The flinch reaction.

'Watch the neck muscles,' said Ernie. 'You can see it tense just before it strikes.'

I started to observe the snakes. Looking for signs that signalled a strike made it more comprehensible and more interesting. But I was surprised at the speed of the strike. It wasn't lightning fast, but if you weren't quick you'd be caught.

'Snakes strike with speed, but their general rhythm is slow,' Ernie explained. 'Imagine the way a fly views a human being, how slow we must seem. It must really surprise a fly when it gets swatted. Compared to the snake, we're like flies.'

Ernie told me he had gone to university full of high hopes. 'I thought it would be full of people with a burning interest in animals, like me. But what I found was nice people who just wanted to get jobs.' He had worked in several zoos, but he preferred Howlett's. The animals had plenty of space and could choose whether they were on view or not.

'What's the worst thing about pythons?' I asked.

'When they shit on you. It can be very liquid, white urea mixed with black faeces. Sometimes they spray it all over you, very pungent. And a fifteen-foot python can produce a lot of crap.'

'What happens to the bones?'

'Digested, everything is digested. Chain will eat a chicken

and all that comes out the other end will be the quills of the feathers.'

'And if it ate a man?'

'You'd need at least a twenty-five-foot snake to eat a man. But if it did, there'd be nothing left except your gold fillings and maybe your wristwatch.'

Ernie kindly drove me to the station in his beaten van. I told him I was planning a book about snakes. He didn't seem disconcerted by my ignorance. 'It's good not to be a specialist. Specialists can often miss the obvious. Because things are connected, aren't they?'

Of the few books that touch even tangentially on snake hunting, those of C. J. Ionides stand out as the real thing. Ionides was an Englishman of Greek descent who, after a varied career as a soldier and big-game hunter, settled in 1950s Tanzania as a professional snake hunter. Completely eccentric, he insisted on being wheeled through the bush in a converted wheelbarrow because his gammy leg made walking difficult. He used his reputation as a witch doctor to keep his servants in line. When one employee consistently embezzled money, Ionides told him it would have to stop or else the man's penis would drop off. The money was quickly returned.

It was from Ionides that I learned the last-ditch protection against an attacking snake: ram snuff down its throat. Because the chemo-receptive Jacobsen's organ is so efficient at detecting chemical traces, the nicotine is absorbed almost instantly, killing the snake very quickly.

I went out and bought some snuff, Irish High Toast from George Smith and Sons in the Charing Cross Road. It was, the shop assistant assured me, the strongest snuff on the market.

*

I went to see Colonel H. again to sound out his views on snake hunting. He was looking out of the window at a thrush on a small bird table in the garden.

'See that fellow there? Comes here at the same time every day. Set your watch by him.'

He moved slowly back to his armchair in front of the blaring TV set. On a side table was a small statue of a laughing Buddha. It was the only artefact the Colonel had retained. Apart from this and the 1930s Homburg on top of the wardrobe, the room, in its bleak nursing-home function-ality, could have belonged to anyone.

The Colonel was in good spirits. Another friend had died, a fellow army officer from his Indian days. 'I'm one of the last, y'know,' he announced cheerfully. He was not without sentiment, but he hid it well and had no fear of death.

'Malaya's the place for big pythons. I saw one caught once by staking a pig inside a bamboo cage. The beggar can get in, but with the pig in his tummy he's too fat to escape through the bars, so to speak.'

He told me he'd caught a python, *Python reticulatus*, he said, by shooting through the branch of the tree the python was resting on. He'd been out looking for epiphytic orchids at the time, and when he found them, he blasted them from their treetop positions with a shotgun loaded with heavy ball. Colonel H. always had a gun handy, even when he was 'unarmed'. Unarmed simply meant 'not heavily armed'. Shot-guns didn't count, and when he drove through the Malay jungle in his pillarbox-red jeep, he'd blast away at jungle fowl as they flew up from the road. He explained why the jeep was red: 'CTs [Communist terrorists] know who I am. Khaki jeep could be anyone. They leave me alone, I leave them alone.'

'But weren't you at war?'

'Absolutely.'

25

It was a stupid question, Colonel H. was one of those people who are always at war.

The Colonel agreed that Amazonian green anacondas were a sideshow. 'Malaya's your place, by which I mean the whole archipelago. Never been attracted to South America for some reason. The Dusun of North Borneo are the people for you. Best python hunters in the world. Eat them for breakfast and sell the skins afterwards. Warrior people, of course. Know their onions, do the Dusun.' Knowing your onions was the highest praise you could expect from the Colonel.

The thrush had flown from the bird table and a blackbird had taken its place. There was a long silence as we stared at the bird pecking at a string of nuts.

'Has a beautiful song, the blackbird. People will tell you the song thrush is better. But the blackbird is really the best.'

He gave me a rare smile and I left.

When it came to snakes, I most definitely didn't know my onions. But after reading everything I could find about big pythons, especially the reticulated python (so called because of the pattern of diamonds on its back), I realized that the only way to find out about hunting snakes was to hunt them.

I was still undecided when I received a call from Paul Raddatz. Perhaps he took me more seriously than I did myself. He told me he had confirmation of a new thirty-foot python in a cave in Indonesia. He was trying to muster media interest before he went out to capture the thing. He wouldn't tell me where the cave was, but I guessed Kalimantan, the area from where he operated his snakeskin-collecting business. It was as if he'd thrown down the gauntlet. The race was on.

Previous travel had taught me the importance of certain key items of equipment. They don't even have to be that useful, they just have to inspire confidence when you're at the lowest ebb, alone, wet, mosquito-bitten and wishing you were having beans on toast while listening to Radio Four in a warm English kitchen. The important thing is utter reliability. A hi-tech walking boot that comes apart at the seams, a tear-proof cagoule that is shredded by falling into a thorn bush, a clever stove that leaks fuel and explodes, melting your dome tent into a piece of hard plastic the size of a burned-out matchbox car; these are not the tools you want for a serious endeavour.

My four tools of preference were: 'The Tool', a Leatherman combination pliers, knife, file, scissors and screwdriver; a pair of Zeiss folding binoculars; a leather-covered surveying tape I'd been given by Colonel H., twenty-five yards long when extended and essential for officially recording snake lengths; and a three-cell Maglite high-powered torch, of the kind used by the New York Police Department as a combination cosh and flashlight. At the last minute I also packed the ornamental kris, the engraved Malay dagger I had from Colonel H., and though it had little use, I valued it as a talisman.

Although rucksacks and sleeping bags and special boots have their uses, I wanted to avoid looking like a tourist. And you can usually buy what you need in the last town before the place where there are no towns. Besides, every time I went into a camping shop I had a bad experience with the staff. They persuaded me to buy stuff whose utility I seriously doubted. I bought a lot of small camping accessories designed to make life both easier and more complicated at the same time. And after a lot of dithering, I bought some chloroquine malaria pills. I had little faith in them, but being a weekly dose and not Larium, they seemed the least likely to give me Gulf War syndrome or some other neurotoxic side-effect.

Reticulated pythons are sufficiently aggressive to make them an unpopular subject for study. Far less is known about them than about other giant snakes. In the league table of dangerous snakes, retics are second after venomous snakes and anacondas are fourth after Indian pythons. This has earned them a certain privacy denied to more passive species. The great herpetologist Frank Wall said that reticulated pythons favoured only the densest jungle, while the equally respected Stanley S. Flowers claimed they needed to live near humans, relying on domesticated animals as their fodder. I decided to investigate both habitats – densest jungle and populated areas. I planned to move on whenever the trail grew cold, hoping that if I went to enough places known for long snakes, I'd sooner or later get lucky. This went against Ionides' advice never to go looking for snakes – wait until they find you.

My idea was to put out the word as I went along, in case there were locals who wanted to help. I had no idea what I ought to pay for a giant snake caught for me; it was another thing I'd have to learn on the job. As Ionides said, 'There is no textbook on snake catching. I learned the hard way with thirteen bites, each a mistake of some sort.'

The night before I left I got into what Colonel H. would call a funk. What would I do when I actually came face to face with a snake that was big enough to eat me? My rudimentary plans included going to Malaysia, where a friend from university had promised to introduce me to his uncle who was an expert in snakes, and to smooth my way into joining the Perkhidmat Jabatan, the municipal snake catchers of Kuala Lumpur. I had read about twenty-foot pythons being found in the sewers of Bangkok, so why not KL? Wading through a Third World drain seemed as good a place to start as any. Somehow it was less frightening than the jungle, which I knew was my ultimate destination.

I tried to calm my nerves by drinking stiff shots of Jameson's and reading Alfred Russel Wallace's book *The Malay Archipelago*. Wallace spent nine years in what is now

28

Malaysia and Indonesia, collecting animals for sale in Europe. This was how he subsidized his travel and work as a naturalist. Wallace was more interested in animals than in people, or rather he wrote of people as he did of animals, his tone general, treating people as examples of a subspecies rather than giving an account of the characters he met. But he recorded almost everything he saw, and though I skipped a bit over the long lists of woodpeckers and their Latin names, it was fascinating reading. The book has additional interest because it was during this series of voyages that Wallace came up with the mechanism of evolution. As a concept, evolution was not new. Rumi, the Sufi poet, expounded it as an explanatory theory some six hundred years before Wallace was born. But it took the new universal scientific culture to convince the world of its importance.

Evolution without a mechanism requires there to be some supernatural plan, some objective measure of betterness that encourages, or provides a morphogenetic template for, the lower to become the higher. There has to be some sort of magnetic pull towards improvement, otherwise wouldn't everything just stay the same? The nineteenth century saw the triumph of the mechanical solution, just as ours has seen first the electrical and finally the electronic solution. A society that had been revolutionized by mechanical devices became adept at searching for mechanical explanations of the world. Malthus proposed that since populations grow exponentially but food production can only grow arithmetically, the only brakes on overpopulation were famine, disease and war. This mechanical explanation has since gone out of fashion. No one talks much about Malthus any more.

But Wallace had read Malthus, and during a fever-ridden stay on Ternate Island in the Moluccas, he came up with the theory of evolution. In a feverish flash he connected the thousand upon thousand of beetles he had collected, all the same species but exhibiting considerable intraspecies variation, with the inexorable laws of Malthus. If one variant was more successful at feeding and breeding, that variant would proliferate. And Wallace was confident that this could account for different species as well as change within a species, because he had seen intraspecies variation as wide as differences between species.

Both Darwin and Wallace collected beetles in their youth. Although English and American children seem to have long lost this interest, beetle collecting is very popular among Japanese schoolboys even today. Perhaps the clerkish, assiduous, obsessive temperament you need to collect beetles is the same you need to make your nation a great economic power. Both being beetle men, the two Victorian scientists had an unstated respect for each other, which tipped in Darwin's favour because he was the older, the more 'establishment', the nobler born and the better known. Wallace, in short, worshipped Darwin, even dedicating *The Malay Archipelago* to him.

Darwin, though an obsessive worker, was a gentleman who never had to earn a penny in his life. Wallace was a self-educated animal collector who spent nearly twenty years in the field, bringing back from his Malay trip alone an incredible 126,660 specimens. That's an awful lot of mounting and stuffing. In fact, not allowing for illnesses and days off, he collected an average of thirty-eight specimens a day, every single day, for nine years. I was only looking for one, and I thought that was a big deal. No wonder we lost the empire.

The sheer volume of wildlife Wallace observed makes him a hero to naturalists. It does not necessarily mean, however, that he originated the theory of evolution. But the dark events surrounding his first letter to Darwin, explaining the contents of his feverish dream in Ternate, have led many to suspect that Darwin wasn't quite the gentleman history has portrayed him as.

Exhibit A: On 8 June 1858, Darwin wrote to his friend and confidant Dr Joseph Hooker that he had worked out 'the keystone' of the theory of evolution. On 3 June, Wallace's brother, who lived in Leicester, received a letter from Wallace posted at the same time as the Ternate letter to Darwin, who lived in Kent. If anything, living closer to London, Darwin should have received the Ternate letter before 3 June. He claimed he received it on the 18th. Mysteriously, the letter later disappeared, making this kind of cross-checking impossible. No other letters of Darwin's have been lost except those surrounding the fateful discovery of evolution.

Exhibit B: In a letter to Sir Charles Lyell, one of the few that did survive from that period, Darwin suggested they publish Wallace's Ternate essay, but added that this would mean 'all my originality, whatever it may amount to, will be smashed'.

Exhibit C: It was a year before Darwin published his theory of evolution. The joint paper read out by Darwin at a Linnean Society meeting without Wallace's permission contained nothing new by Darwin, but what Wallace said was revolutionary. Wallace found the solution to the problem of how species diverge. Darwin had not been able to solve this. Wallace's letter from Ternate contained the essay: 'On the Tendency of Varieties to Depart Indefinitely from the Original Type'. In it he outlined how it is environment which determines whether a variation predominates, so demolishing the immutable nature of a species. This is the engine of the theory of Natural Selection. As this was supposed to be a joint declaration of a theory discovered by both, why did it take Darwin another year to formulate his version?

You get the impression that Wallace was such a nice chap that he really didn't care if Darwin got all the credit. Perhaps the bitchy world of modern science could learn a thing or two from Wallace. When he came back to England he immersed himself in countless other areas of activity: phrenology, votes for women, and campaigning, way ahead of his time, against the false claims made for inoculation.

Wallace had encountered a huge python a few weeks before he came up with his theory. It was on the island of Ambon and he was saved from being bitten only by the energetic efforts of a native from Buru Island. The snake descended from the rafters of his hut, a twelve-footer 'capable of much mischief', before being grabbed and dashed against a tree stump by the Burunese. According to Wallace, the people of Buru know how to handle pythons because their island is composed mostly of marshy swamps teeming with snakes. It was another clue. I looked up Buru in a guidebook. There was only the sketchiest of entries. Buru was now a penal colony, a modern Indonesian Devil's Island, probably a perfect choice with all its swamps and snakes. Access would almost certainly be denied. I made up my mind to visit the place.

In the end Samia was very good about what she saw as my last *Boy's Own* adventure before marriage. She said she too often had 'doubts'. 'I don't,' I announced, anxious to reassure.

On the evening before I left we had a fine farewell dinner. Samia restrained herself until the last, saying only, 'Please catch your snake – but don't catch another woman!'

Sometimes I wondered what it would be like never to date another woman in my life. Strangely, it didn't bother me now that an adventure was in the offing. In the weeks of preparation the thing had taken on a more serious hue than I intended. I *had* to catch the snake. I thought about Wallace, spending nine years in the bush. I only had four months, because of the wedding. It made my stomach tighten with anxiety as I thought about all the holes in my flimsy plan.

The snake was already inside me, coiling and uncoiling in my guts before I left.

When I was putting on the welder's glove, Ernie told me an odd story about a previous underkeeper at Howlett's reptile house. 'We took on this lad because he liked snakes and reptiles. I think he had a pet monitor lizard of his own. We had him feeding this lot [the thirty small pythons] but the fact that they kept striking at him seemed to get him down. He complained he wasn't sleeping well. Then he developed asthma. He'd never had asthma but working with snakes brought it on. In the end he asked to leave, he couldn't take the dreams.'

'The dreams?'

'Well, nightmares really, every night he had nightmares about snakes. I don't recall the details, but it frightened the devil out of him. Used to wake up wanting to scream but not be able to because of the asthma.'

I fell asleep and did not dream and when I awoke it was dawn and time to leave. But in the taxi to the airport I thought about snake dreaming, about waking up alone and fighting for breath and not being able to scream.

TWO

Miss Revlon Asia Is Unavailable

Everything has to be paid for, and without the fear
you wouldn't have the excitement.   *C. J. Ionides*

Harun was having another heart attack. It was the second
that day. The first had been in his chauffeured Daimler,
stuck in the interminable traffic that clogs all routes into
Kuala Lumpur.

'The problem with these detachable collars,' he said, wrest-
ling with his shirt collar, 'is that they're really difficult to get
off when you're having a heart attack.' He smiled wanly.
Although his mop of curly hair was now grey, he still had a
boy's face. We were on the twenty-seventh floor of a skyscraper in central Kuala Lumpur looking out over the work
in progress of the city. A giant crane swung its arm in a slow
arc towards us and I thought in its metallic stupidity it would
smash through the window of Harun's plush private office. I
flinched, but Harun didn't notice. He was too busy lighting
a Camel cigarette. It was early afternoon but he was already
on his second pack. Behind his head was a framed Miles
Davis poster which I remembered from university. 'I had to
get rid of Marilyn,' he said.

Harun is one of the most indefatigable smokers I know.
He has always been committed to smoking, refusing to
give up even in the wheezy depths of a bronchitic cold or
during such healthful activities as between lengths while
swimming in a pool. But even now he kept his cool. He
was talking about his 'coronaries' (pounding heart, loss of

34

breath) but he never even mentioned cigarettes, not even obliquely.

'One of the other partners,' he said, more relaxed now that his collar was loose and hanging at a drunken angle, 'just dropped dead the other day. Massive coronary. He was very cheerful and positive right up to the end. He didn't have a red face or complain of chest pains or anything. The only clue, which I noticed a few days before, was that he got out of breath very easily. He'd climb a flight of stairs and he'd be breathing like someone who'd just run a mile. Apparently breathlessness is a key indicator.'

'You're not going to have a coronary,' I said.

'I hope not,' he said, refixing his collar. 'But believe me, things have changed since you were last here. KL is a very stressful place to be.'

He was right, Kuala Lumpur had changed. The skyline had been jacked up with tall buildings and the roads were packed with brand-new Proton Sagas, Prime Minister Mahathir's car of the people, and a Mitsubishi copy known also as a *poton haga*, Malay for 'cut price'. Daily smog, known as 'the haze', was causing a record number of bronchial infections. Portable cellphones, known as 'handphones', were a necessary status symbol even for those who couldn't afford a Proton Saga. The old easy-going Malaysia had in five years become a roaring Asian tiger.

'The haze is the price we pay for good sunsets,' Harun said with a smile. I felt he'd said it before. 'And let's face it, though trees are nice, isn't it a bit high-handed to stop us cutting ours down after you chopped all yours down a thousand years ago?'

'It wasn't a thousand years ago,' I said defensively.

'Well, whatever. The point is, we need timber exports to fund growth.'

'You mean washing machines for people who used to be happy washing clothes in the river?' I snapped.

35

'Exactly. Though, to be fair, most of the rivers are too polluted for washing now anyway. By the way,' he was baiting me now, 'I've just been working on a project which will turn an entire island into a cement factory. Imagine that – a solid cement island producing nothing but cement.' He raised his hand to stop my objection. 'And we need cement, we really do. Last month there was a crucial shortage. Cement bags were changing hands like, like gold dust!'

I wanted to puke, but I was staying at Harun's house, so I asked him for a Camel cigarette instead.

Harun's uncle Izham shared my misgivings about Malaysia's 'progress'. 'We have gone down the tubes for sure,' he said. 'Siltation is a major problem. So many reefs are destroyed that the fish have nowhere to spawn. We are storing up trouble, you are right.' He was a university lecturer in biology, though his speciality was animal parasites. Izham was a tall, wiry man with quick gestures and a kind, wide-eyed expression, though he had a double eye blink which took over his whole face from time to time. Dressed for preference in tracksuit and training shoes, he always seemed to be running somewhere. He agreed to take me for a walk in the jungle, to help me get used to it and give me the benefit of his wide knowledge.

Izham had grown up in a village near the Thai border. He had practised *silat*, and showed me some snaky foot moves that characterize this Malay martial art. He had stopped Thai boxing at fifteen: 'My father very sensibly knew that after we are fully grown we hurt each other too much in boxing.' His father had been the village schoolmaster and all his nine sons had made good careers for themselves. Izham's elder brother, Harun's father, had been a diplomat, but now he was a businessman and very wealthy.

The jungle was less than a mile away. Izham lived in a suburb of Kuala Lumpur which bordered on a large pocket of unmolested forest. As we shouldered our small rucksacks, he tapped his and smiled, showing me there were several cans of cold beer inside. Mine was weighed down by my notebook and Wallace, a worthy tome and useful as something to sit on in an emergency. On the way to the jungle I saw a run-over snake in the dust and hoped it was a good omen.

Izham explained that this was original but 'managed' jungle. Some of the very biggest trees might have been cut down, but many remained, some well over a hundred years old. Off the path it was not, in most places, very overgrown, another sign that it was old jungle. The path was wide and paved, which gave the forest the appearance of an ornamental park, reminding me of one I visited as a child in Galloway, Scotland, which had been full of exotics, grown because of the warm Gulf Stream. So my first sight of the jungle made me think of home.

There was a sound of leaves crunching under an animal's tread. Izham stood high to look over a low bush and excitedly pointed to a big lizard. It stopped, looking over one shoulder and then another, before it meandered away. It was a monitor lizard, about four feet long, the biggest lizard I'd ever seen wild, but only lunch for a big python.

Izham told me how to distinguish the sound of a crawling snake from an animal. 'If a leaf or stick breaks, then it's an animal. But if it's the sound of a stick rubbing, then it's a snake.' He told me how to find fighting fish in a stream by the bubble of air over a sunken sago log. 'If a fighting fish loses,' he said, 'it will lose all brilliance of colour for many weeks. Even fish hate losing!'

I was excited to be in the jungle, but it didn't strike me as real jungle, despite the heat and the ever-present mosquitoes. There were meranti trees with flared buttresses (used as boat frames, said Izham) and creepers hanging down that were strong enough to swing on like Tarzan, but if you took away the strong creepers and the big buttressed tree trunks we could have been in a dark wood in England on a very hot and sticky day. Even the smell of the place was not as jungly as the 'jungle' glasshouse at the Botanic Gardens in Oxford. There were monkeys and lizards and we heard a hornbill calling in the distance, but if I hadn't been with Izham I wouldn't have noticed any of these things. I consoled myself by recalling Wallace's first impressions of the jungle in Brazil. He had expected it to be teeming with wildlife, but in his first few days he saw nothing. Colonel H. had told me, 'If you want to see things in the jungle, stay quietly in one place and wait for animals to come to you.'

Despite the paucity of wildlife, as we tramped on and the paved path ran out, I began to fantasize about finding a thirty-foot python on my first day looking. It is this kind of wild hopefulness that causes me to buy lottery tickets. We came across a patch of disturbed ground, as if someone had been scratching with a hoe. 'Wild boar,' said Izham, and looked around like a hunter.

Suddenly we were on a grassy hill planted with nutmeg trees. 'This isn't the jungle,' I said. Izham confessed that it had recently been landscaped in. He suggested we sit down and drink a beer.

It was early evening, not yet dark, and Izham grew philosophical. 'I have been giving considerable thought recently to whether it is better to travel hopefully or arrive.'

'Travel hopefully,' I said without thinking.

'Yes, I thought so too, but when I started to think I realized it was very hard to do, in practice, I mean. You cannot treat it as a consolation prize if you fail to arrive. It's much more than that. You have to run the risk of losing sight of your goal by making as much of the journey as possible. Sometimes, often, you have to risk being blown off course.'

'How do you mean?'

'Well, the question I'm now asking myself is: how much does travelling hopefully *reduce* your chance of arriving?'

'Why can't you do both? Travel hopefully *and* arrive?'

He smiled and blinked his whole face quickly and smiled again. 'Yes, I used to think that when I was your age.'

We opened more cans. Although Izham was a Muslim, he declared that Koranically speaking only date wine was forbidden. 'And I *never* drink date wine!' He chuckled, springing another ringpull.

We carried on walking, through high elephant grass. Izham pointed out a prickly rattan whose name in Malay meant 'to hook you back'. We stopped for a final beer by a lake, which, Izham said, the British had discovered when flying over it in the 1920s. 'So before that time, this lake did not exist!'

It got dark as we looked out over the lake. The jungle began to get noisy, but not deafening as I'd been led to believe. Izham pointed out a frog making a noise which I had thought to be that of a bird. We watched the glowing bodies of fireflies and he indicated the reflecting eyes of a moth, close together. Eyes further apart meant a monkey, and very far apart was a tiger.

We got back to the road and walked to a payphone. Izham didn't like handphones. He called the second wife to come and pick us up. As we waited, he said, 'After long thought I decide it's better to travel hopefully than arrive.' Then he added, 'It doesn't matter if you don't get your snake, you know that?'

The Shogun leaped into pole position at the lights. Zaki, Izham's son and my driver, told me he wanted to help me find my longest snake. He shook the steering wheel and made Beavis and Butthead noises, just to show me how impressed he was. 'Wow, snakes! Hey, far out, I mean, seriously cool. Let's stop at the Hard Rock. I want you to meet Fat Carl.'

The Hard Rock Café, Kuala Lumpur, is not the kind of place you go to buy Hard Rock T-shirts. Like the electricity box outside my house in London, the Hard Rock has somehow become the place where the local kids hang out. Harun thought himself too old for the Hard Rock, but Zaki loved it. With a three-hour happy hour every day of the week, the bar area was packed, frenzied and good-natured; it felt like being in an English pub at Christmas. Zaki told me it was a good place to make snake 'contacts'.

Zaki had just finished starring in a wristwatch commercial which involved him paddling through surf in a canoe. 'But in the final cut, they only showed my wrist and the face of the girl on the beach. My head was cut right out.'

'That's good,' I said. 'It means you're not getting overexposed.'

'But I want to be overexposed! Here, meet my mother and Ally.'

Ally was Zaki's prize possession, a blond-haired English model, his girlfriend. She was accompanied by Zaki's mother. 'I often come here,' his mother told me. 'I can never be bored watching people.'

Zaki and his mother were very close. She approved of Ally's looks but thought her weak-minded. Ally had an extraordinary pair of breasts that somehow got into everybody's face, but when I averted my eyes I quickly concluded that she was, in fact, weak-minded. She didn't like hot food, mosquitoes, men ogling her, air conditioning, the heat, getting up early, alcohol, smoking, Malaysian money or photographers. Ally really knew what she didn't like. I tried to avoid the crush around her breasts; somehow their magnetic curvaciousness was causing a log jam in the bar, people making a pilgrimage from right across the room for a closer

40

look. It was like one of those wildlife documentaries showing the intense competition for an African waterhole at dusk.

Elbowed out of the way by a new admirer, I started a conversation with Johan, a lonely Finn. He was interested in Zaki's mother, and had already bought her a drink. Johan was tall, heavily built and very blond with a small ponytail. He designed hospital interiors and he assured me he 'loved women'. 'You see that woman over there?' He pointed across the bar to a Malay or Thai woman in a red jacket. 'She comes here every night. I told her she was a beautiful woman, but I cannot pay.'

'Why not?'

'It is not my way. So I come here every night and look at her. See that one over there? I look at her too.' Johan told me he was married with four daughters. They were coming soon from Finland to visit him. 'I would like to bring them here to meet you,' he said, 'but they don't like such smoky places.'

Fat Carl then appeared, beaming like an outsize greedy chipmunk. He had a bulky kaftan-clad body and an immaculate beard on the widest jowls I'd ever seen. He was Eurasian-Malay and spoke beautiful English. He stopped and talked to every second person, often just a few well-chosen words. Fat Carl knew everyone but there was nothing in his languid carriage that suggested a man 'working the room'. No conversation lasted longer than Carl wanted. Not just a master of the entry word, the casual comment, he was equally gifted in the departure line, the 'excuse me' that did not signal rejection but rather reward for having talked at all. Fat Carl assumed a confidential tone with me, quite different from the mocking humour he directed at Zaki. 'The Malays,' he confided, 'have an absolute horror of snakes. They loathe them. The traditional Malay house, as I am sure you will have seen, is a dark, windowless dwelling, raised off the

41

ground. An architecture of fear – fear of tigers and fear of snakes. It's no longer polite to dislike tigers, poor things, so this centuries-old hate-filled passion is directed at snakes. You have met Raja Ula?'

'Who?'

'A self-styled Indian snake charmer who calls himself the Snake King. As we speak he is probably being stung by one of his thousand pet scorpions!' Carl laughed his rich baritone laugh and explained. 'The Malays are obsessed by breaking records. We have the tallest building, the highest flagpole, the largest mosque. It's one of Mahathir's complexes and he's passed it on to the whole nation. This poor little Indian has set himself the challenge of spending a record number of days in a glass cage with a thousand scorpions. They sting him regularly, I understand, but his heart is set on the record. I believe it's still going on at one of the large hotels.'

Zaki stood impatiently at the edge of our conversation. 'Yo, Carl!' he said.

'Ah, Junior,' said Carl, 'you must take Robert to see our scorpion man.' And with a delicate eliding movement of his bulk, Carl had disappeared into the crowd.

'He likes to call me Junior,' said Zaki, as if I'd just found out some secret that needed explaining. Then a new idea took hold. 'But Rob, I've just been talking to this guy. He's been in prison, you know Pudu Jail, the one with the world's longest mural around its walls? They shut it last year. But this guy's got connections. Talk to him. But whatever you do, don't mention Pudu Jail!'

I slid in next to the man from Pudu Jail. He was Malay with a handwoven hippie rucksack, a pointed nose and long, greasy hair. I didn't like his eyes, but he laughed manically, showing me he was here to have a good time. Before he spoke, I felt sized up. I didn't like that.

'So my little friend here tells me you're looking for snakes?'

42

'Big snakes,' I said. 'Pythons.'

'Well, you've come to the right man, because I can get you anything you want. Anything this dirty town has to offer, I can get it. Girls, pills, grass, E, acid, Thai sticks, you name it—'

'Can you get me a gun?'

'You want mine?' He laughed some more. 'I like you,' he said, showing me his beer glass was empty.

'These snakes,' he said a moment later, receiving his beer with a nod. 'Like, how big do they have to be?'

'I only want one,' I said, 'but it must be over thirty feet long. That's nine metres. There's a prize being offered by an American zoo.'

'How much is the prize?'

I thought fast. 'Twenty thousand dollars.'

'I'll drink to that. But this nine-metre snake must be like a freak, right?'

'They do exist, I'm sure of that.'

He wrote down the details in a small book. 'You know what they call me?' he said without looking up.

'No, what?'

'They call me "the chosen one", because,' and here his voice dropped several tones, 'I was in Pudu, you know Pudu Jail, for possession of, get this, three grammes. Enough for two joints! I mean, everyone smokes, but it's me they have to make an example of. Ninety-nine times out of a hundred you give the cop a fifty and you're off. Not me, I was chosen!

'Pudu is the real story, man. I can tell you stuff that'll make your hair stand on end. You know how they say when a man goes to be hanged he doesn't make a noise? That's bullshit. I've seen guys crying and screaming – and they let you hear, they want you to hear – just minutes before they put the noose on. Twenty men in a room and one bucket to shit in. I learned to make fire like Stone Age man, a razor blade and a nail, and keep it burning for eight hours in a piece of burned cloth in your pocket. If you want things in Pudu, you trade "spring cigarettes". I was good at rolling those – it's like a one-metre-long cigarette rolled in newspaper, then you cut it up with your razor.'

'Where did the tobacco come from?'

'It comes, man, it comes.

'Mahathir chose me, man, and I suffered. I suffered for one year. And somebody will kill that man because of the shit that he's done. You know the haze? You know that's caused by the new airport they're building? Malaysia is fucked, man – you heard it here first!

'Call me, man, that's my wife's number. She's a lawyer, but it's cool.'

Then the chosen one started to dance in the cramped available space near the bar. He danced an intense solitary dance with a cigarette in his mouth, his hippie rucksack on his shoulder. He didn't look at me again and I slid off my bar stool out into the night.

I took a taxi to Bangsa. Harun looked washed up at the bar, tearing the cellophane off his third pack of Camels.

'Where you been?' he grumbled.

'I just met "the chosen one".'

'You mean some religious nut?'

'Something like that.'

I perched on a high stainless-steel stool and allowed Harun to summon a whisky on the rocks.

'I've been thinking about our conversation. You know my firm has done the legal work for the Bakun dam?'

The Bakun dam was a byword for ecological disaster. A useless hydroelectric project in the forests of Sarawak, Borneo, it was commissioned, I suspect, because it would have been, at the time, the biggest dam in the world.

'I didn't know that,' I said.

'There were meetings,' said Harun, 'when I could have voiced my disapproval. I could have said we shouldn't do this. But I didn't. I said nothing. But it wouldn't have made a blind bit of difference. Some other firm would have done the work. I still feel bad, though.'

'Have a drink,' I said.

'The thing is, the firm we're dealing with, who got the overall contract, also got the timber concession for the dam area. The value of the timber alone means they're in profit even before they start building the dam.'

'Maybe they'll run out of cement,' I said.

I followed up Fat Carl's suggestion and made an appointment to meet Raja Ula, King of the Snakes. He had finished his scorpion marathon but was coming in the following week to talk to the hotel about merchandising deals. Next to his scorpion cage his snakes had also been on display, including several long pythons. Long snakes have always been money spinners. In 1805 George Wombell bought two reticulated pythons for seventy-five pounds and in three weeks had made his money back by advertising them as 'the longest snakes in the world'. Neither of Wombell's snakes was more than twenty-five feet long.

I was also trying to contact Suleiman Sharifa, the head of the Perkhidmat Jabatan, the municipal snake collectors. The phone line to the snake depot was idiosyncratic at the best of times. I rang and rang, but only about one call in ten ever got connected. The rest were killed by someone picking up the phone and immediately slamming it down. For a day or two I went crazy, ringing about forty times an hour. Even when I got through Suleiman was never there. This sudden crazy impatience was, I now see, the first sign of snake fever.

Days drifted by at Harun's palatial house. Sumi, the Indonesian maid, brought me coffee as I read accounts by nineteenth-century travellers interspersed with occasional chauffeured trips into town. I kept the ceiling fans on full blast as I paced the marble floor trying to will things into action.

One day Harun came home from work and asked, 'How would you like to meet Miss Revlon Asia?'

'Fine,' I said, forgetting for several seconds that I was on the verge of marriage. Being in another continent from your loved one, I had discovered, has that effect.

Harun's wife was designing sets for a dance extravaganza entitled *Scintillations*, and Miss Revlon Asia had agreed to dance the main female role. 'Certain critics,' said Harun with due deliberation, 'have pronounced her the most beautiful woman in the world.'

I was about to hunt my first snake. Suleiman had called back and I was now speeding through KL's back streets on a snake call-out with the Jabatan boys. There were five of us in a Toyota minivan. Suleiman's three assistants, one Chinese, one Malay and one Indian, were all very friendly, and kept offering me Gudam Garam clove cigarettes. I sat next to Suleiman, who was driving, and he briefed me on what to expect.

'This is in one of our high-class neighbourhoods, la. There are trees and suchlike, many places for snakes. We have heard it is a python, but people always say python. Python, la!' he shouted over his head to the boys in the back and they burst into uncontrollable laughter.

We roared through the gates of a large house in the Bukit Tunku district. A gaggle of excited servants gathered around Suleiman, who was broad-shouldered and had a moustache, but he ignored them as a teacher ignores schoolchildren. Somehow he ascertained everything he needed to know without seeming to ask questions. The lady of the house, a sedate woman in her fifties, politely ignored me, as if it was normal, now Malaysia was a roaring tiger, to employ white trash to deal with snakes. Suleiman bowed his head a fraction and explained to her what we would do.

The Chinese, who had a disconcerting walleye, hefted the Bygon tank out of the minivan. Bygon is a multipurpose insecticide, and Suleiman assured me that snakes didn't like it either. I thought about my snuff, and wondered if the Bygon acted on Jacobsen's organ in the same way. 'It will not kill, la,' said Suleiman, 'but snake become very poorly.' It was the Indian's job to manage the snake pole. This was a long tube of metal with a short tube welded alongside it. A blue nylon rope went in a loop through the tubes to make a noose. It was the Malay man's job to hold a smaller snake pole and to hand out Gudam Garam cigarettes at strategic moments. I was thankful I had been given no job.

We went through the well-tended garden. The lawn was bright green, colourful shrubs crowded each side and tall palm trees stood further back. The garden was on several levels, and we descended steps that became increasingly damp, towards a hoop-shaped swimming pool reflecting light in lazy brilliance.

Almost hidden was a low bunker-type building that housed the swimming-pool pump and served as a changing room. Suleiman went through the peeling metal door to investigate. Then he called, 'Mr Robert, come forward! It is a cobra.'

Feeling sheepish and somewhat nervous, I pushed open the door. If I was to be reincarnated as a mongoose, now was the time – they are twenty times more resistant to cobra venom than other mammals of equivalent size. It was gloomy inside but light came in from the other end which opened on to the pool. Suleiman held up his finger and pointed. I heard a sudden hiss and he took a step back. The snake was in the washbasin in the far corner and I just made out its tail hanging over the edge. Unable to contain themselves, the team came into the room. The Chinese had the Bygon tank on his back and a long spray nozzle in his hand. He nodded at Suleiman and blasted the basin with Bygon. I inched forwards with the Indian and just as he was about to noose the snake, which was coiling and uncoiling in discomfort, I realized it was about to strike. The Indian pulled back and then in an instant moved in and had the cobra, which was about three feet long, dangling from the noose. Assisted by the Malay, who brought forward a blue PVC sack, the Indian quickly bagged the snake.

Outside, Gudam Garams were handed round. The lady of the house sent down soft drinks and the servants kept their distance, looking fearfully at the now still bag.

'You know how I know it is cobra?' asked Suleiman. 'After I open the door, I tap the wall. When they hear that noise, a cobra always hisses. You know cobras from the hissing.'

I felt sick, what with the soft drinks and all the clove cigarettes. I knew then that I didn't like venomous snakes. Pythons are my kind of snake, I thought, I'll stick with them. My only consolation was that I had known when it would strike. I was learning to read snakes and that gave me a small measure of comfort. I wondered what would happen to the cobra when they got back to the Jabatan headquarters. I wasn't going back with them so I wouldn't see for myself. Suleiman had earlier been evasive, implying that some snakes were released into national parks and others given to zoos. 'Even after they've been Bygonned?' I asked. He smiled jollily in reply. 'The cobra will find a new home, do not worry.'

In previous eras cobra venom has been highly valued. A highly modified form of saliva, it was used as a cure for angina and as an analgesic for advanced leprosy. Now that we have other drugs, cobras are not so popular. Rattlesnakes, too, had their day. Dr 'Diamond' Self of Texas kept an epileptic free of fits for two years by administering minute doses of diamondback-rattlesnake venom. Asthma responds to sand-viper venom and Russell's-viper venom is a coagulant used in the treatment of haemophilia, tonsillectomy and dental bleeding.

'OK, this is the deal,' said Harun. 'I've arranged for us to meet Miss Revlon Asia at this new gallery in Bangsa. It's a private view of sculpture by a guy who recasts bits of Proton Saga in stainless steel and gold.'

'Sounds terrible.' I wondered what would happen when I met the most beautiful woman in the world. I was glad I wasn't yet married and at the same time consoled myself with the thought of Harun as chaperone.

'You're right, it does sound terrible.' Harun looked crest-fallen. 'But let's go anyway,' he added.

I got in touch with Sri Gobind, who had organized the publicity for Raja Ula's scorpion extravaganza. He was very smooth on the phone and invited me to the Metropole Hotel to meet the Snake King and his manager. 'But I must warn you,' he said, 'he's a very ignorant fellow and speaks no English.'

The Snake King was heavily built with a huge, confident stomach draped in a flashy open-necked black shirt. He had a gold entwined-snake medallion on his hairy chest. He was bearded and regal, except for his penetrating nose picking, which he indulged in when Sri Gobind's translations took up too much time. The manager was also fat, but shifty and weak-chinned. Sri Gobind was extremely well groomed, about thirty, with a Mont Blanc pen in his shirt pocket and a handphone clipped to his belt. We sat round a circular conference table in an anonymous meeting room at the Metropole. The King lounged back in his plastic chair and his stomach bulged over the table top.

The details of the ordeal were impressive. The King had spent twenty-one days in a glass cube ten foot by eight foot with five thousand scorpions. His meals had been provided by the hotel where the record-breaking attempt had taken place. Twenty-one days with five thousand scorpions had smashed the previous world record, held by an Indonesian – a meagre fifteen days with 2500 scorpions. The glass cube had been air-conditioned and the King had a mattress to lie on. On average, he had been stung nine times a day. Sri Gobind emphasized the magnitude of the achievement. 'An ordinary fellow, you or I, for example, would be feeling extremely woozy after two or three bites. Nine would most definitely kill you. Most definitely. And Raja Ula – ' here he gave a respectful nod to the King, which was regally acknowledged – 'had nine bites a day, every day for twenty-one days. He is the most bitten man in the world.' The King rolled up his shirt and revealed the scarred balloon of his stomach. For some reason, most of the stinging had occurred there, which was fortunate, as he had plenty of protection.

'How does he feel after all those bites?'

'He has headaches and chest pains all the time,' said the manager triumphantly. 'But he has been brought up in this way of life, it is what he knows.'

I looked at the King with genuine respect. It was hard to imagine a more unpleasant way to earn a living than suffering headaches and chest pains and just waiting for the next scorpion to sting.

'And scorpions are very stupid,' said Sri Gobind. 'They are not like snakes. They cannot be charmed. It is in their nature to sting. They have no respect for Raja Ula.' He nodded again to the King. 'And the flash cameras excite them to sting more. When the press come, Raja Ula is stung repeatedly, repeatedly.'

I wondered if Raja Ula had had to undergo a scorpion version of 'a good stinging' in his youth. Had he built up his immunity this way?

Raja Ula answered in detail. He had not been the strongest

boy but he made up his mind when he was young never to admit to feeling fear or pain. The first time a scorpion stung him, he was surprised that he did not die. But he was happy that others respected him for laughing at the pain. He believed that more people die from the shock of snake bites and scorpion stings than from the actual venom. With scorpions he had, he was sure, built up an immunity. With snakes it was not possible. Perhaps he had inherited some immunity. He had been bitten four times by cobras, once spending ten days in a coma. His arm became gangrenous, but he insisted that it not be amputated. 'A snake king must have two arms,' he said. The arm healed. 'The liver is strong in my family,' said the Snake King. 'But the mind is also strong. A snake tries to kill the mind first.'

'What is your favourite snake?'

'Cobras. They are the most intelligent.'

'Do you handle pythons in your show?'

'All the time. I have two pythons, both of record length.'

'What kind?'

'Burmese pythons.'

It is very rare for a Burmese python to be longer than twenty-two feet, but they are the easiest to tame and the most good-natured.

'The thing is,' I said to the manager, 'can you find me a python that's longer than thirty feet?'

'No problem,' said the manager without missing a beat. 'In fact, last week I was offered a python that was thirty-five feet long.'

'Thirty-five feet? Are you sure?' My heart was racing and suddenly I was absurdly pleased with myself. This was it!

'I measured it myself. But it was so big we need a crane to lift it.'

A crane to lift it!

'Don't worry,' I said, in a voice squeaky with greed, 'I'll hire a crane.'

'No problem then,' said the manager.

'No problem,' I said.

There was a hurried consultation between Raja Ula, Sri Gobind and the manager. Sri Gobind spoke. 'These fellows want to know, what is the bottom line for them?'

'Twenty-five thousand US dollars,' I said. 'And you can split it any way you like.'

Sri Gobind translated the amount into Malayasian ringgit. The room suddenly went very quiet.

'When you want this snake?'

'As soon as possible.'

'Give me one week.'

Inside I was shaking hands with myself with glee.

Now that I was on a roll, I looked forward to meeting the most beautiful woman in the world. Raman, Harun's driver, chauffeured me to the gallery. Harun was going to meet me there from work. I was feeling expansive and chatted to Raman in the rudimentary Malay that Sumi, the house-keeper, had been teaching me. Raman said, 'Mr Harun is a very good boss, a number-one boss. He said, "Take care of this car as if it was your own." I do not have a car. I have a bike – but it is dirty! Malays say that if you take too much care of your own things you cannot take care of other people's things. I say to myself, if I take care of this car it will be happy with me. It will like me for that and do well for me.'

At the private view I looked for pieces of Proton Saga, but Harun had been mistaken. This was a show of paintings made to look as if they were scenes in the viewfinder of an automatic camera. I swooped on a glass of white wine, regretting it almost instantly. In the ever-present heat of tropical KL, wine always made me feel ill straight away. Beer was different, as long as it was cold beer. Whisky was best, drunk straight, preferably after the sun had gone down. I understood now why all those planters preferred the hard stuff.

In a suave movement of pale blue I saw Fat Carl at the far end of the gallery. Harun was late. I wondered whether Miss Revlon Asia was already in attendance. I spoke to a supercilious, balding young man from the British Embassy, whose insistent English accent and pale, sweating neck brought home to me that I was abroad. I wanted to like him, perhaps even to make friends, but two Englishmen abroad, if they are not friends immediately (usually because of some shared mishap), are forever caught in the endless circling of suspicious old dames. In an obvious move I refilled his wine glass from an attendant's bottle, and escaped to find more. Carl's kaftan, hemmed in a subtle shade of purple, swept past me as I stood aimlessly at the wine table. He raised his eyebrows, gestured at the two wine glasses he had in his hands and moved off with a seigneurial smile.

Harun arrived, but seemed tense and distracted. I looked at him, the casual, laid-back Harun I'd known at university, grown socially hypersensitive. His unlined face was the same, only the greying bouffant gave any outward sign of change. 'By the way,' he hissed, 'the market crashed today. I doubt if too many pictures will be sold.'

'When's Miss Whatshername arriving?' I asked.

'Maybe she's gone,' he said, grimacing at his Rolex.

'Harun, what on earth are you doing here?' A young Malay man with frameless glasses gave him an amused look. Harun made a hoarse laugh. Continuing his joshing tone, the man said, 'Why don't you just go home?'

Harun laughed again and then stumbled. I wondered if he was having another coronary. 'I feel odd,' he said. 'Let's go.'

'But we only just got here. What about you-know-who?'

'Please,' he said.

Outside in the balmy heat he recovered and explained, 'That guy, Kumir, when he asked why I was there, I suddenly

53

felt he'd seen right through me. That he knew I was a complete phoney. Sorry.'

'Wasn't he just joking?'

'Not him. Anyway, it freaked me out.'

Suleiman called and told me he'd caught a python. 'Not a big one, but it is *ula sawa batik*.' A reticulated python. I jumped in a taxi to visit the Jabatan HQ.

Behind the garbage trucks and greasy wheelie bins was a lawn of closely mown weeds. The walleyed Chinese, with considerable flourish, emptied the familiar blue PVC sack on the ground. Out came a beautifully patterned reticulated python, about ten feet long and probably a year old. It lay on the lawn without moving, still recovering, no doubt, if recovery was possible, from a hefty dousing in Bygon.

Suleiman used the long snake pole and slipped the noose around the head of the dozy snake. Then he handed me the pole and I prepared to do the same. It was a bit like one of those fairground games where you have to hook a plastic duck floating in a tank of water. When I got close with the nylon noose, the snake, which I suspected of being dead, moved its head just enough so that the noose did not lodge. I tried again. The snake moved again. I kept trying and the snake kept moving. Then, without warning, the Chinese swooped down on the snake, grabbed it behind the head and shoved it into the noose for me. I tightened the rope. My first python. 'That's how it's done,' said Suleiman. Despite the help I'd received it felt good, but I resolved to hire a team at the first opportunity.

After a round of cigarettes, which I felt it was my duty to hand out, I asked what would happen to the python.

'Do you want a pet?' asked Suleiman.

'If it was three times longer,' I managed.

Without bothering with the bag or the rope, the Chinese man picked up the snake and, holding it behind the head and a little further behind, carried it to the edge of the lawn to a rusted forty-gallon oil drum. He dumped the snake inside. The pretence of releasing snakes back into the national parks was gone.

'We caught one python, eighteen feet, we gave that to a zoo,' said Suleiman.

'Was it difficult to catch?' I asked, eying the drum.

'No, it was very sleepy – it had just eaten eight ducks!'

The Indian man dropped three pieces of cut-up lorry tyre into the drum. Then he doused the snake and the pieces of rubber with petrol. He soaked a piece of rag in petrol, borrowed my lighter, lit it and dropped it in the drum. It was a hot day, but I felt the sudden heat of the almost invisible flame ball. The drum was heavy, but you could hear the noise the snake made as it banged against the sides, burning alive.

Sumi, the Indonesian housekeeper, had seen my kris while cleaning my room. She told me it was *tuju*, a magic kris. I said that was unlikely, as Colonel H. had been given the kris by the father of a Malay soldier he'd put on a charge for being drunk on duty. If anything, it was probably an *un*lucky kris. No, she said, she could tell, it was charged with magic.

Sumi was perhaps thirty with a wide, toothy smile. She came from a village in Sumatra where they knew all about krises. In her village there was a *bomo*, a magician, who could make a kris come alive and kill someone in the night. We both had a good laugh at this, though it made me uneasy. Sumi was unperturbed. In a moment she was back watching her favourite soap opera on the television, squatting three feet from the screen. She always watched soap operas when Harun and his wife were out of the house.

Sri Gobind had a proposition, a private deal, but he couldn't use the office phone, his co-workers might be listening. He, the Snake King and the manager would pick me up and drive to the manager's bungalow, which was in a distant suburb. He hinted that the thirty-five-footer had been located.

There was a lot of joking in the car when the Snake King complained that no women were interested in him. 'It is since his display,' said Sri Gobind. 'They think he is full of poison. Perhaps they think they'll be poisoned, or give birth to a scorpion.'

'Even my wife thinks so,' said the Snake King in a matter-of-fact way, as if this was just a necessary but unpalatable part of the job, like fire fighters complaining of the inconvenience of working nights.

The manager was driving. I sat next to him, and the Snake King and Sri Gobind were behind. He whispered to me through the hole in the headrest, 'I tried at first to be an honest businessman, but I got nowhere. I have a degree in law but everyone is a lawyer these days. I have concluded that I must be dishonest in future. I do not want to be, but it seems I have no choice.'

It was an astonishing assertion to make, considering we were on the brink of a 'deal'. I wondered if it was a perverse gambit to make me trust him.

We drove on and on, past new developments of high-rise housing and estates of identical red-roofed, white-walled bungalows. Malaysia was gripped by a building frenzy. No wonder there were cement shortages. A more worrying side-effect was the recent dengue-fever epidemic. Pools of stagnant water on building sites were a perfect breeding ground for infected mosquitoes. Two of Harun's friends and his next-door neighbour had all caught dengue in the last month. The safety of the big city was an illusion. It was almost certainly healthier deep in the jungle.

Sri Gobind continued his sales pitch. 'I have not told the hotel about the big-snake project. I have also not informed them about organizing a scorpion show in England. Do you think Channel Four will be interested?'

I was impressed that he knew about Channel Four, but I couldn't see a fat man being repeatedly stung by scorpions as anything more than a bizarre filler on the news.

'What about a hotel show?' asked Sri Gobind.

'Maybe,' I said. 'But English people don't usually visit hotels to see venomous snakes and scorpions. It's a new concept.'

Sri Gobind agreed it was a new concept. Bit by bit he explained that it was also an unsuccessful concept, at least in Kuala Lumpur. The show had cost twenty-five thousand pounds to mount (I found this hard to believe), but only five thousand had been taken. The scorpions alone cost a pound each, and they'd used ten thousand.

'I thought there were only five thousand?'

'They were not strong scorpions. At first many died. We did not broadcast this fact. But we still have two thousand left, in a room in the hotel. That is another problem. You cannot release two thousand scorpions just anywhere.'

I wondered about the hotel. Surely there were regulations about keeping scorpions in hotel rooms?

'How much did the Snake King make?' I whispered back through the headrest.

'Actually nothing,' said Sri Gobind. 'We told him it would be good publicity. That is why he is concerned about T-shirt sales. That is the only way he can make money out of this thing.'

I'd seen the T-shirts. They were certainly eye-catching, if not repulsive, though I couldn't see many people actually wanting to wear portraits of an overweight Indian entwined by venomous snakes with several scorpions sitting on his head.

We pulled up in front of a dilapidated bungalow. The

57

drive was stacked with wooden crates. The manager took me to a crate four feet long, three feet deep and two feet wide. That might sound like a big crate, but for a fully grown python, it isn't. Behind the chicken wire, which fronted the crate, the python, a Burmese, was immobile. It was in poor condition, with bald patches showing grey where scales had been lost. I guessed its length from the size of its head to be no more than twenty feet.

'There is your thirty-foot snake!' The manager beamed.

I couldn't believe they'd try such an obvious rip-off. I thought there had to be another angle, like T-shirts or publicity, but there wasn't. Colonel H. would probably have fed Sri Gobind and the manager to the python. Instead I succeeded in becoming rather petty.

'What about the thirty-five-footer? The one I need the crane for?'

'That is coming too, perhaps next week.'

'Well, let's get this one out and measure it,' I said, though I didn't have the tape with me.

'This snake is too dangerous,' said the manager. 'It can easily eat a man.'

'No, it can't,' I said.

'Yes, it can,' said the manager.

'No, it can't, its mouth isn't big enough to get past a man's shoulders.'

'Yes, it is,' shouted the manager.

'No, it isn't,' I shouted back.

The King of the Snakes mimed, rather well, a man being eaten by a snake. He volubly explained in Tamil how this snake could eat me alive. Big bully, I thought.

'This snake can really eat a man,' Sri Gobind said earnestly.

'How do you know?' I said. 'Have you seen it?'

Sri Gobind didn't actually say yes but I knew he wanted to.

58

'I'm sorry,' I said, 'but this snake isn't thirty feet long.'

'It is.'

'It isn't.'

'It is.'

'All right, let's measure it.'

'It is too dangerous.'

'It isn't at all dangerous. It's a Burmese python, and a knackered one at that.'

'It can eat a man.'

'No, it can't.'

'Yes, it can.'

The King of the Snakes started to poke around in another crate with a small metal stick, hooked at one end. He brought out a thin, green cobra, which hissed and rose up from the stick, hood flaring.

I tried to concentrate on the hissing, which was more of a prolonged 'heeeshh' sound. Snakes have no vocal cords. (Professor Owen in *The Anatomy of Vertebrates* wrote, 'The true "chordae vocales" are absent in serpents, and the voice is reduced to a hissing sound, produced by the action of the expired air upon the margins of the glottis.') But talk about high-pressure sales tactics. I thought for a moment they were going to threaten me with instant cobra death if I didn't back down. The King took another stick and played the cobra back and forth. He was good, I had to admit. He had the rhythm of the snake, hooking it away just as it tried to strike. His movements were easy, almost automatic, but his face showed real concentration. Once the snake came too close to his head and he moved it back very quickly. This was not a devenomed snake charmer's pet – it was deadly.

'This cobra is full of venom,' said the manager.

'I'm sure it is,' I said.

Somehow this implied threat diffused the argument about man-eating pythons. Sri Gobind started another long discussion with the manager and the word 'T-shirt' came up in most sentences, as well as '4 per cent', a lousy percentage for T-shirt profit by any standard.

It was left vague as we got back in the car. The thirty-five-footer was promised again, but with little conviction. 'It is always the bottom line with these fellows,' said Sri Gobind through the headrest. I kept quiet, watching instead the endless lines of bungalows we drove past, the new developments.

If you've seen the movie you'll know the line when Paul Newman reveals a card bluff and announces, 'Sometimes nothing is a real cool hand.' Well, I had nothing and it wasn't cool. I sulked indoors at Harun's, under the churning fans, avoiding even the garden and its threat of dengue. Sumi made tea and fried-batter delicacies and told me she knew of a *bomo* living in the Indonesian community some way off Jalan Damansara. She could take me, but I had to tell Harun.

Harun didn't laugh when I told him. 'It can be serious shit with these people.'

'Sumi said they can value my kris for me.'

'What*ever* you do,' he said, 'don't take the kris.'

The next day I took the kris with me for the *bomo* to value. Raman drove Sumi and me to the Indonesian shanty town in Harun's Daimler. Raman told me there was a *bomo* in his native village in Tregannu, who would be much better than Sumi's *bomo*.

Raman parked the car some distance away, and Sumi and I walked towards the corrugated-iron shacks. We crossed over an open concrete drain clogged with plastic bags and walked past scrawny chickens and a goat feeding on kitchen scraps. Sumi was holding on to my arm, but released it as some men appeared. She ignored them and we ducked into a darkened hut with a cleanly swept wooden floor. A blue cloth hung down covering an inner door. I sat on a plastic chair in front of a Formica-covered table. Sumi ducked through the hanging cloth and called the old woman, who came out drying her hands on her apron and smiling. She had grey frizzy hair, pinned on top, and a face lined with smile lines. She went back through the door and after a long while came back out with three glasses of tea. We all sat down round the table. She told me she could read palms, give me a lucky charm or put a curse on someone who had tried to harm me. She explained that they had to have really tried to harm me, otherwise it would backfire on me, because she only practised white magic and was not a *pawang*, a black magician.

I thought about putting a curse on Sri Gobind for wasting my time, but it seemed a bit harsh. I reached into my shoulder bag and brought out the kris. 'Is this *keris bertuah*?' I asked. 'A fortunate kris?'

She hardly looked at it. 'That is a tourist kris,' she said. 'It is not special.'

'It's over a hundred years old,' I said.

'It is old but it is nothing. Maybe it's lucky for you, though,' she said smiling.

She then inveigled twenty ringgit (five pounds) out of me and read my palm. She guessed my age correctly and said that my job involved television (looking at a word-processor screen all day, perhaps). She was right that I wasn't married and added, almost as an afterthought, that this year would be a lucky year to get married. Sumi beamed at me as this was related. The *bomo* was wrong about my number of siblings and told me that I suffered back pain, which I don't, though she offered to cure it. Sumi told her I was looking for snakes and the *bomo* said if I dreamed of snakes it would be lucky for me. This coincided with Japanese views on snake dreams: to dream of a white snake is considered a portent of wealth in Japan. She told me I'd wasted many chances but that my career was looking good. All in all, it was one of the more

61

lacklustre palm readings I've ever had. (Once I had my palm read in Japan, and the reader wrote out my father's name correctly transcribed into Japanese syllables.)

It was now dark and the generators in the settlement were starting up. We were about to leave when a younger man, whom I took to be a son, came in. He had a moustache and wore a sweat-stained singlet and baggy trousers. After speaking to the woman, he politely asked me to show the kris again. He unsheathed it and told me that for a kris to be lucky it had to be *tjatjap*, the blade when forged dipped in the entrails and brains of a snake.

Sumi screwed up her face in disgust.

'Yuk,' I said.

The young man reached down and softly held my hand. I thought it meant more palm reading. Instead, his attention was fixed on my flashy Seiko watch.

'How much for your watch?'

I misunderstood him and told him, 'I paid a hundred dollars. You can get them cheaper here in KL.'

'No, your watch. I'll buy it. Three hundred ringgit.'

'You can get them cheaper—'

'OK. Five hundred ringgit.'

Though this was double its value I didn't want the hassle of having to buy a new watch. 'No,' I said.

'One thousand. My last offer.'

Suddenly it was worth the hassle. 'OK,' I said, unbuckling the clunky steel bracelet.

'But you have to give me kris as a present.' He said this forcefully, as if the whole deal was concluded. He was looking at me now and not smiling.

'The kris is not for sale,' I said.

'I don't buy kris, I buy watch. Kris is present.'

'Kris is not present,' I said, beginning to dislike him.

He breathed out heavily. 'Fifteen hundred.'

'No deal, no present. Watch only.'

62

He looked disdainfully at my watch. 'I can buy watch like that in market.'

'Well, why don't you?'

He turned without speaking and left. Outside I asked Sumi what it had all been about. She didn't answer until we had left the encampment. 'This is proof,' she said. 'You cannot buy magic kris, it has to be a gift.'

Back in the car, Raman asked whether the people who lived in the shanty town knew where Sumi lived. Her friend knew but she wouldn't tell the *bomo*. Good, said Raman, otherwise they might try to come and steal the kris. Sumi said they wouldn't dare steal it because it was a magic kris. Raman berated her for her stupidity. Magic krises always had curved blades, he explained.

'Whatever you do, don't tell Harun about this,' I said. By now I too was at least half convinced that there was something magical about the kris. Colonel H. would, I'm sure, have mocked me for such thinking, but he wasn't above a bit of superstition when it suited him. In the old Oxfordshire house there were only two human statues: Laughing Buddha and Saluting Man. Saluting Man was carved out of jackfruit-tree wood by a Naga craftsman. He had a spear in one hand and saluted with the other and on his head was a hat made from the skin of a red tiger.

The WWF knew nothing about red tigers, but Colonel H. insisted they lived deep in the jungles of the Naga Hills, 'too far from a town for these environmental johnnies'. The red tiger is slightly smaller than the Bengal tiger and instead of having yellow and black colouring, it is red and black. The hat on Saluting Man was a piece of aging tiger skin, reddish orange and black.

When Colonel H. left his house I was surprised he did not take Saluting Man with him. They went back a long way and Colonel H. would refer to the statue as if it knew things obscure to mere humans. When Colonel H. got rheumatism in his hand, he said that a deep crack had appeared at the same time in the spear-carrying hand of Saluting Man. These things are linked, he'd say.

When I was young, Colonel H. had explained the kris to me in frightening detail. He said they were used for executions because a good kris wielder could stab a man without drawing a drop of blood. He led me to believe that the Malay distaste for seeing blood was connected to running amok. 'Too fastidious. A bit like Japs. Have to let off steam somehow. Of course it's also genetic.' Colonel H. was a great believer in genetics for generalizations about races. When it came to individuals he was more canny. 'Bad blood' or 'inbreeding' could crop up in any genetically pure strain, as could 'one-offs' or 'singular exceptions' in races lower down the Colonel's genetic top ten. 'Warrior' races were always preferred to 'gentle people', especially if their warrior skills were used to fight oppressors like the British. In common with many of his generation he had a particular dislike for the Germans, though the Japs 'knew their onions'.

Once, before the television set blew up and we were reduced to sound only, I had been watching *The Banana Split Show* at the Colonel's. During one regular feature called 'Danger Island' ('O-oh, Chango, It's Dan-ger Island'), four white adventurers battled each week against thousands of coal-black cannibals in sub-Rider Haggard situations of extreme implausibility. I loved it. As a horde of cannibals streamed across the screen, Colonel H. commented, 'They're the good guys.' 'No, Grandad,' I said, 'it's the other men.' He repeated his statement, which for a young lad was utterly incomprehensible: 'No, the black fellows are the good guys.'

The word 'racist' meant nothing to him, and as his greatest kindness and affection were reserved for those he considered beneath him, the term does not easily apply. Isn't racism about hatred and separation rather than love and tolerance?

And though he would never admit it, it was love that the Colonel felt towards 'his people'.

It was the charity preview of *Scintillations*. Everyone who was anyone, and quite a few who weren't, gathered at the huge estate of Hijjas Kasturi, the leading architect in Malaysia. Harun borrowed his father's Mercedes 500 to drive us to the event. We followed the Swedish ambassador, who drives a Volvo, down the long private road through tamed jungle to the magnificent modern palace created by Hijjas. There was some confusion about parking and I noticed that the British ambassador, in a Rolls-Royce with Union Jack pennants, was the cause of the traffic hold-up.

The modern skyline of Malaysia's capital owes more to Hijjas than any other person. Apart from the Twin Towers, he and his firm have designed almost every tall, big or simply very noticeable building in Kuala Lumpur in the last thirty years. I was keen to see his own place, for though I did not actively dislike Hijjas's public buildings, I've noticed that all too often the most experimental architects live in the most conservative dwellings. They reserve their experiments for the public.

Hijjas's palace did not disappoint. Huge and modern in a Frank Lloyd Wright kind of way, it had two vast sloping roof structures connected at ground level by a roofed but open walkway, an airy modernist cloister with high pillars which fronted a split terrace, down which poured a three-hundred-foot cataract of water. This flowed into two large pools, Olympic size, though full of koi carp and dotted with lilies. It made me feel, when standing on the cloister, that I was in a modern parthenon, made more splendid because it was a private residence.

There were other buildings discreetly located in the grounds. An all-glass motor museum contained Hijjas's

Jaguar car collection, complete in every respect, Harun assured me, from the first SS to the latest XK8, with a rare Le Mans D type and a Mark II used in a film by Bob Hoskins. There were servants' quarters, guesthouses, a complex of offices for 'working at home' and an underground art gallery for promoting local artists, which was his wife's passion. One room of the underground art gallery was reserved for Hijjas's architectural models, a showcase of his creations that so dominated the city.

A fifteen-minute excerpt from *Scintillations* would be danced along the wide causeway that separated the two pools. The five hundred or so guests shoved for viewing space along the cloister. The space was further limited by the classical Indian drummers who were partnered with a jazz ensemble to provide music for the extravaganza. I got the impression that being deprived of standing room was a rare experience for most of the guests. I wasn't surprised to see Fat Carl, in a beautiful white kaftan trimmed with gold, but I was amused to see Sri Gobind lurking behind the drum kit with an Indian girl.

He blundered towards me when he saw me. 'What are you doing here?' he asked.

'What are *you* doing here?' I countered.

He muttered something about publicity and wanting to see Hijjas's house.

'Any news on the snake?' I said.

'To tell you the truth, I think those chaps are barking up the wrong tree. Their hands are full with T-shirts, they have no time to go snake hunting.' Sri Gobind's Mont Blanc was displayed prominently in his well-ironed shirt pocket. For some reason it intensely irritated me. 'Do you want me to introduce you to some girls?' he asked.

'No,' I said, 'I already have a date with Miss Revlon Asia, reputedly the most beautiful woman in the world.' Which wasn't entirely true, the date part, I mean, but Sri Gobind was the kind of weasel you can only get rid of with superlatives. In any case Harun had tentatively promised a meeting after the performance, which counted, I thought, as a kind of date. It would be a test, confirming for me that I was right to be getting married and not pursuing other women.

As the band tuned up, I spoke to Zaki about my plans. I explained that Sarawak or Sabah in Borneo were better places to hunt snakes than peninsular Malaysia. I said that I was interested in meeting Penan tribesmen, who reputedly have the greatest knowledge of jungle lore among any nomadic forest dwellers. I had read a lot by and about Bruno Manser, who spent six years with the Penan and helped them organize resistance against the logging companies. If there was one foreigner Mahathir loathed, it was Bruno Manser. But Manser lived like a Penan for six years and left only when he heard his parents in Switzerland were ill. Manser was no tourist, nor a man on sabbatical from a centre of learning; he was, perhaps, a modern-day version of Colonel H.

Lickspittling anthropologists in cahoots with the Malay government scorned Manser's studies and his encouragement to direct action. Deals cut between university departments and logging companies made the Penan tribal areas off limits to journalists, a situation which suited both organizations. Meanwhile the logging and desecration of their fragile way of life continues. I didn't know this for sure, but I guessed it was closer to the truth than the Penan people embracing bulldozer culture with open arms, enjoying forced relocation to shabby concrete encampments and welcoming the wanton destruction of the trees they worshipped.

Zaki nodded as I ranted against Mahathir and his shameless modernization programme. He was less sure when I got on to tribal people.

'The only thing I know about the Penan is that they have like this weird coconut hairstyle.'

'Uh-huh?'

67

'Yeah, like this guy came to my school and played Penan music. He was Malaysian, but he had a coconut.'

It was true that Manser also favoured a Penan hairstyle.

'If you hang with the Penan, you'll end up with a nut cut!' Zaki said with glee.

'Why go to Borneo?' asked Harun.

'I've got to get into the jungle,' I said.

'They're pretty hard on activists in Borneo right now,' said Harun.

'I'm not an activist,' I said.

'I know, but if you go to Borneo you might become one.'

The lights dimmed, the tabla drummers started drumming, the spotlights swept the causeway and the performance started.

'Which one is Miss Revlon Asia?' I whispered.

'The one wearing that jellyfish costume,' said Harun.

I should have guessed. She was outstandingly beautiful, and graceful too, considering she was dressed as a jellyfish.

At dinner I sat opposite a Norwegian paint millionaire who'd just opened a plant in Malaysia. He was a big man with a red face and at first he beamed with charm, being most solicitous of his Malay hosts, Harun's mother and sister and Harun himself. He reserved a different behaviour for Europeans.

'You won't find what you're looking for,' he said bluntly when I explained my quest. Perhaps being a boss made him think he was an expert on everything.

'Oh, really?'

'You're looking in completely the wrong place.'

'Where do you suggest?'

'South America.'

'Anacondas are fat but they're not long,' I said.

'The longest snakes aren't in Malaysia,' he said.

'They aren't in South America either,' I replied. Deadlock.

68

'You know, Rob's thinking of going to Borneo, but I'm trying to persuade him otherwise,' said Harun.

Taking in the grand sweep of the place, Harun's mother said, 'All my children studied law. I do wish one of them could have been an architect.'

The paint millionaire went off to refill his plate.

'What's his problem?' I said.

'Paint fumes,' said Harun.

Miss Revlon Asia appeared at our table. She still wore her dance make-up, though she had shed the ungainly jellyfish costume. There was a perfect regularity about her Eurasian face, and her body could not be faulted. But as introductions were made, I realized how strongly she craved attention. The applause of the audience had not been enough. In a way this was a nice thing because it made her human and vulnerable. But someone who is too eager for attention brings out your human desire to starve them of it. As Harun would say, my small talk evaporated. Married life would be easy at this rate, I thought.

Sri Gobind cornered me at the buffet, in front of a huge curry tureen. He had dripped curry on his shirt, though the Mont Blanc was unscathed. 'I don't mind you dating Malay girls,' he said.

'Thanks very much.'

'You're an educated man. But what I hate is when I see a Malay girl running after' – he thought for a moment – 'a cobbler from Manchester who hasn't had a bath in five days.'

'I agree,' I said. 'Unwashed cobblers are the worst.'

Harun made a last-ditch attempt to persuade me not to go into the jungle to look for a giant snake. 'It's a harsh environment. There are leeches, mosquitoes, poisonous spiders and thorns. Everyone who goes into the jungle gets crucified by the thorns.'

'But you told me you've never actually been into the jungle.'

'I know,' said Harun. 'But I've hovered over it in a Super-Puma, checking out timber concessions. It's a dangerous place.'

I couldn't help but smile.

'You can't make mistakes there,' he pleaded.

The party was winding down. I slipped off to have a look at the underground display of Hijjas's architectural models. Down a wide flight of concrete stairs I entered the glass-doored gallery. The air conditioning hit me and made, as it always does for a few moments, a delicious change from the heat outside. I wandered alone in the deserted gallery, getting tiny electric shocks off the carpet as I touched the glass display cases. So many buildings, so much white concrete, cantilevers, steel and glass. So much impudence in the face of nature. How could it last?

THREE

Dung Sniffing in Borneo

Pythons bite like dogs.   *C. J. Ionides*

'KK,' said Roy Goh, the *Borneo Post* crime correspondent, 'used to be a *really* dirty city.'

We were driving in Roy's 1974 Datsun through the outskirts of Kota Kinabalu, the capital of Sabah, North Borneo, on our way to an illegal drinking establishment. A friend had recommended Roy as a useful snake-hunting contact in Borneo. We drove down a street of prostitutes, then Roy doubled back so that we could take in a street of transvestites. 'Even now there are more TVs in KK than you'll ever see in KL,' he said proudly. 'By the way, how's your BM?'

'What?'

'Bahasa Malay, the Malay language.'

'Oh, that. Not too bad. I can get by,' I said.

Roy liked acronyms, shortcuts, being nippy. He had a fat body and a big moon face, which surprised me, because he didn't have a fat voice on the phone. He moon-smiled at me with nervous sympathy as he flicked through the gears and downloaded information. On the back seat was his flashpack and battered Nikon. Roy was the sole recorder of crime in North Borneo. It was night-time, but his face glistened with exertion.

'The worst thing I covered was a landslide. A whole village of Indonesian migrant workers buried in mud, 138 killed. I had to photograph people having mud sucked from their lungs, but everyone they sucked who I photographed was

71

dead.' He shook his head, lit a cigarette and threw the gold pack back on the dashboard. Then he apologized and offered me one. 'B&H,' he explained. He shook his head again. 'I still have dreams about that mud slide. Bad dreams.'

Roy was twenty-four, Christian, part Chinese, part Kadazan-Dusun. I picked up on that, and asked if he was related to the snake-worshipping Dusuns.

'The problem is, the British called everyone in North Borneo Dusuns. The real tribe live near Mount Kinabalu, but they're market gardeners, not snake catchers. I'll ask my dad, though, he should know.'

We drove past Roland Ng's cybercafé and the Tungnan bookstore, which earlier that day I'd discovered actually sold sporting goods; this was confusing because Longbee Wholesale of Sport and Stationery sold clothes and Tai Sen Electrical was a laundry. KK was hotter and steamier than KL and I'd spent a lot of the day going into shops which weren't what they seemed.

'How was your day?' I asked Roy.

'Pretty busy. Two murders, a robbery and a case of cheating. Murder victims both immigrants, one Indonesian, one Filipino. It sounds bad, but it's statistically true: 95 per cent of crime in Sabah is caused by illegal immigrants.'

'How about the cheating?'

'That was a Malay guy, a legal immigrant.'

We pulled up at the illegal drinking den, which was a big veranda with heavy wood tables and chairs. David, the Christian Indian owner, brought us ice-cold cans of Carlsberg, all stamped 'No duty paid in Malaysia'. They came by speedboat from the duty-free island of Labuan, a few miles off the North Borneo coast, and were half the price of legal beer.

We drank a lot of beer with Roy's friends, and when the conversation lapsed they started to poke fun at David, calling him a *kiling*. The word comes from the noise made by the chains of indentured rubber tappers, brought from India by the British. Malay Indians hate to be called *kilings*, but David laughed gamely. They relented and said he was 'a black Indian with fair legs'. David dutifully rolled up his trousers to show that his legs were, indeed, lighter in hue than his face.

'Tell me,' said David earnestly, 'is Cliff Richard still young?'

'He looks young,' I said, 'but I think he's fifty.'

'Is he married?'

'No, in fact, I read somewhere that he lives alone and is celibate.'

The drunken Kadazans laughed uproariously but David ignored them. He showed me a cassette of Cliff's hymns. 'Is this how he looks?' There was a picture of the ever-young Cliff strumming a guitar in a nativity scene.

'Yes, that's how he looks.'

'Then he is still young!'

A cousin of Roy's, who had a Charles Bronson moustache and a seventies-style long haircut, asked if I was married. Earlier he had been obsequious, but after several beers his manner became boastful, interspersed with tiny burps.

'No, I'm not married,' I said.

'Best way.' Burp.

'But I'm getting married when I go back to England.'

He raised his eyebrows ironically. Burp. 'Do you know the only way to keep a marriage alive?' Burp.

'No.'

'Adultery.' He took a long slug from his beer and burped again. Burp.

Peter, a tall man, part Kadazan, part Indian, part Chinese, was keen to interrogate me. 'Where are you from?'

'England.'

'What town?'

'London.'

'I hate London. It's so cold and unfriendly.'

73

'Been there, have you?' I said.

'I was a student, for two years.'

'Bad place to be a student.'

'It's a bad place, London.'

'When were you a student?'

'Seventy-seven, seventy-eight.'

The conversation had dry-docked. I took a sip of beer and hoped Peter would shut up. He must have had a terrible time in London if it was still bothering him twenty years later. 'One thing, though, that TV programme *Mind Your Language* is true. I liked that show.'

Mind Your Language was a comedy set in a language school, made in an era when racial stereotyping was uncomplicated ground for a comedian.

'I liked it too,' I said.

As the Kadazans got drunker, the conversation went through a maudlin phase.

'What is there to do except drink and tell stories?' said one.

'I'd rather save one man than fail to save a hundred,' said Roy, still haunted by his landslide experience.

'I just realized,' said another, returning from David's garden, 'I prefer pissing to drinking!'

It was really time to go home. The only snake information I had gleaned was that a large python had been washed up recently on Pulau Banggi Island off the north coast of Borneo. 'Maybe twenty feet long,' it was agreed. Reticulated pythons are well known for their ability to swim oceans. The first animals to repopulate Krakatoa after the devastating 1883 volcanic eruption were reticulated pythons which had swum hundreds of miles across open sea. Because of their elongated single left lung (the right lung is rudimentary and nonfunctioning) which runs most of the length of their body, snakes have both a built-in buoyancy aid, and, in comparison to other animals with lungs, a huge air capacity driving a very oxygen-efficient system. All snakes can spend a considerable time under water without breathing, many in excess of half an hour, so swimming is an activity that holds no fear for them. As a reticulated python also holds the world record for going without food – 679 days – a long sea crossing presents few problems.

As he drove me home, Roy catalogued the range of crimes he usually reported on. Today's murders had been unusual; most often he had to report on cases of cheating, but there was also a problem with fish-bombing (dynamiting reefs to catch fish) and shabu, meta-amphetamine addiction. There was solvent abuse among Filipino children and cough-mixture addiction among the Malays. Recently, he said, there had been a fresh outbreak of buffalo-dung sniffing.

'Buffalo-dung sniffing! Come on, Roy, you're kidding!'

Roy didn't smile. He was serious. Kids of all ages were loitering behind buffaloes just waiting for them to drop their load. 'Then they crowd in and inhale.'

'Inhale what? Methane?'

'It's very addictive, whatever it is. They're thinking of bringing in new laws to stop people letting their buffaloes wander anywhere. It's too much of a temptation.'

The next day I got a telephone call at my hotel from Wallace Wong, a cousin of Roy's. 'Are you named after *the* Wallace?' I asked.

'Of course,' he replied. I felt this was a good omen. Wallace told me he'd just heard from a friend at the National Parks Department that they'd confiscated a big python. 'You're welcome to it,' he said.

'How big?'

· 'Big.'

I felt the familiar rush of excitement. It made it easy to ignore the wall of heat as I strode with purpose out of the air-conditioned hotel.

Wallace Wong was Borneo's first and only deer farmer. He had trained in Australia and New Zealand, and he still had a certain antipodean prickliness about him. He was suspicious of me until I revealed I'd once eaten a chocolate-coated bumblebee (during a school science lesson). He hadn't been impressed by crocodile or ostrich meat but the bumble-bee did the trick. Wallace was three-quarters Chinese, and told me, 'In the Canton snake market, reticulated python flesh is more expensive than prime beef.' As a child he had suffered from asthma, but he'd been cured by being fed whole monkey minus only its fingers, toes and innards. Asthma ran in the Wong family. 'I'm now buying flying foxes for my son, they're supposed to be a better cure than monkey.'

'You could always try sand-viper venom, in minute doses, of course,' I said.

Wallace nodded, as if he was willing to give anything a try.

I had been collecting snake cures for a while. Python flesh was supposed to cure tuberculosis and Pliny wrote that snake fat, rubbed into the head, was a cure for baldness. Snake gall was said to cure the bites of mad dogs, though this was probably a mimic cure for the regularly successful, though unproven, method of treating a snake bite by using the gall of the snake that has bitten the human. Snake excrement also has a long and interesting history. In his memorable 1862 work *The Excreta of Reptiles in Phithisis etc.*, Dr Hastings wrote, 'I only seek to prove that the excreta are the most powerful auxiliaries in rectifying the range of corruptions yet discovered.' Python excreta was good for relieving tuber-culosis and could be taken internally as long as too much nausea did not result. Dr Hastings employed a 'strange man' who frequented London zoo to scrape up the snake shit from cages.

Wallace wanted me to help him design a zoo. His friend,

who was a deputy minister in the Parks Department, wanted Wallace to implement his plan for a Borneo wildlife park. 'Let's face it,' said Wallace, 'a park will eventually be the only place to see animals. In a couple of generations there won't be any trees left in Sabah.' But Wallace knew only about deer. I was to be the snake expert and the chief contact for other zoo experts in England. I told Wallace about Ernie and he got excited. He thought Ernie was just the right man for the project.

With Wallace referring to me as a snake expert, I wondered how I'd shape up handling the big snake caught by the Parks Department. Ionides wrote, 'Handling snakes requires maximum concentration, and it always helps of course to have a thorough knowledge of the snake you're dealing with.' He pointed out that too much pressure on the snake's head can cause the bones, which are not closely knit together, to flatten out, allowing the snake to jerk free. Another problem was securing the snake's body. 'Unless the body is also held firmly certain snakes will start gyrating, whirling around from the neck until they break free.' As a piece of general snake-handling advice, Ionides suggested that snakes with a tight skin, like cobras and vipers, should not be held too rigidly at the head. Snakes with slacker skin, like pythons, can be held much more rigidly.

Wallace met me at the Parks Department headquarters. We went in to see his friend, the deputy minister, who sat behind a huge desk in an office. The deputy minister was a Malay; Roy had told me you had to be, to get on in public-service jobs. He had wet, rubbery lips, and when he stood up I was surprised at how short he was. We went downstairs and clambered into his chauffeured Land Cruiser which was parked outside. The tiny deputy had to make a considerable high step to get into the front. We then drove, chatting amiably, around the building and into the car park beneath the building. After our twenty-second drive the chauffeur pulled up behind a pick-up truck. The snake was in a bag in the back, the minister explained.

I approached the pick-up thinking, Well, of course it won't be that long, but what if it is? What if it is? I had to restrain myself from running like an excited child. Then, about three yards from the tailgate of the shiny new burgundy pick-up, I saw blood dripping on to the oil-stained car-park concrete. I looked over the tailgate and the metal runnels of the pick-up bed were awash with thin, red-brown blood. There were two supermarket plastic bags in the back. Cautiously I lifted one open. Chopped into two-foot-long steaks was a python, its markings still beautiful, but smeared with blood.

'Oh, dear!' said the deputy minister. 'I thought it was alive.'

The confiscated python would have been about twenty feet long; not long enough, but it still made me sad to see it so neatly chopped.

Roy's father was an expert on the jungle and the wildlife in the jungle. He was an official hunter, responsible for culling elephant if they got out of control and ran amok. He told me he had once driven over a snake that was stretched full length across a road. At first he thought it was narrow tree trunk. Only after driving over it did he realize what it was. I have heard similar stories from Japan and North America. Another version is sitting on a log for lunch or a smoke when the snake suddenly comes alive. Not that I disbelieved Roy's father, it's just that his story had the form of an urban myth. He cautioned me about reticulated pythons in general.

'They have about a hundred recurved teeth, two rows each side at the top, one at the bottom. The strike can be vicious – a slashing bite that can sever arteries and tendons.' Roy looked on with pleasure at the prospect of a slashing python bite. His father continued, 'This python has the longest teeth of any nonvenomous snake, and in the Bornean jungles it's an alpha predator, whatever man may think!'

'You saw that picture, didn't you?' Roy chipped in.

I thought back to the infamous *New Straits Times* photograph of 1995 – a dead man with his head and neck totally inside the distended jaws of a twenty-two-foot python, its fat coils enveloping him in a body-length death grip. The blood that stained the seemingly headless torso was particularly offputting. I grinned and waved my hand in a way that was intended as casually dismissive. 'He was probably asleep when that snake caught him,' I said.

Roy's father nodded politely.

Deep down I started to get snake fear for the first time. It was little consolation to hear from Roy's father that the constricting muscles of a snake are not used for defence – a big python will strike like any other snake, with coiling and crushing reserved for potential meals and not aggressors. But the fear still lodged on the idea of a really nasty bite.

The tension in the air was broken by Roy's mother bringing in some rice wine for me to try. 'Now they're all Christian in the jungle you can only really drink this stuff in town,' said Roy's father.

He told me, and Roy immediately agreed, that the place I should visit to pursue long snakes was Long Dao, a remote Lundaiya tribe village very close to the Indonesian border. The Lundaiya tribe were former headhunters, converted to Christianity in the 1950s. They used to worship snakes and one old man in the village still wore a python-skin vest rather than a football shirt.

Roy's father had visited the village four years before. He gave me a photograph of a family he had stayed with, the Balan family. One of the sons played for the first division Sabah side; football was keenly followed in the village and he was Long Dao's most famous son. Roy's father told me to give the photo to old man Balan. Then I could stay with him. 'But you'll have no problem about where to stay, everyone will want you to stay with them. Remember, though, there's no smoking or drinking allowed in Long Dao, now that they've become Christian.'

Roy and his father gave me advice on what I should take as a gift for the headman, since the usual gift of tobacco would now be highly inappropriate, if not insulting. They thought metal dishes, bars of soap and towels would go down well as gifts for anyone I stayed with. When Roy's father visited, he had handed out piles of his children's old clothes.

Then I had a brainwave. 'How about taking a football as a gift for the headman?'

Roy and his father thought it was a good idea but they warned me that footballs were expensive in Kota Kinabalu. But my mind was made up; somehow I knew the football was a perfect gift.

'Remember,' repeated Roy's father before I left, 'only smoke in the jungle, and *never* mention rice wine.'

In KK none of the sports shops sold footballs. I took a bus out to Penampang, a place famous for its weekly *tamu*, or market, where everyone from the outlying jungle came to buy and sell their wares. I did not find a football, but the variety of goods on sale was intoxicating. There were eels in plastic bags, rubber boots and chainsaws, gamelan cymbals and desiccated warty toads, tables laden with nuts of all kinds and others selling only rambutan, something like a lychee in a prickly outer shell. Several traders arranged their goods on a mat on the ground. One toothless old man with a wispy white beard and almost shut eyes had in front of him a vast variety of jungle woods, herbs and dried seahorses. He was also selling silver Straits dollars, all mysteriously dated 1925 and still a currency in the remotest parts until recent times. These were possibly silver, but had certainly been cast by some inventive craftsman long after 1925.

I asked if he had any snake cures. He held up what looked like a dried root, and told me it was a cobra's penis. All male snakes actually have two penises close together, called hemipenes. The act of sex is made more interesting by the snake's hemipenes turning inside out just before insertion. This exposes sharp spikes that fix inside the female's body. If the female tries to escape, the male is simply dragged after her, his tail pulsating, a sure sign of sexual excitement.

In a small glass jar the aged trader had several grey stones. They were bezoars, concentrations of hardened material usually found in the stomachs of ruminants. The old man gestured, spoke rapidly and held one up for me to see. '*Ula batu*, snake stone,' he kept repeating, claiming that the stone was made from concentrated snake venom. I shook my head and pointed to my stomach. He shook his head and said that the stone would glow red hot if a snake approached me. I had heard that bezoars were sometimes rubbed on snake bites to draw the venom off, but a glowing stone was a new one. I haggled viciously and, after storming off several times, bought my very own snake early-warning system for two pounds.

Back in Kota Kinabalu I found what I was looking for the moment I stopped looking in sports shops. In a shop sign-posted as a bookstore I bought a top-of-the-range leather football, imported from England and fake-signed by Manchester United football team. The headman will probably declare a national holiday when I hand that over, I thought with glee; or hand me the keys to the village and make me an honorary member of the tribe. I felt the football was my lucky talisman; it would carry me through the leap of faith needed to strike out for the jungle village.

It took three hours to get by fully laden taxi to Sipitang, a coastal town with a narrow beach littered with rocks and plastic bags snagged between rocks. Half the journey, along the suggestively named Jalan Pimping from KK, had been on dusty, untarmacked road, with the driver slowing for each hidden hole and sump-grazing rock. He knew the route all right and was trying to shave minutes off, overtaking logging trucks with considerable faith, powering blind into their following dust cloud and then out the other side, tucking in neatly to avoid head-on collisions. He dropped me next to a VW camper, anxious to be off, assuring me that this spot was the right one for Long Dao. Roy had told me there was a logging road which stopped at Long Siau, ten miles from Long Dao. From there I could walk or take a boat. 'But boats will be expensive,' he warned.

It was blindingly bright and hot and the spot next to the VW, where I stood with my bulging, football-carrying hold-all, was without shade. Thankful at such times for being a smoker, I took in the surroundings under pretence of lighting my ninth before last cigarette. Nine cigarettes to go before abstinence (I intended to hold my four cigars as a survival aid for forest use only). I didn't want to be tempted in the village, cause discord and perhaps suffer punishment. Whatever ex-headhunters do to people who break their tribal laws, I didn't want to find out.

Across the dusty road were low, open-fronted shops. In front of the one right opposite, on the raised wooden pavement, stood a few old men, talking and looking at me in a way that made it clear that foreigners didn't come often to Sipitang. I went over and made contact, offering cigarettes, politely declined, and asking for buses to Long Dao. A woman who was shopping came to my rescue. My Malay, aided by a dictionary, was producing amusement but few results. She spoke some English and my problem became hers. People stopped to talk to her, and soon we were the most interesting thing on the street. Agnes quickly told me her name. Agnes was a Christian, a Sabahan Baptist, and she was glad to discover that I too had been brought up a Protestant. She asked if I was married and I said yes. It was part of my tribal acceptance strategy. I didn't want to invite matchmaking, or incense men into believing I was after their women.

A major hurdle was discovering what kind of vehicles went to Long Dao. The VW camper couldn't, she explained. A four-wheel drive rumbled past; that couldn't go either. Then a pick-up. 'Like that, but tall,' she said. When a Toyota Hi-Luxe went past, sitting like a boat on its high-sprung suspension, she pointed and grew excited and even asked the driver if he was going in the Long Siau or Long Dao direction. He was not, but at least I now knew what to look out for: Hi-Luxe pick-ups with enough ground clearance to drive over a tree trunk.

Agnes's husband came along carrying two shopping bags. He had a scraggly beard and sinewy arms with blue ink tattoos of centipedes. Gruff but helpful, he went off to find a Hi-Luxe he thought was off to Long Dao. Agnes bought me a Coca-Cola, which I knew to be an expensive drink, but I hadn't a hope of paying. She handed out peanuts and we shelled happily on to the wooden pavement. People of all ages, though mostly villainous-looking, tattooed young men, oddly contrasting with the softly feminine Agnes, joined us for a time in eating peanuts and pondering the problem of getting me on my way. But even the tough-looking men were gentle in their manners and polite in their greeting and leaving. Descendants of a warrior people, I could hear Colonel H. saying.

Two hours passed easily. There were several false alarms as we flagged down Hi-Luxes. One was even going to Long Dao, but they wouldn't let me ride in the back when they saw I was a foreigner. I pleaded, but with a resigned placidity. Waiting by the road, I had complete faith that something better would turn up.

Agnes's husband returned. He reported that a man called Nelius was in charge of transport to Long Dao and that he would be around later. Hovering behind Agnes's husband was a short, slight young man who by his diffidence made it hard to tell if he was part of the team effort. I said hello and he told me his name was Lite. After several minutes it became clear that Lite was there to look after me until the man Nelius was found. Lite, who came from Long Dao, thought we should go to a different part of town to wait, so we left at a quick pace. He offered to carry my heavy bag, but I insisted and Lite did not argue.

We went to Chicken Wing McDoodle's, which, being the only place serving Western food, and twice the price of other joints, was *the* place to be seen at in Sipitang. Lite revelled in the meagre luxury of McDoodle's with its air conditioning and green plastic tables. He told me he always came here when he came to Sipitang. I picked at my wings, knowing that this would be my last Western food for a long time. It was a pity it was junk food, but Roy had told me I'd be eating sticky rice and snake meat in the jungle, so I made the most of it.

Roy's father had instructed me on the etiquette of the Lundaiya people. Don't come to the point too soon. Explain where you've come from. Eat what's offered, and whatever you do, don't refer to the three-day rice-wine-drinking orgies that went on before the Christians got hold of them. I didn't tell Lite about my pythoneering; I'd come to that point later. Right now I was keeping it simple, following Lite's lead, saying only that I wanted to visit his village.

My afternoon with Lite had a dreamlike quality. It was like a return to boyhood, hanging around town without much to do, not talking much but agreeing mostly, no struggle for dominance, things done because they're the obvious thing to do, a few good laughs, no agenda but no boredom either. In fact he reminded me of a friend I'd had when I was small.

He had the same startled-rabbit look and brush-cut hair a little long at the back. It came as a shock when he told me he was twenty-six.

Lite always asked me if I wanted to do something just before we were about to do it. I always agreed, and this was how I found out what would happen. Slowly things began to fall into place. The Long Dao football team had come that day to play against a team made up of those who had been born in Long Dao, but had left the village to settle along the coast. The village team would return home the following day. Nelius was the football team's manager, which was why he knew about transport. Lite was staying at SFI, which sounded like a shop.

SFI, Sabah Forest Industry, was a model housing estate for the thousands employed in the logging trade. Lite's uncle worked there and had a neat bungalow. We turned up there, with others we'd picked up along the way, in a minibus shuttling the short distance to and from town. The roads and dwellings were all the same and SFI was a huge place, a mini-town in its own right. There was a horrible stink of putrid seaweed which Lite told me was caused by the paper mill, which stood like a monstrous concrete cathedral, with glinting metal silos and smoking chimneys, right in the heart of SFI. Lite said I could stay at his uncle's that night, and he was happy when I said yes and dumped my bag in one of the back rooms.

In the front room, decorated with Tom Cruise posters and football trophies, tough-looking young men with tattoos came and went, carrying football boots. The tattoos were often of centipedes or insects, well drawn in blue, logging tattoos, Lite explained. He had none. Lite didn't like logging and had only worked once, for eighteen months at a resort hotel up the coast. He'd been a car jockey and then a barman, and he'd really liked that. But working every day had got him down, so he drifted back to the village where life revolved around fishing, swimming, a little hunting, and football. He was so self-effacing it took a while for me to realize that Lite played for the Long Dao team. He hadn't wanted to tell me outright for that would have been a boast. To play for the team was to have warrior status, no subject for idle self-aggrandizement.

Lite and two other players polished their boots and we set off for the match. The stadium in Sipitang had concrete seating in terraces. The teams got changed on the terraces. They had excellent kit: boots of professional standard, shin guards, numbered shirts, and a football that rivalled my own in quality. Two linesmen and a ref were correctly attired in black. This wasn't village football as I knew it. I'd thought Lite might ask me to play, to make up the inevitable lack in numbers, but I couldn't have been more wrong. There were six subs eagerly warming up and awaiting their shot at glory. A short-sighted foreigner whose main skill was performing deeply unprofessional fouls: no chance. It was also hot, even though it was late afternoon, so hot and so humid that I doubted if I could have lasted even twenty minutes of serious footballing exertion.

The terraces filled up, the teams finished their kick-about and the match began.

Both teams were very good – amazingly good, considering that only five hundred people lived in Long Dao. In England, being serious about football is being serious about supporting a football team. Village football is just a way of blowing off steam. Things were different here. There was a purity and grace to the way they played which suggested ritual rather than giving the other side a good hammering. It reminded me of the way the Japanese play rugby – a little too conscious of the way they look, a little too stylized. But the tribesmen were polite and good-humoured. Fouls were apologized for. Questioning the ref was shouted down by the other players.

A tussle for the ball which became an intricate tangle of legs produced laughter on both sides. The players were keen rather than aggressive, and none of them was lazy. I was sweating just sitting in the shade. At half-time they looked exhausted and each gulped down pints of water.

In the second half they slowed down, but still played well. Lite was a competent rather than excellent player. The Long Dao goalie, who I'd noticed had snake tattoos all over his body, had a tremendous boot. With considerable style he could loft the ball almost into the opposing penalty area. Later Lite told me he had tried out for the Sabah team but there had been 'problems'.

I discovered what the 'problems' were talking to Mr Nelius, the team manager. A dapper man, with shiny polished leather shoes and ironed slacks, a rather high voice and a know-all's demeanour, Mr Nelius was not the kind of man I would have expected the team to take seriously. But quickly I realized that Mr Nelius called the shots. He had made the team as professional as possible, he said, but there was one thing he could not stop. This was the 'problem'.

'What is it?' I asked.

'It is beer drinking,' he explained.

I pictured an orgy of celebratory quaffing after the match; in fact, given that I'd been led to believe drinking was *verboten*, I began to look forward to it. 'Celebrating their victory, I suppose?' I said.

'No,' said Mr Nelius. 'They do not drink after the match, they drink *before* it.'

I verified this as I went with the team for a round of 'mellow browns' after the game. The Long Dao originals had won 1–0 and we gathered in a café to celebrate. A mellow brown was a brown banana milkshake, refreshing enough, but unsatisfying, you might have thought, for tattooed former headhunters. Not at all. They all equally drank their mellow browns which Mr Nelius paid for. Maybe the goalie (who was an unrepentant drinker, hence his problems at the Sabah team trial) went off later and got drunk on his own, but I never found out.

I was pleased to discover about pre-match drinking. It confirmed my suspicion that the match was, in fact, a substitute head-taking raid. In the past young warriors would work up steam for a raid by drinking rounds of rice wine. The footballers were doing the same. Mr Nelius, being more staunchly Christian, wanted it to stop, but I liked the idea. Apart from Lite and two others, the football-warriors also smoked and I took this as an opportunity to smoke down to my last four cigarettes.

What happened next was a sleight of hand, or a devious piece of social manoeuvring. Mr Nelius intimidated Lite into giving up his new friend, me. It made me pretty sick to see Lite pushed around by Mr Nelius, but I was caught in Japanese politeness mode, triggered by Roy's father's insistence that I respect their customs. It's dangerous ground because it takes a while to sift out the customs from the simple human foibles. And you're going to make mistakes anyway. I think now I shouldn't have bothered.

First stop was a cinema which showed films on a video projector. It was called a minitheatre. There was a programme, but as we were the only customers, the Chinese owner showed us the last half of a Steven Seagal movie and the first half of a Hulk Hogan movie where Hogan had been hypnotized into believing he was Santa Claus. It was very possibly the worst film I had ever seen, but fortunately someone had lopped off the ending. I wondered if the minitheatre specialized in semi-double bills, because neither Lite nor Mr Nelius seemed to think it at all odd that we were leaving without seeing a complete film.

Lite deferred totally to Mr Nelius. It reminded me of a Japanese martial-arts disciple and a teacher: the same respect, the same silence unless spoken to, the same allowing the big man to pay. And Mr Nelius was anxious to pay, first for the films and then for a huge sweet-and-sour-sauce-covered fish we ate in a Chinese restaurant. Lite always served himself last and dutifully refilled water glasses when they were empty.

Mr Nelius was not only the manager of the football team, he was also the headmaster of the village school. As he dabbed sweet-and-sour sauce daintily away from his face, he informed me he was also a member of the church committee, head of 'internal security' and, ominously, head of the anti-smoking campaign. He was most proud of being head of internal security.

'What kind of internal security problems do you have, apart from the smoking?' I asked.

'Stealing chickens,' he said. 'We have had several cases of chicken theft recently.' For Mr Nelius, burgeoning crime was a sign that Long Dao was at last becoming really civilized.

Mr Nelius told me his younger brother Fowzi was 'head of tourism' in Long Dao. Since the first Hi-Luxe-passable road link had opened three months previously, Mr Nelius was anticipating an upsurge in tourism. The opening of the road coincided with the departure of an anthropologist who had been staying in Long Dao for a year studying Lundaiya language and customs. So I was sandwiched between the academics and the sightseers. I'd have to move fast; jungle life was changing with the times.

Both Lite and Mr Nelius spoke highly about Mr John the anthropologist from Manchester, England, who not only became a fluent Lundaiyo speaker, but was also good at football. I was beginning to hate him already.

We were driving around town in Mr Nelius's Hi-Luxe, me sitting in the front, poor old Lite exposed to the elements out back. We drove to Lite's uncle's and Mr Nelius got out and went and had a long conversation with Lite. Miserably

Lite came round and told me there was more room at Mr Nelius's cousin's, which was where Mr Nelius was staying, and where I was supposed to be staying. He went in and got my bags. At Mr Nelius's cousin's I was given a bed while the others slept on the floor. I was guest of honour because Mr Nelius was fitting me up to stay in Fowzi's new rest house, the first rest house ever to be built in Long Dao, in anticipation of the coming tourist boom. In Mr Nelius's eyes I was good material for the minister of tourism to cut his teeth on, and I would be the first person to rent the guesthouse (which at two pounds a night was cheap, I had to admit). To celebrate the deal, Mr Nelius cracked open some milk drinks which had been donated to the school. Taking milk from the mouths of infants, I began to wonder just how corrupt Mr Nelius was.

Nelius deemed it unsafe to have more than four on the back of his Hi-Luxe, so ten had to go on the back of the other one. I was in the front, which was dull at first, but when it began to rain and all the others had to shelter under pieces of ripped plastic, I was glad to be in the high cab. Nelius was a cautious driver, avoiding with care the overburdened logging trucks which drove down the middle of the dirt track which went the seventy-six miles to Long Dao. In dry weather the trip took four hours; in wet weather it could take days. We stopped at a river and I ate for the first time traditional Lundaiya food, pieces of meat and sticky saltless rice wrapped in a palm-leaf package. Each man wolfed down two packs of rice, except Nelius, who sat somewhat apart, eating, I noticed, a takeout from Chicken Wing McDoodle's.

We passed some areas that had been strip-logged for the paper mill. There was nothing standing except a few stumps and thin trunks with a chewed-off look in a root-strewn expanse of churned-up laterite soil. It looked as if the First World War had been fought there. But the paper logging soon gave way to areas that had been logged for big trees only. Both Nelius and I smiled when we saw a logging truck lying stricken on its side, rear wheels and axles hopelessly bent and the dark-skinned crew sitting in the shade smoking. One jumped up as we drove past, but Nelius ignored them. 'Indonesian drivers,' he explained.

Fifteen miles from Long Dao the logging ended and the road cut through virgin forest and small paddy fields cut by the villagers of Long Siau. Nelius hoped that it would stay that way. Despite his love of Western accoutrements, he didn't want logging to reach Long Dao. 'When the trees go, everything goes.' Admittedly there was an element of family interest at work – he realized that tourists would hardly be enticed by picture-postcard views of the Battle of the Somme.

The last fifteen miles were the toughest. Deep streambeds bridged simply with bundles of logs wired together slipped and trembled as we crawled over in the lowest gear. In a long stretch of deep mud the second truck was bogged down several times and the football team all had to get out and push. We splashed past them, Nelius honking the horn.

The only vehicles in Long Dao were three Hi-Luxes which were parked on a bluff overlooking the green sweep of the river valley. Huts roofed with tin stood around a village green. Buffaloes grazed. The longhouse where the old headman lived with several families was opposite the neat white church. We walked past the wooden school building to Nelius's hut. Outside every hut was a solar panel, a gift from a Sabah politician who needed tribal votes.

'Did you vote for him?' I asked.

'Yes,' said Nelius.

There was even a solar-powered streetlight at the edge of the green, there to illuminate the wooden duckboards that ran between ponds full of chirping frogs.

All the huts were six or seven feet off the ground, and you reached the veranda up a small ladder. Inside his hut Nelius showed me his solar battery cupboard and the solar light bulbs in every room. Drinking tea, we awaited the arrival of the head of tourism.

'Shouldn't I go and pay my respects to the headman?' I asked. This had been one of the instructions I had imbibed from reading about Bornean tribes and it had been reinforced by Roy's father.

'He is at the church now,' Nelius told me, 'it is better to see him tomorrow.'

Then I asked Nelius about the sign on the post outside the village which announced a one-thousand-ringgit fine for a first smoking offence and a five-thousand-ringgit fine or two years in jail for a second offence. Five thousand ringgit was more than a thousand pounds, equivalent to several years' wages for most Malays. Despite this astonishing disincentive I had already seen several men smoking inside the village.

'It is difficult to enforce the no smoking,' said Nelius. 'The young men want to smoke so they smoke. But I have stamped it out in the school and the clinic.'

Fowzi, the head of tourism, arrived with a deferential and yet canny air. He was a slim young man with big-knuckled hands from working in the fields. He announced that he would take me up to my rest house, which was awaiting its first tourist on the top of the hill overlooking the village. He shouldered my bag and we headed up the grassy path. Nelius made the surprising announcement that it was the first time he'd visited the rest house, a three-room bamboo structure on six-foot stilts. It had a tin roof.

Fowzi chipped a piece of resin off a big lump in the fireplace and quickly used it as a natural firelighter to start a fire. There was no chimney in the main room, but the wood was a special hardwood that didn't smoke. Split logs of firewood were stacked on a rack over the fire and somehow this absorbed what little smoke there was. Coffee was made, black with sugar and lots of grounds, and we sipped contentedly on the veranda, watching the sun go down behind the lines of hilly forest. The trees went on for ever, in successively more misty lines, like the screens on a stage, somehow two-dimensional. No one spoke for a long time, but it didn't matter. A few solar lights twinkled down below, a dog barked and then was silent. It was all very peaceful.

FOUR

The Headman Is Hiding

In different circumstances, I dare say, I might have
become quite a distinguished juvenile delinquent.

C. J. Ionides

It was cold. Light in cocktail-stick-thin strips showed
between the split bamboos that separated me from the misty
jungle-clearing hilltop outside. It could have been North
Wales. Hey, I thought the jungle was meant to be hot, hot
and steamy. But this was not the case, not at night, when I
shivered on the wooden sleeping platform, using a mosquito
net as a blanket and wearing two of the T-shirts I'd bought
as gifts for the welcoming villagers I was supposed to be
meeting.

It was so cold that I could not lie in bed. To use the
outside jakes required a slippery trip down a back ladder and
a fearful tread through long grass to a vertical hut, whose
door was so low that I could see over it as I squatted. When
it's cold, fear of predators, vermin, venomous insects and
snakes becomes less intense. I could kid myself that they
were not there. Because I think of them as sneaky, and
anything with half a brain would not have been loitering on
that hilltop in such cold conditions.

But I was wrong. A jet-black hornet the size of my
Leatherman Tool perched on the wooden pole that supported the washing platform tacked on the back of the
hut. The hornet wouldn't let me ascend the ladder that led
over the platform (also floored in split bamboo) through the
back door into the hut. It kept dive-bombing and buzzing

me. In the end I walked from the shithouse right around the rest house and up the front ladder, but the front door was locked from the inside. In a rage I also noticed the beautiful misty morning and the way the river forked at one end of the village. The name 'Long' means the junction of two rivers. There was continuous barking from several locations down the hill, hidden in mist. A lot of dogs in Long Dao.

Round the back I just ignored the hornet as it nuzzled my hair. I hadn't been stung for a long time, probably the last time I was visiting Colonel H.'s hives nearly twenty years ago. Any immunity would have long worn off.

It was six thirty in the morning and time to light the fire, necessary at least to drive out the cold that gripped me throughout the night. Chipping the resin was difficult, but once done and lit with my lighter it burned like a gas flame. However, it did not set alight the hardwood, which pays for its smokelessness by being very slow burning and difficult to light. The resin went out several times and I cursed with frustration. My hands were black with soot and so were large parts of my forehead. I chipped off more resin, big crystalline chunks of the stuff – a pyro's dream – and split the wood with the parang I had bought in Sipitang just before leaving. Eventually a fire burned and the kettle boiled. Coffee was made and I was happy. This simple Boy Scout preparation cost me nearly an hour.

The snake totems stood outside the house of the python man. His son, the goalie who liked to drink, charged me a couple of pounds to take a photograph of him wearing the python-skin vest. It was a fascinating throwback to an era which passed in Europe with the ancient Greeks. At that time the uniform of the old snake cults was reinvented as the clothing of a warrior of a new religion of light. Plutarch wrote of them, 'The men of old time associated the snake most of all beasts with heroes.' Wearing the vanquished snake's skin is the origin of the term 'speckled hero', the snakeskin itself being speckled in pattern, and worn by the Apollo cult's heroic warriors. It demonstrated their triumph over the more ancient snake cults, a case of the vanquisher copying the uniform of the vanquished. A more recent example of this is the bearskin guard's hat that the British copied from the vanquished Russians of the Crimea.

In some ways it's not accurate to say the snakeskin-wearing hero tradition has passed in the West. In the David Lynch film *Wild at Heart* the hero pronounces, 'This here snakeskin jacket is a symbol of my individuality and belief in personal freedom.' Marlon Brando, always synonymous with the rebel hero, is mythologically clad in a snakeskin jacket in the 1950s film *The Fugitive Kind.*

I later verified that the main traditional Lundaiya costume was made of bark. I suspected that the python vest was for ceremonial purposes only. But now that Christianity had arrived, the light religion which had displaced the previous animal-worshipping cults of the Lundaiya, it could be worn as a sign of a warrior. Python man was, comparatively speaking, a modern warrior. He was not afraid to wear the snakeskin since he had Jesus on his side. The old bark-wearing Lundaiya would have eaten snake (as they do now) but they would not dare tempt the snake gods by wearing their clothes as medals or fashion accessories.

The old python man himself was hard at work in his field. When he came back he was glad his son had worn the python costume. I got the impression, which Fowzi encouraged, that the goalie was a loafer, and any activity, even posing for tourists, was better than doing nothing. The old man said he had made the vest himself many years before, and it had always been the only one in the village. With Fowzi translating into Lundaiyo, I explained my interest in pythons, especially very long ones. Apart from telling me he had caught and eaten one a few days before, the old man had little to tell me. I had a bar of soap and a metal dish with me, but I felt foolish handing them out. In the four years since Roy's father had been to Long Dao, a money economy had got going, making soap and dishes, though welcome, not nearly as welcome as cash. I had paid the son and that was enough.

Fowzi told me another hut had totems but the man who lived there had one eye and was a little crazy. This hut was on the outskirts of the village and did not have solar power. As we approached, two barking dogs came out and then slunk back. In place of conversation I had started a ritual of asking Fowzi the cost of everything. 'How much?' I asked.

'A good hunting dog can cost four hundred ringgit,' he said. This was nearly a hundred pounds.

'How much is a bad hunting dog?' I asked.

'There aren't any,' he said and smiled. 'Bad dogs are killed and eaten.'

Old One Eye worked away on his porch, weaving with great dexterity a basket with shoulder straps. Because of the way he held his head, his good eye seemed to have moved to the centre of his face, twinkling and grimacing like a large marble held in swivelling place by eyelids like walnut shells. The eye flickered up and down and saw everything and it echoed in some way the knotty pieces of wood, the serpent totems made from wood deformed by spiralling creepers, which had led me to the old man in the first place.

This hut was old One Eye's. Apparently he had only recently put up the snake totems, in imitation of the python man. Because of the overwhelming Christian devotion of the tribe, totems were only tolerated in the village as part of the new drive to get tourists. Somehow I couldn't see how old One Eye would help the tourist trade: he was grotesque to look at and more intent on basket weaving than answering my questions about snakes. But I saw he had a clove-cigarette pack on his porch, so I offered him one of my last cigarettes. He lit it, puffed noisily and swivelled his eye up to gleam at me.

At this stage in our relationship, Fowzi was a very conscientious translator. This is what old One Eye had to say: 'There used to be many big snakes in this place but because we eat them now there are only small snakes. We eat them too! If you catch one, wrap it in clay and bake it in the fire. The big snakes are in the forest. These people are frightened of snakes.'

'Do you know any special ways to catch snakes?' I asked.

'Shoot them.'

'I want to catch one alive.'

'Why?'

'For a zoo.'

'Are you doing "research"?' He said it in English.

'Yes.'

He laughed and told me about John the anthropologist who had come to the village and questioned everyone about their families and recorded in detail the stories known only to the old people. Unlike Fowzi and Nelius, he did not appear overly fond of John. Perhaps the anthropologist had not spent enough time listening to the old man, preferring instead the comfort of the headman's longhouse where he had stayed while he was in the village.

'He came and wrote down the stories, but now those stories are dead.'

I thought he meant that the stories were dying out but he corrected me.

'Those stories are not told because we now have the Bible. That is the living story.'

'But it is good to know the history of the tribe,' I protested.

'It does not matter. Now we have television. That is more interesting!'

'But what about jungle knowledge? Using plants as medicine, for example?'

'That is another subject. That knowledge, the thing that is useful to a man, he already knows.'

It seemed a marvellous defence of ignorance. I wondered briefly if old One Eye had heard of Socrates.

'It is true that the names of things have to be learned, but that is easy. But sometimes different plants are used for the same sickness. No one teaches you what plant to use. That you know already.'

'Do I know it?'

Old One Eye laughed at the idea. 'You know many other things.'

'But how do you know the things you have always known?'

'I dreamed them.'

Then the old man took up his basket and started to weave again. As we walked away, I asked Fowzi how he lost his eye.

'A bear scratched it out.'

I told Fowzi we needed to assemble a team, men who knew how to hunt and weren't afraid of snakes. Fowzi looked doubtful. 'I am not afraid of anything but now is a busy time for planting rice. Last year the government sent rice to the village because the paddy fields flooded and the rice plants were destroyed.'

Fowzi, it seemed, had killed snakes, including a python he said was thirteen feet long. He had never taken one alive, and looked to me to provide a methodology of capture. Ionides had favoured park-keeper-style metal grabs, but he mainly caught venomous snakes, where keeping your distance was essential. Rolf Blomberg, a Swedish naturalist, favoured forked sticks and rope lassos. In my plan I hoped to be able to surprise the snake while it was resting after a meal. At this point a rope loop, guided through a bamboo or other hollow tube, could be secured around its neck. It would then fall upon any helpers to wrestle the snake into being tied either lengthways to a long pole, or plopped into a suitably large crate.

We sat talking on the veranda of my hilltop hut. I told Fowzi he should call it the Bamboo Hilton. He had never heard of the Hilton Hotel chain and when it was explained, he rejected the name as confusing for tourists. His sense of humour, I realized, did not extend to his business. He changed the subject by asking me about my 'wife'. 'Do you have children?' he asked.

'No,' I said.

'I have three,' he said.

'Bad luck,' I said.

'No! It is good luck. It is you who have bad luck!'

'All right, good luck then.'

He looked at me suspiciously. I averted my gaze and took in the panoramic view of the river and the peaceful village. It was time to haggle. I told Fowzi I was not a rich man, not like the Germans who had flown in and been taken on a jungle expedition six months before. I now understood I was not the first visitor Fowzi had guided, but he assured me I was the first he had handled since going professional. I didn't like the sound of this. He assured me that being a professional meant that he wouldn't have to cut any trip into the jungle short in order to look after the farm work. He now had an arrangement with someone else to do that. After my experience with the avaricious Snake King, I was keen not to be cheated. When Fowzi mentioned a modest sum for his daily hire, including food (about fifteen pounds), I remained silent. Then he asked me again about my ideas for improving tourism in Long Dao. I wondered if it was flattery, but Fowzi seemed deadly keen. He whipped out a worn red cash book and a pencil stub and started to take notes.

'What is a jungle camp?' he asked.

It was a surprising question, but I quickly realized Fowzi was intent on providing tourists with the experience they wanted rather than the genuine thing. I drew for him a mini-village of lean-to huts. He explained that when Lundaiya go into the forest they just build a sleeping platform.

'But what is "jungle survival"?'

That was harder to convey, since he knew more about it than I did. He seemed a little unsure as I sketched in what to him was just a normal hunting trip. He then told me he had built a raft for the Germans, having seen a picture of one in a 'jungle adventure' brochure on a visit to Kota Kinabalu. 'Lundaiya only use log boat or plank boat,' he explained. 'The Germans are very tall and strong but they walk too slowly in the forest,' he said. I made up my mind not to be a jungle slowcoach.

Just before he left, Fowzi dropped his price by a quarter. 'Because you have helped me become more professional,' he said.

The great snake hunt was beginning to take shape. Fowzi told me that snakes go to waterfalls and mountains to commune with spirits. I told him that we should also consider where a large snake can get ample food. Caves too, I knew from my reading, would be a good place to go hunting. Fowzi clarified his position on waterfalls and mountains: 'The snake goes there from time to time, but it does not live there all the time.' I sensed that he was dubious about catching a snake when it was communing with spirits.

Fowzi told me he had once killed a snake, and when he came back to pick it up, another snake was attempting to mate with it. He'd killed that too. It is true that female snakes become particularly passive when they are receptive to mating, but it was the first time I had heard of the extreme passivity of death being mistaken for a come-on.

101

My strategy for the jungle was to cover as much ground as possible. If we found a likely snake site we would stake it out for as long as seemed appropriate. We decided to make a wide sweep through virgin forest, crossing into Kalimantan (illegally, in my case), taking in a place that Fowzi said contained many deer and a hilly region with caves. The nearest village in Kalimantan, also Lundaiya, was five days' hard walk from Long Dao. Fowzi said people sometimes made that hike to get duty-free cigarettes and visit relatives.

'How many days would the Germans take to get to that village?' I asked.

'Many weeks,' said Fowzi.

Every morning Fowzi brought me fried banana fritters and brewed up coffee. For lunch and dinner he alternated wild boar with venison stew. He served ferns on the side as vegetables. With everything we either had packets of pudding rice prepared by his wife and wrapped in a banana leaf or the same rice boiled on the fire.

I still hadn't told Fowzi about my football, but I kept pestering him to arrange an introduction to the headman. I'd been several days in the village and I still hadn't handed over my photograph to Mr Balan. I had convinced myself I shouldn't do this until I'd made contact with the headman. Apart from old One Eye and the python man, Fowzi seemed to want to isolate me from the other villagers. From Fowzi's inadequate directions I eventually found Lite's house, but he'd gone on a fishing trip, his smiling father told me. I trudged back up the hill to the lonely splendour of my bamboo palace and waited for Fowzi to bring supper and news of the great snake hunt recruitment drive.

'It is difficult to get good men in Long Dao,' whinged Fowzi, smearing his sooty hands on his sagging tracksuit bottoms. 'The men in Long Dao have no vision!' Fowzi was a fan of Prime Minister Mahathir, who originated the slogan '20:20 vision for a technocratic Malaysia by the year 2020.' 'I have Vision Long Dao,' said Fowzi, his eyes gleaming with can-do mania. 'We will build tourism, start a coffee plantation and increase basket production.' Then he paused. 'Who is WWF?' he asked.

I told him about the World Wide Fund for Nature. He told me that WWF wanted to stop logging before it got to Long Dao. Would they help the villagers? Fowzi demanded. I didn't know, but 'at least someone is on your side', I said.

Over the days we spent planning the trip, various men had dropped by, ostensibly to have a word with Fowzi. They came with their dogs, rangy, wiry men, older than me, smiling, yet wary, always polite. I wondered if they were all recruits.

'OK, just how many men have you managed to round up?' I eventually asked.

Fowzi looked shifty. I braced myself for another speech deploring the villagers' lack of vision. 'They go to Sipitang,' he said. 'They know the outside world. But when they come back there is only here for them. They forget the outside world. Like Lite, he only goes fishing or swimming. They don't want to work. The old men are better. They respect me for what I am trying to do. They are prepared to work hard like me—'

'How many?'

'One.'

'One?'

'One, but he is a very good man.'

For former snake hunters, the Lundaiya were surprisingly reluctant to go out hunting snakes. It seemed that instead of me selecting them, they were selecting – or rather, not selecting – me. I seriously wondered whether three of us would be enough to capture a thirty-foot python weighing over three hundred pounds. We might capture the snake but could we carry it? I made a deal with Fowzi that if we caught the snake, one of us would come back to the village to get help. He assured me that once it was caught, everyone would help out. He explained that people would have no choice in that case. To prove it wasn't all vain talk, Fowzi took me to see his uncle, who laid out several python skins for inspection. A skin can be stretched up to 20 per cent after removal, but these were still impressive skins. One was twenty-eight feet long. His uncle had shot the snake after he'd found it gorging on a deer caught in a trap.

'Where did you catch it?' I asked excitedly.

He gestured vaguely. 'Nearby. But it is the only *ula besar*, big snake, I have seen in my life.'

Lite came to visit me one morning and brought some freshly killed venison in a blood-smeared plastic bag. He smiled his shy smile and asked me if I wanted to go swimming with him. I instantly agreed and we trotted fast down the hill, wetting our feet in the dewy grass, to the place where the two rivers joined. 'This is my favourite place for swimming,' said Lite. We stripped off, down to undershorts in my case, and swam in the quite cold river. Lite dived under and went a long distance holding his breath. I didn't follow him, cautious as always and remembering the case of Brad, an American I met in Tokyo who spent three days in Indonesia, swimming in a delightful river on one of those days, before returning to Japan with an annoying earache. The earache got worse and worse, moving through a muted tinnitus to a continuous sound, he resignedly told me, resembling the noise made when you upset a pile of saucepans. After scans and probes had gone the full distance to Brad's eardrum, the doctors could only shake their heads. Certain pills they gave him diminished the noise, but Brad now found he was losing his balance. When I last saw him, he grinned with touching optimism and told me they were pretty sure it was some kind of rare boring insect that had penetrated into the Eustachian canals of his middle ear. 'We're kind of waiting now for it to either make a right turn into my brain, or a relatively harmless left turn into my sinuses.'

I kept my head above water.

Lite took me to a shallower, gravel-bottomed part of the river, which was much warmer, and we floated contentedly. I saw no fish and Lite told me you had to go an hour by boat from the village to get good fish. There were water snakes, though, he said. Compared to rare boring insects, water snakes are nothing. In freshwater rivers there are no poisonous water snakes in Borneo. And even the highly toxic sea snakes with their black and yellow markings are deadly only if they bite you in the narrow skin between the fingers and toes – their mouths are simply too small to get a grip anywhere else.

Lazing in the water with Lite, I was struck again by how similar this jungle setting was to other places I had already visited. The river, with its gravel and weeds, was very like the lower stretches of the Tech River in southern France. The hill that overlooked the village, with its knee-length meadow grass, was similar to any overgrown hillside in rural Surrey. The cropped grass field around which the church and the longhouse were arranged was like any village green in Olde England. My trip to Long Dao, with its woodfire cooking and rural pursuits, was more like a trip back in time than one in space.

We came out of the river dripping and sat for a while in the sun. I admired Lite's plank-sided dugout, which had cost considerably less than a good hunting dog to have built. The bottom section was half a hollowed log, with planks to build up the sides, bow and stern.

On the subject of the headman, Lite explained that the old headman had recently been deposed, or made way for another, it was hard to tell. I decided to quiz Fowzi and Nelius about this.

I had met Nelius on several occasions since arriving in the

village. Each time he had urged me to watch Long Dao's single satellite TV set which was installed in a hut called the community centre. It was the only broadcast TV in Long Dao, and on any evening as I went past I could always see a few souls sitting on scruffy chairs watching Astra TV or some such rubbish. To my mind it was too close in my memory to the college TV room of my university days, a room I managed to avoid for three years. A few of the rich villagers, those on a government salary like Nelius, or ex-government employees, like the aging sergeant major who claimed to remember Colonel H. from his time in KL during the Emergency, were wealthy enough to have video recorders driven by solar power. When Nelius eventually sensed I hadn't come twenty thousand miles to watch satellite TV, he took to trying to entice me into his house to watch a video. He had the latest Bond movie, more my class of viewing, he hinted with his knowing smile. As head of internal security Nelius had his blind spots – it was a pirate copy from Sipitang.

My two-man snake-hunting team was ready to move. Fowzi had persuaded Baru, a cheerful villager with a walleye and a gun, to accompany us into the wilderness. The gun was very important. Fowzi didn't have one. Even Nelius wasn't entitled to a hunting gun, though in times of national emergency he was entitled to a 9-mm Browning and an M-16, which were issued by the army in Sipitang. There was a quota for gun ownership in the village, which Nelius administered. In reality people just borrowed guns when they needed them, and it was Baru's father's gun we would be using.

I briefly met Baru's father, who had a bad limp. Strangely, this too was the result of an encounter with a bear. He told me he had seen snakes drinking at the udder of a goat.

Milk-drinking snakes occur in stories in every continent

106

where snakes are common. In fact the restricted snout of a snake makes sucking, as opposed to biting, virtually impossible. Snakes that have been 'milked' of venom are sometimes restored to strength by being drip-fed milk, though this may be sympathetic magic because some evidence suggests that snakes, like domestic cats, have problems digesting milk.

Baru had once been the pastor of the Long Dao church. In his mauve underpants and splayed bare feet, grinning a gap-toothed smile and looking two ways at once, he was not an obvious churchman. Now he was a general-purpose villager again, farming, hunting, fishing and trapping. He was keen to come on the great snake hunt because Fowzi had said he could try out his new fishing net upriver.

What would Colonel H. have made of my army of two (former) headhunters? Not much, probably, compared to his legion of Nagas, armed with flintlocks and spears and eager to hack the head off any Japanese foolish enough to get caught. Recruiting an army of headhunters requires more than just money. You have to have enough charisma to make them want to follow you into the jungle. It helps if you're offering something of status. I realized I was behind the times. I would have had no trouble in recruiting a football team to play against some touring foreign side.

Fowzi assembled food, ropes for snake capture, cooking pot and kettle. He and Baru carried the gear in two rucksacks made from a board with cloth shoulder straps. Woven rattan sides and an adjustable front flap made this a light and versatile pack. When I tried it on I was surprised at how comfortable it was. The straight wooden board, because it didn't cling to the back, was a lot less sweaty than an ordinary rucksack, which was what I was carrying. It was just a day sack but in it I put all my key items of equipment.

The night before leaving I laid them out on the floor of the bamboo rest house both to calm and inspire me for the toils ahead. The leather-covered surveying tape recalled a previous era of colonial exactitude, measuring up an empire with sweat pouring down your brow. 'The Tool' was a piece of American ingenuity, a can-do problem-solver made to the rugged standards of the frontiersman. The big Maglite torch was a precision instrument owing something to the hi-tech materials that evolved from the space programme and the gritty reality of urban cop power. My Zeiss binoculars had something of the tank commander about them. Finally, my magic snake stone and the secret power of Irish High Toast. I wrapped the snuff in two small plastic bags, not wanting it to become ruined in the damp of the jungle. I had left the kris behind in KL for safekeeping. It was a casual decision which months later I did not regret.

In another plastic bag I put my current notebook. At the back I had copied various quotations germane to the snake hunt. When snake fear arose I could always contemplate the no-nonsense approach of the 1930s big-game hunter Jim Frey:

> The capture of pythons is a very unexciting and ordinary sort of business. A number of traders set off to find a suitable specimen. When they come across a great snake peacefully digesting a huge meal, its stomach vastly distended, they just put it in a sack, and the great reptile offers no resistance whatever to the indignity.

Fowzi popped in to let me know he'd just been praying for the success of our hunt at the church. There were church services, of an informal kind, every evening for an hour or so. Men gathered after the service to discuss things on the church veranda. Fowzi also told me not to tell anyone we were off the next day on a hunt. It was bad luck to do that, he said.

I was quite firm with Fowzi and he reluctantly took me to the headman's house. I had the football in a plastic bag.

Fowzi knew about the football and had immediately suggested I donate it to the football team run by his brother, but I instinctively rejected this suggestion.

The headman's house was a small and dilapidated hut on stilts, not at all like the lavish longhouse of the former headman. The headman's wife was a wary, tall stick of a woman. She told us the headman was out visiting, and it was too late to track him down. Fowzi promised to arrange an interview as soon as we returned from our hunting trip. 'The headman is also a partner in the tourism business,' said Fowzi. 'He will not mind that you have not visited him.'

In the early evening dark we passed a group of young men, some smoking, standing around the gated entrance to the village green. Half hidden in the dark, with body tattoos and eyes catching the available light, they had something menacing about them, but then I recognized two or three from the football team. Fowzi strode past, scornfully ignoring them. It was a calculated insult but the young men remained silent, cowed by Fowzi's self-confidence.

'Why don't you speak to them?' I asked.

'They have no vision,' said Fowzi, his face set in grim determination.

FIVE

Civet Cat for Breakfast

There is in each of us, to a greater or lesser degree,
the instinct to hunt. How he hunts is personal to
the hunter.
                                                    C. J. Ionides

'What's this?' I pointed my spoon at the pot bubbling on the
early morning fire. Fowzi mumbled indistinctly but I knew
the second I tasted that nauseous, faintly perfumed chewiness
with a hint of burnt fur: civet cat. We had been in the jungle
less than a week and already I loathed the taste of civet cat.
Apart from rice and two tins of sardines with black-eye beans,
it had become our staple. If only I had brought a bottle of
Lea and Perrins Worcester sauce with me, it would have
made all the difference.

We had left the village at six in the morning, walking in
line past the last of the solar huts, over the river on a bridge
that swayed increasingly as we made our way across, magni-
fied our footsteps and sent them singing along the taut wires
of the bridge, the fast-running river far below the yawning
gaps between planks. Fowzi went first, me next and Baru
third. I waited until Fowzi was across before I started, but
Baru was unconcernedly right on my tail, doubling the bridge
swings, or so it seemed.

I had made the decision, long ago, that I would keep with
my jungle guides, come what may. Now I was having to keep
up, I reviewed the sense of my decision. I knew from past
efforts that lagging would feed any despondency. I knew too
that the sight of Fowzi standing nonchalantly at the top of

every incline, waiting for old clumsy slowcoach, would be hard to bear. Harder, really, than the rough and tumble of keeping up.

Over the bridge we were now moving swiftly through a dark grove of bamboos. Thick on the ground was the brown mulch of bamboo leaves, covering, sometimes to a depth of several feet, the collapsed and rotten trunks of fallen or chopped bamboos. Standing on these wooden tubes I enjoyed feeling them split and flatten to the ground. I was following Fowzi blindly at this stage, hardly noticing whether there was a path or not, picking my way on and over the rotting bamboos. I wondered if there were pythons lurking under the mulch. Somehow being on the hunt for snakes made me less frightened than if I had simply been taking a walk through the jungle. But hunter or not, all alpha predators deserve respect – I trod as carefully as I could.

Baru kept up a lively discourse, talking volubly over my head to Fowzi, who talked in swifter, lower tones; perhaps I should have felt ignored, but I didn't. I was glad to have good reason not to speak, comfortable with my own thoughts in the cool of the early morning.

At the edge of the grove Fowzi broke off from the path and started knocking with the back of his parang on the lower sections of tall bamboos. When he heard the right noise, he cut a hole in the bamboo and handed me a straw made from a much thinner bamboo tube. I drank from the pint or so of water accumulated in the lower part of the trunk. It was cold water, without taste, no different from tap water. Then Baru started knocking at bamboos and, after Fowzi told me water is only ever in the first two or three sections off the ground, so did I. My parang was cheap and heavy, shiny-bladed in a sheath I had made myself from wood bound with nylon string and gaffer tape. My inventive, but shoddy, workmanship had been politely admired by Baru. He and Fowzi had parang sheaths made from grey plastic drainpipe, heated over a fire and flattened to make a hard-wearing envelope for the parang's blade.

After putting holes in a good few more bamboos than necessary, we shouldered packs and came out of the grove to follow a high path along the bank of the river. The path was narrow. Forty feet below was the river, undercutting the bank so that the edge of the path crumbled into a loose vegetation hiding the space below. Despite fears of thorns or insect bites I gripped at grass stems and tree roots on the side away from the drop off. I lost my footing once, sending a footprint-sized load of gravel into the torrent below. Down on one knee, with Baru embarrassingly gripping my trouser waistband, all my faith in the wiggly tree root I had one hand on, and sweat in two huge tear-shaped drops inside my specs, I told myself off for being careless, too long in the city, not properly warmed up.

We followed the big winding curve of the river, getting a fine view of the fast-running shallows, sun sparkling off water into the distance, able to get that commanding feeling of walking high up along the contour of a hill, enjoying the reward of altitude without suffering the cost of an uphill or downhill struggle.

The path edged away from the bank and lined itself up on the two haphazard bamboo logs that lay horizontally as a bridge across the gully. There was very obviously no hand-rail. Fowzi started off, with more caution than usual. Remembering the way Baru had tailgated me across the last bridge, I stepped up on the two poles. Fowzi signalled back to me to wait. Halfway across, the bamboos sagged and wobbled with each step he took, duck-footing his way along the bamboo poles. Now Fowzi was on the uphill stretch towards the other side. A fantastically loud creak, like the prelude to a break, made him stop and look ominously round. Baru grinned wildly in encouragement. Moving very much more slowly now, Fowzi made it to the other side. Baru made a noise like a cheer. I stepped up gamely.

The gully was a muddy trickle through rocks, a good thirty feet down. The poles stretched ahead about thirty feet across the chasm. By length and width those bamboos were almost identical in size to the snake we were hunting. Inching forward with a caution that made Fowzi look reckless, I reached, quite easily, the creak point in the middle. It wasn't just the offputting sound, it was also the fact that a gap was opening up between the poles that made things more unnerving. If I fell I knew I would probably break something. Despite trying to rationalize the gully as shallower than it looked, every time I risked a glimpse between the swaying poles, I was shocked that, yes, it really was that deep.

My first thought on reaching the other side was: I hope we don't have to come back over that bridge.

Baru, with set grin and a show-off's confidence, crossed the bridge in rapid steps that made me think he was foolish rather than sure-footed.

Now we were all across it was as if we'd finally escaped the extent of the village. Without exchanging words, Baru handed the single-barrelled shotgun to Fowzi, who slung it over one shoulder. A nylon belly pouch full of twelve-bore cartridges was also transferred to Fowzi's waist. Each cartridge was going to cost me an extortionate pound sterling, though Fowzi had assured me they were all brand new and not refilled with black powder and small stones, which was the condition of some cartridges he'd used. Stripped of his gun, Baru started to whistle tunelessly, but this, like the earlier over-my-head conversation, he soon gave up.

My feet became dewily soaked after a fast traverse through a new kind of forest, thin, tall trees with flowers growing everywhere, the path merely a long indentation in the ground cover of stalks and thin leaves. My boots were holding up well, despite being several sizes too big. Too big is always better than too small, as long as you have plenty of pairs of socks to fill them out. Otherwise you get the skin on the top of the big toe pinched off by the loose leather of the boot. Very soft leather is much less likely to pinch, and these boots were very soft, though dilapidated and in places torn. I had taken them from the Bamboo Hilton where they hung on the wall, discarded by a member of the German expedition. My own boots I had increasingly had doubts about as I got nearer and nearer the jungle. A cheap version of Timberlands, they were neither as comfortable as I expected nor as rugged as I needed for running up and down rock-strewn gullies. Though I love boots, and can quite easily see why the great Victorian explorer and polymath Sir Richard Burton should have acquired over a hundred pairs of boots by the time he died, I have very rarely found boots that fit me comfortably. American boots I have found the worst, being far too narrow for feet as wide as mine. Boots sold in England, especially the current trend in nylon training shoes with sewn-on scraps of leather and a semblance of ankle protection, are worse than useless, being too narrow, too artificially arched and too low on the inside. Continental boots are better, simpler and more sensible than the Anglo-Saxon boot, bigger and wider and altogether bootier. The German discards were not a disappointment. I counted myself lucky to have found them. If I'd worn my other boots I'd have been squelching along in two dripping sops by now, the thin leather of the uppers as waterproof as a wick.

Fowzi and Baru both wore rubber one-piece football boots. Known as *adidas kampong* because of the three side stripes in imitation of an Adidas boot, the boots were more like galoshes with studs. But studs were not to be sniffed at, now that we were going up and down muddy tracks. Fowzi wore two flour sacks over his feet as protection against leeches. He tied the sacks just below the knee. He wore no socks, or rather the sack acted as a sock. Baru, too, wore no socks. He did not have flour sacks either, and after walking through a patch of damp lilies he stopped and pulled a small leech from his foot. Watery blood seeped from between his toes and his look of concentration at removing the leech changed, when he saw my riveted, horrified gaze, to one of gap-toothed amusement.

In Kota Kinabalu, Roy had tried to scare me with leech stories, but I had been acclimatizing myself to leeches for a long time, ever since seeing a Shell oil-exploration film in the early seventies at school. In the film the field geologists burned leeches off with their cigarettes. In fact, as I remember it, they used a leech attack as an excuse for having a smoke. This film served to emphasize the necessity of having cigarettes in the jungle. The geologists explained to the camera that pulling a leech off without first stimulating it with fire meant the teeth of the leech would be left behind in the skin, where they would fester. In France, while walking in the wooded gorges of the Pyrenees, I had suffered one or two small leeches. I had dealt severely with both with the glowing nub of my Gauloise filterless.

Leech protection, now that I was down to carrying only a clandestine pack of big cigars, would have to be more efficient than the casual attitude of the hobbit-footed Baru. My ripstop cotton trousers had double-stitched seams and ties that served to close the trouser bottoms. Because of the giant German boots I wore two pairs of thick socks. To further seal off the nether regions I tucked the trouser bottoms into the socks. Any leech breaking through that lot deserved all the blood it could get.

I felt close to collapsing from exhaustion when we reached the top of a muddy incline and several huts came into view. We had been going for about an hour. My thin cotton shirt (sensible long sleeves as protection against mosquitoes) was completely wet. I even wrung a few drops out from each sopping armpit. Even the cuffs were drenched. Fowzi and Baru had T-shirts on underneath their shirts. We stood outside the huts and I changed my shirt. I only had two, which looked like a bad miscalculation. I draped the wet shirt over the rucksack. Because we were in a real clearing there was at least some sunlight to dry it out. This was Baden-Powell's method for 'avoiding fever in the tropics': always keep a dry shirt on your back by rotating your shirts and using the sun as a permanent tumble dryer. This method may have worked on the veldt (it worked in the mountains of Europe anyway) but it did not work in the Borneo jungle. I did not realize it, but this patch of sunlight was the last real glimpse of the sun I would see for over three weeks. And when there is no sun, nothing can dry in the palpable humidity of the forest.

These huts were made from sawn timber and stood about eight feet off the ground. The heavy planking gave an appearance of farm sheds raised high off the ground to store a tractor or a harrow underneath, but under these sheds were dogs always trying to scratch first one ear, then another, and chickens and fishing nets with small plastic doughnut-shaped floats. Nailed to a shed wall was the skin of a deer; white and bloody it buzzed with flies.

There was no solar power but the roofs were still covered with corrugated tin. Carrying each piece of roof from Long Dao, over the bendy bamboo bridge and along the river bank, must have been an effort.

An old man with repaired glasses shouted harshly from his lair above the ground. Half his doorway, at the top of a bamboo ladder, was blocked off by a board and his bleary, bespectacled face peered out over this makeshift door.

Fowzi disappeared into the old man's hut to discuss the snake situation hereabouts. Baru and I went next door, where the old man's tubby daughter laid out on the floor an early lunch of monkey, deer and wild boar, all in bite-sized chunks on red plastic saucers. With growing unease I realized that the headless human form sitting hunched on the sideboard was the charred remains of the monkey I was experimentally chewing on. All three meats tasted very similar to me: chewy, chewy, chewy, like my idea of rehydrated pemmican.

The tubby daughter, in a long, torn, dirty T-shirt, poured out home-grown coffee. Next to where we sat bobbed a smooth bundle suspended by an engine-valve spring and a piece of rope. Her son or daughter was absolutely silent, and only when the tubby woman bobbed the bundle did I realize it contained a child. Baru and I took it in turns to also bob the bundle.

Several green ammo boxes were stacked up against one wall of the hut. They were British .303 Bren-gun ammunition boxes, dating, I guessed, from the time of the *konfrontasi* between Malaysia and Indonesia, when the Malay army were supported by British troops at potential hotspots such as the Borneo border. The boxes now appeared to contain old torch batteries.

I said no to another helping of fried monkey and when Fowzi stuck his head through our door I asked him in English if these people had been expecting us. 'Oh, no,' he said. 'But these people always have some food ready – how do you think she became so fat!'

The old man said they had killed a three-foot python a few days ago. It had made a nice soup. He had heard of a long snake living a long way off in the jungle. 'In the same place that I said,' said Fowzi.

'What place was that?' I asked.

'The place of the shouting monster,' said Fowzi.

'Oh, the shouting monster,' I said. 'I thought the shouting monster was actually a kind of monkey?'

'I am not sure, but maybe he could also be a kind of snake?'

117

It seemed that Fowzi was asking for my interpretation of Lundaiya mythology. What had actually happened earlier was that I had allowed my excitement at hearing about the shouting monster (a kind of sasquatch) to be too obvious. Anxious to produce a trip 'professionally' tailored to my requirements Fowzi almost redesigned his mythical monster to suit me. But the promise of fifty thousand dollars made me more hard-headed than usual. I cross-questioned Fowzi's description of likely terrain with the penetrating scepticism of a weary copper.

This collection of two or three huts was the last outpost of Malaysia before the border with Indonesia. We walked around a hot field of maize, a sunken rice paddy, over an incongruous barbed-wire fence and then we were in the forest. 'This is virgin forest,' said Fowzi.

The now accepted absence of wildlife, the lack of under-growth and bushes, and big buttressed trees much less common than I expected, made the forest, in the rare flat stretches we encountered, like any English wood. The only difference was the amount of treefall and rotting wood. Everything in the forest was either dying or shooting up through the mulch of decomposing matter. The rainforest was like one big steamy compost heap. When we had to hop over a tree blocking the path (which was often), first Fowzi and then Baru took two or three swipes at the log. Not enough to clear it, but when each traveller takes a chunk or two out of the tree, eventually the path is clear again. It is like mountaineers placing a rock on a cairn. The path, too, was hardly noticeable. It seemed magical the way Fowzi found his way, especially when there appeared to be several routes to chose from. This was the *main* route from Long Dao to Kalimantan, I had to keep reminding myself, and had been for centuries, yet it was so indistinct and overgrown that it gave the impression of being an abandoned path that was hardly significant in the first place.

But the flat sections were all too rare. Mostly we went up and up knolls and then down and down to ditches carrying rocky streams or just mud. Sometimes there was a long stretch of just going in and out of deep gulches, pulling our way up the side using tree roots. I long ago gave up being picky about foliage grab handles. I fell down several times on this, the first day in the jungle, but made light of it since the tireless and unforgiving way Fowzi climbed hills (and didn't wait at the top for me) put me in danger of appearing in his mind in the same category as the Germans. Baru also fell down a good few times, once tobogganing down a steep slope on his rump past both me and Fowzi, his face knotted in competition between worry and the kind of glee associated with village idiots.

We stopped for a rest around eleven o'clock in a clearing dominated by a low clay mound. I didn't know what the significance of this mound was until Fowzi asked me, in a way that anticipated some reaction, to walk around the mound and see what it was. It took a while for me to get it. The mound was built in the shape of a forty-foot crocodile. Baru told me with some pride that it had been a place where the warriors of the village had come to stick spears with the heads taken in battle still on the sharp end. Very *Lord of the Flies*, a row of spears topped with heads dripping blood from their severed necks. They stopped coming here after the war with the Japanese, said Baru. They had taken heads then. One of the rivers we would later cross was known as English River because Lundaiya had sheltered English people there when they had fled from the Japanese.

The crocodile motif is common from New Guinea to the Nagalands. The Lundaiya could only have encountered crocodiles on their trips to the sea, since in Long Dao there are none. The common cultural artefacts, religious objects, rituals and dances among headhunters as far apart as India and

119

Polynesia have been well documented, by John Austin-Coates among others, that curious old mandarin of the old British Empire and a close friend of the irrepressible American inventor Buckminster Fuller. In the past Lundaiya had traded in cowrie shells and worn hornbill feathers in their headbands, both practices followed by tribes far separated from them by mountains and sea. There must have been some great migration in the past, whose origins were then long forgotten. Or, more plausibly, this migration was just part of a continuous cycle of interaction and movement between tribal groups, which are never so static as we like to believe.

I asked Fowzi if John, Long Dao's tame anthropologist, had believed the Lundaiya had always been in the area where they now were. He was examining a hole in one of his flour sacks at the time. 'I don't know,' he said. Then his tone grew confidential, as if being in the forest allowed him to speak his mind, something he had to watch when he was in the village. 'Whatever John found out is only part of the truth. He came to Long Dao and said he would find out from everyone. But he only stayed at the old headman's house, you know, the big longhouse. He only got that family's view of Long Dao. But there are several families in Long Dao. He only lived in one place because it was the most comfortable!'

'Did he ever go into the forest?' I asked.

'Only twice! In one year!' Fowzi snorted. 'I took him but he made me march by his compass, straight up and straight down hills.'

It sounded like what we had been doing.

'Without taking the path, it was very tiring. Today we only go up as far as we have to, then the path goes around the hill. John made me go over the hill. So many hills.'

John had given Fowzi his compass. It was a cheap imitation Silva walking compass, and Fowzi treasured it though he told me he never used it, nor ever would, because it was just too tiring.

Before we left the crocodile mound, both Baru and Fowzi pissed without ceremony on its algae-covered legs. After buttoning up, Baru drew his finger across his throat and pointed at the mound. There was such glee on his face that this normally sinister gesture seemed as friendly as a wave. And yet when Baru was a little boy his father and uncles had been busy cutting off heads with probably the same outrageous good humour.

I prepared again for more footslog and falling over, hoping we had not much further to go. My shirt felt wet and slapping, chill, for the minute before it started steaming.

Two or three hours later we arrived at a ramshackle pile of logs which Fowzi euphemistically called the 'hunting lodge'. He and Baru quickly repaired a sleeping platform about a foot off the ground. Over the top they slung a polythene sheet to keep off the rain. Several ants found their way into Fowzi's shirt sleeves. He scratched at the redness and then asked me if I had any medicine.

'What kind of medicine?' I demanded.

'Cream?' he said lamely.

'No,' I said, 'I don't have any medicine.' It was my turn for revenge. 'Don't you know any plants that can cure that rash?'

'Yes,' he said distractedly, perhaps remembering he was the jungle supremo, 'plants.' He tugged up a clump of weeds, apparently at random, and rubbed them into himself. 'Plants are OK,' he said, 'but cream is better.'

Baru went down to the river to set his net. Wearing only his soiled pink underpants, he dove and swam to fit the net across the cold and fast-flowing river. When he came back he asked me for some aspirin because his 'head was pain'. I told him sternly that I had no aspirins, especially not for meagre headaches. I couldn't believe it – the tough jungle dwellers had either been perverted by pill-popping visitors or they were complete hypochondriacs, viewing Western medicine as more potent than their own. Perhaps the remarkable pharmacopoeia of jungle tribes is less a reflection of medical skill than a response to hypochondria in the rainforest.

Knowledge of medicinal plants is not always passed down conventionally. Many indigenous forest dwellers report that they dreamed which plant would be a particularly good cure. Darwin's father, a nineteenth-century physician, employed a similar method. He found that if a patient craved a certain food or plant, and it was proved they had not heard about it from another, then its prescription often provided a complete cure.

It is a healthy tradition. The founding father of medicine, Aesculapius, was visited in a dream by a snake sent by Apollo to teach him the value of medicinal herbs and plants. In this myth we can see that Apollo, having vanquished the threatening Python, the old chthonic ruler, now employs his old enemy as his messenger. Aesculapius was said to return to this world himself as a snake, visiting and impregnating at night many women who slept in his temples. He was said to father thousands this way, including Alexander the Great.

In the epic tale of Gilgamesh, Gilgamesh longs for the herb of immortality which grows at the bottom of the waters of the dead. He manages to take the plant, but when he jumps in the water to refresh himself, a snake steals it.

The connection between snakes and medical knowledge is contained in the story of Cadmus, who, along with his wife, was returned to this earth as a snake to cure human ills. Porphyry wrote later that medical skill could be gained by eating some part of the snake, a common and fundamental primitive dogma, perhaps a confusion with listening to the snake dream that is an emissary of the hidden, but know-ledgeable, unconscious.

Baru quickly recovered from his headache and made a fire, at which he was expert. He was full of boisterous good humour, tempered by a certain shyness and a desire to be helpful. It was impossible to dislike him. He told me the net he had set was a new one, made of nylon with weights fixed beneath it and floats on top to provide a suitable trap for fish. I asked him why he had not completely blocked off the river with net. He explained that if a log is floating down, a net secured at one end only is less likely to be damaged. Fish, it seemed, did not probe forwards to see if there was some barrier, they simply swam and got their fins caught in the fine mesh and this was their downfall.

The noise of a shot made us both look up from the fire and stare off into the encroaching gloom of the forest. Baru smirked meaningfully and poked at the fire, anticipating a deer fest as the evening's entertainment. When, about twenty minutes later, Fowzi returned empty-handed, we were both disappointed. Fowzi mimed a deer showing its hindquarters to him and this was all he had to shoot at.

I thought sadly about the deer running around with pellets in its bum, but the sadness quickly passed when I realized we would be eating tinned fried dace in salted blackbean sauce. It had an odour I hadn't smelled since opening a friend's fridge and discovering a small portion of fur-encrusted fish curry several weeks old.

Before eating, Baru said grace. It was a very long grace for such a meagre meal. I began to ponder the disadvantages of having a pastor as part of the snake-hunting team.

The air was so still it was possible to have several unpro-tected candles burning away, one on each corner of the sleeping platform. I scribbled in my notebook by their light. I was glad we were sleeping off the ground, relatively safe from nocturnal snake intrusion. The old cowboy trick of running a hairy rope around camp to deter snakes may work, but not because snakes dislike crossing hairy ropes. The real function is to spread the smell of humans, which some snakes instinctively avoid. Insects and frogs provided a wall of sound which rose and fell in time with some ancient cycle of the virgin forest. The air was warm but cooling perceptibly and I buttoned my damp shirt up to my neck. Baru played with my Maglite, flicking its beam on and off at the jungle on the other side of the ravine opposite. He and Fowzi loved the way the beam could be focused to a spot. It was also a much more powerful torch than their own, a cheap, plastic two-cell job. Again I felt that faint surge of proprietary pleasure that comes from being a passport-carrying representative of the wicked West, source of all techno-marvels.

Fowzi had supplied me with a thin orange bath towel. He had earlier referred to it glowingly as a 'blanket', and as the chill of night came upon us I could hardly hide my disappointment. I had expected something thick and woolly, like an ex-army blanket. I set up my mosquito net and crawled under the towel, with my nylon poncho on top and the rucksack as a sleeping bag for my feet. Baru donned a balaclava that seemed to have ears, and lay like a contented gnome next to me. Fowzi too had extra clothes on hand to ward off the night cold. I mentally prepared myself for another good chilling.

About ten o'clock I woke up. Fowzi and Baru were hovering by my net. 'We're going night hunting,' said Fowzi.

'Good,' I said.

'Do you want to come?'

'No.'

They crept off and I lay listening to the rising and falling of insect sound, the sudden inexplicable noises of movement in the undergrowth that made me hold my breath and listen intently, and twice, the shocking far-off crash of trees falling.

I understood for the first time Bishop Berkeley's obsession with falling trees. If a tree falls in the forest and no one hears it, has it really fallen? All over the forest, miles and miles from us and any civilization, trees were falling, unheard. The extreme aloneness of our situation struck me, but it was the reverse of loneliness. It was a kind of heroic oneness with things. It was what I knew I sought, the opposite of big-city isolation where one is reduced to an insignificant tag. Here in the jungle I was existing on full strength; trees falling depended on me for their reality, and listening to the trees fall I felt, for a brief while, the marked and primitive joy of custody of wild places.

A gunshot, five minutes, and then another, nearer. I almost dozed off and then the hunters returned. Fowzi, with amused indifference, flopped a dead creature down next to the fire, an animal that looked to me like a thin domestic cat. I took a closer look. It had striped fur along its back, a bushy tail like a fox and a raccoonlike snout, with the bodily proportions of a healthy tabby. Civet cat. Related to the skunk, a fact whose importance would loom ever larger as our days in the forest went by.

With a disgraceful lack of ceremony Baru threw the civet cat on the fire and, using its tail as a handle, burned all its fur off. Well, never all, he always left some, perhaps behind the ears or under the belly, to add an extra something to any civet-cat dish we might eat. Using his parang he first cut a log in two to make a clean chopping board, then the cat was quickly butchered, and everything, bar its tail, was popped into the big pot ready for breakfast.

Before dawn Fowzi was blowing the embers alight and preparing a meal. The hacked-up pieces of cat were first fried with ten unchopped cloves of garlic and a little salt. Then, reaching into a secret pocket, he produced a tiny sachet of Aji no moto, Japanese monosodium glutamate. He sprinkled a few grains with a knowing flourish, as if this would make all the difference, as if he had in his hands the key to successful civet-cat cuisine. After a quick frying, water was added to make the inevitable soupy stew. The head of the civet cat looked mournfully up at me out of the milky, greasy soup. With a relish which I tried hard to share, we breakfasted on the rubbery hide and odiferous flesh of the cat. Civets, like skunks, have scent glands which perfume their meat with a flavour similar to that same high rot you can smell at a fruit market after a warm day's trading.

Even Ionides' diet would have been preferable to civet cat. He always ate the same thing every day, a diet honed by the demands of travel in the African bush. For breakfast he had a single sausage and a cup of diluted coffee essence. For lunch a lump of charred goat meat mashed with a boiled potato and 'gravy'. For dinner, tinned cheese melted on bread and another cup of coffee essence with four sugars. Delicious.

After breakfast (why *after*?) Baru checked his nets and found five fish called *talamuk*, each weighing between two and four pounds. They had barnaclelike pustules on their noses and thick, bloated lips. I found myself cheered by Baru's enthusiasm as he speared each fish on a swiftly cut twig and set it to roast in the fire. We ate one each as a breakfast supplement and saved the rest for lunch. Before leaving, Baru tied the civet cat's bushy tail to a stick to make a ramrod for the gun. His walleye swivelling sideways with glee, he cleaned the gun. At least no one could complain we'd wasted any part of the beast.

As we left the hunting lodge I saw written in charcoal on one of the supports in English: 'Lite is arrive here 4\7\96.' Fowzi explained scornfully, 'He arrive here last year for two days, that is the first time he come here in his life.'

After walking a few miles, I realized I'd left my hat behind. 'Don't worry,' said Fowzi. 'There is no one but us in this part of the jungle. We can get it when we return.'

126

It was only a red baseball hat, but I was rather fond of it. I'd secretly hoped it would become part of my snake-hunting image. Ionides had had the most famous snake-hunting hat, a type known as a 'double *terai*' with two crowns and ventilation space between. It was purchased in 1923 and given to Ionides by a game scout in the 1940s. He was still wearing it twenty years later, though impromptu use as a snake glove had so worn it that it gave Ionides something of the aspect of Piltdown Man. He declared, 'No one dares touch it – for it's impregnated with poison from the fangs of innumerable snakes. It's one of the things that's helped build up my reputation among the natives as a character to be respected.'

That day, Fowzi and Baru took it in turns to miss deer. The technique for not bagging a deer is as follows: First find yourself in a camouflaged spot halfway up a hillside with a commanding view along the contour and down the hill. Make sure, by sucking thumb and holding it in the breeze, that the wind is blowing towards you. Take a thin leaf, tear off each end and fold it into a tube. Hold the tube lightly in your hand and blow, making a harsh whooping sound that carries for miles. 'This sound,' said Fowzi, 'makes the deer think a young deer is hurt. But it is not at all the sound a young deer makes. It still works, though.' After anything up to half an hour of leaf hooting, expect to see a deer wander across your sights. Some are small, and some are large with padded-looking antlers, bodies as big as small cattle.

Take aim. Fire. Miss.

Sometimes there were traces of blood, but never much. Sometimes, especially when Baru was shooting, there was no blood, a fact discovered after at least twenty minutes of fruitless chasing around in the undergrowth.

'There is no luck here,' Fowzi moaned as we made camp for the second night and tucked into the remains of the civet stew. As the firelight played on his serious, almost drawn face, he explained, 'I was wrong to shoot the civet cat. Sometimes a cat can also be a spirit. Perhaps such a spirit is stopping our hunting.'

In the morning we discovered python tracks in the mud next to the stream where we camped. Reticulated pythons have been observed to be both nocturnal and diurnal. Perhaps in this part of the forest they preferred the night. In tests carried out, retics refused to hunt for concealed prey in the morning, though they are less choosy about the afternoon. Reticulated pythons are night owls, rising late, leaving the early morning safe for nervous creatures. Gustav Lederer, the herpetologist who made these observations, discovered that a reticulated python can find a dead rabbit, even if it is buried, by following the scent trail, however long, made by dragging the rabbit along the ground. A rabbit in a perforated box also produces enough scent for a reticulated python to find it, even without a scent trail. The key is once again the hypersensitive Jacobsen's organ.

Baru suggested, from the width and depth of the tracks in the mud, that the snake was about ten to thirteen feet long. I wanted to think otherwise but had to agree. And at this stage I had more important things on my mind, such as getting the taste of civet cat out of my mouth as quickly as possible.

I was used now to silent running, creeping up to hide behind a tree as Fowzi, or Baru when he really begged hard, took a shot at some evasive beast. Fowzi had his sights lined up on a family of monkeys in the trees above us. 'Do you want?' he whispered.

I looked at the tender little monkeys and sort of shrugged my mouth, involuntarily getting an unpleasant surge of civet aftertaste. 'No,' I gagged, only just.

By the third day we were down to just the head of the cat, bobbing like a mascot in the boiling stew pot. Even Baru admitted that the flavour (which had grown stronger each day) left a lot to be desired. The only fish we had seen were as tiny as minnows. I tightened my belt as far as it could go.

Around lunchtime, always a difficult time of the day for unsuccessful hunters, Fowzi tugged at my sleeve and made a hushing gesture. He pointed across to a tree whose leaves were shaking. As Fowzi and Baru argued about whose turn it was to fire, I stared hard and made out the powerful form of an ape.

'No!' I said. 'It's an orang-utan. It's an endangered species.'

Fowzi frenziedly loaded up a shell, having tugged the gun away from the disgruntled Baru. 'It's a gibbon,' he hissed. 'Not an orang-utan.'

He was right. It was a large male gibbon, probably at the height of his natural powers. I didn't know whether gibbons were protected or not (they are) but I still didn't fancy offing one for the pot.

'We're in Kalimantan now, you know that?' added Fowzi. Killing an enemy gibbon – very cunning!

'He may have come across the border too,' I said lamely.

'Now is the chance,' Fowzi whispered.

I raised my eyebrows, which was supposed to be a prelude to saying no, but I half knew Fowzi would interpret it as a noncommittal yes. I thought he might miss, but I was also damn hungry. Nothing would have persuaded me to shoot the gibbon if I had been holding the gun, but it's much easier to order deaths than to commit murder yourself.

The gun went off. The gibbon shrieked a horrible screeching, wounded sound, and appeared to crash to a set of branches a few feet below him. As we ran to the foot of the tree there was silence.

'I think he's holding on up there,' I said.

Fowzi nodded. 'He is hit but he is not dead yet.'

'He could be dead and holding on, or trapped on a branch.'

I envisaged the ape gripping the trunk in a bear-hug death grip before expiring and rigor mortis taking over. 'What shall we do?'

'We can wait,' said Fowzi. 'Or come back this way after some time. Maybe the gibbon will have dropped out of the tree to the ground by then.'

Baru took his rucksack and rubber shoes off and said something in Lundaiyo.

'Baru will climb the tree,' said Fowzi.

'Is that a good idea?' The tree looked very tall to me and the long expanse of trunk before the branches spread out had only a hanging mass of thick creepers and tree boles to use as handholds. I knew Baru was made of stern stuff but I didn't want to see him plunge to his death locked in mortal combat with a wounded gibbon.

'Baru will climb up and ... *investigate*,' said Fowzi impressively.

I had to admit that of all of us, Baru, with his muscular arms and prehensile hobbit feet, was most suited to messing around in the treetops. He hovered keenly, waiting for me to OK the mission.

'Can't he tie a creeper round his waist or something? What if he fell?'

'If he falls, he falls,' said Fowzi, rather coldy, I thought.

'*Saya orang lama*,' said Baru, meaning 'I'm an old hand.'

'It'd be better if you were *orang utan*!' I said, but they just looked blank-faced at me.

'OK,' I said. 'Climb the tree.'

With an agility more associated with children on climbing frames, Baru was up and at the tree, pulling on a creeper here, resting his knee on a tree bole there. He stopped and pointed down to one. 'Honey bees,' he said. Fowzi and I both gestured to him to keep going. An impromptu honey-gathering session was bound to end in disaster. Up and up he went and was almost at the level of the branches where we had last seen the gibbon, when he made a sharp cry. Pieces of leaf and twig came floating down from above. There was the noise of tearing and cursing in a native language I could not understand. With all the speed of Jack descending from the beanstalk, Baru plunged down the trunk, barely gripping creepers long enough to slow his rapid descent to earth. His trousers were open and his shirt half off his back.

On the ground Baru tore at his clothes without explanation. He asked for my lighter and torched the inside seams of his shirt and trousers.

'Caterpillar!' Fowzi grinned and so, eventually, did Baru. He rubbed a leaf, taken, it seemed, at random from a ground plant, on the welted rash that stretched from his groin to his chest. Then he put on his sleeping shirt and, eyeing his trousers with suspicion, drew them experimentally over his legs. Fully dressed, he prepared to make a second assault on the tree.

'No more tree climbing,' I said. 'We're wasting valuable hunting time here. We can always come back later to find the gibbon.'

Baru was best at using the leaf to call deer. Everything Baru did, he did with full concentration and pride in achievement. Fowzi and he had, it must be said, a lot of plain bad luck as well as inexplicable failures of marksmanship. Fowzi hinted that my blue trousers were giving the game away by not being camouflaged enough. Sudden wind changes and deer that just turned and ran, as if instinctively knowing they were framed in the sights, had resulted in a few more misses. It was only costing me a pound a shot, but I wondered, if the team had been paying for their own shells, whether they would have shot so many shells off with so little return.

'It is always like this,' Fowzi rationalized. 'Either you kill the first thing and everything afterwards, or you miss the first animal and then miss everything else too.' It was a compelling excuse, but given our lack of luck with merely feeding ourselves, I was beginning to have grave doubts about our ability to snag a huge python.

It wasn't that there was a shortage of game, we were just too incompetent to get it. Baru was blowing away at a leaf when a huge deer wandered into view only fifteen or so yards away. Technically it was Baru's turn to fire, but we had grown weary of his walleye and its deleterious effect on accurate marksmanship. His favoured method was five rounds rapid into the disappearing backsides of a herd of deer. I concluded that his successes, when they came, were just a case of sheer numbers. Fowzi whispered something and tried to get the rifle from Baru, who wouldn't let go. The prize was just too enticing. They squabbled in Lundaiyo. I put my own hand on the shotgun and it became a three-way grapple.

'It's my turn,' I said.

'It's my gun!' Baru whined.

'And I am the guide,' Fowzi explained, 'the head of tourism.'

'You may be the head of tourism, but I'm the bloody client!'

They released the gun. With some awkwardness I located the safety lever on the back, took aim at the side of the black deer, a creature as big as a farmyard cow, and fired. Bizarre though it may seem, at the moment of firing I felt sorry for the magnificent deer, feeling at the time it couldn't be helped.

Just before I fired I noticed Fowzi had both fingers in his ears. A sensible precaution, for the noise of a gun loaded with high-power powder and heavy buckshot was immense. It was a very light gun, a home-made copy of a shotgun made in Sipitang by a skilled metalworker. The recoil was rather stronger than I expected, and I was blown off my feet.

When the smoke cleared, two severe and disappointed faces looked down at me.

'Sorry, lads,' I said lamely.

'It's all right,' said Fowzi, but I knew he didn't mean it.

Baru went off on a fruitless search in case the animal was wounded. They didn't even find any blood. Secretly, I was happy I hadn't killed or even wounded the deer. I was still, despite the gnawing hunger pains, in a soft urban mindset. I would have to pull myself together if I was to grapple seriously with a giant python.

Towards the end of the day a kind of glumness set in as we all prepared ourselves for yet another round of watery civet stew. I wondered if the team might mutiny, though they were just as much to blame as I. Even the gibbon had been a dead loss – when we returned to the tree it had still not dropped out and swarming bees made any further ascent impossible.

Just then Fowzi, up ahead on the path, sighted a brace of *satoh*, a kind of pheasant that has an acutely developed sense of smell. The shot rang throughout the valley and Baru and I rushed up to see if he'd been successful. Grinning with satisfaction, Fowzi held up the dead bird for our inspection.

It was a small bird, revealed after an energetic plucking from Baru to be about the size of a malnourished chicken, but we all believed it signalled the end of the curse of the civet cat.

SIX

Menhirs and *Moomins* –
Stone Dreaming

When I was younger I considered the longest time
it was wholesome to remain anywhere was four
days.   *C. J. Ionides*

When Colonel H. was admitted to hospital, the wooden
Saluting Man statue had mysteriously disappeared.

I was back from Japan for a brief stay, my first since leaving
England to live abroad, and my father told me that he had
gone round to visit the Colonel during a very cold spell just
before Christmas. By now Colonel H., in his late eighties,
had become, to the minds of his neighbours, more than
tiresomely eccentric. On a frosty day he had had a car
collision with another resident of the small Cotswold town
where he lived. Both cars were quite badly damaged, and the
other driver sought to use the Colonel's age against him. He
was a man in his late thirties, an 'executive', the Colonel said,
with a hint of a sneer, with two kids in the back of his
company car. He'd had the bad sense to raise his voice to the
Colonel, using the safety of his children as an excuse to
account for his shock at being in an accident.

Colonel H., who refused to wear a seatbelt, received a
nasty cut on his forehead from hitting the windscreen. Ignoring this, he got out of his elderly Cortina and faced the red-
faced man.

'People like you are a menace ... shouldn't have car ... old—'

'I'd watch your step if I were you, young man,' the Colonel cut in, his voice more chilling than the frosty weather.

'Oh yeah?' But the sight of a stone-faced old-timer who didn't seem to care that there was blood running down his face was beginning to unnerve the man. 'You weren't even wearing a seatbelt, were you?' He was worried now.

'What I do is none of your business. Now run along and call the police.'

'God, I hate the way people like you talk—'

'I'm sure you do.'

The man was about to speak but didn't. He was used to bullying his sales staff. This wasn't going like most conversations should. He changed tack. 'Your face,' he said. 'It's cut. Are you sure you're all right?'

'Don't be a bloody fool, man!' said the Colonel. 'People like me are quite capable of looking after ourselves.'

That wasn't the end of it. The executive persuaded the police, who found witnesses, that the Colonel shouldn't be allowed to drive. It was here he made a mistake. Colonel H. was as shrewd a barrack-room lawyer as they come. He also had daemonic persistence and an attention to detail which made the prosecution look amateurish. He amassed pages of press cuttings proving that the weather had been particularly severe at that time, indulging his macabre sense of humour by red-pencilling accounts where police cars had been involved in fatal skids owing to ice on the roads. He collated weather reports from the meteorological office. He produced large-scale maps with the exact position of the crash marked, showing that the witnesses could not possibly have seen what they claimed to have seen. As a *coup de grâce* he proved, using official performance figures for his car, that it would have been impossible for him to have been going at the speed he was charged with driving at, given the time of acceleration from the last bend.

The case was dismissed and the Colonel kept his licence, but something had happened; perhaps his nerve was gone, or that bump on his head affected him after all.

My father found him shivering on the stairs wrapped in the curtains run up years before from blankets from the Himalayan principality of Swat. He'd been there a day and a night and was suffering from hypothermia, having taken another crack on the head falling down the stairs. Barely conscious, he said, 'What are you doing here? Best leave me to die.'

They took him to a low-key kind of mental-health unit. Technically he was now no longer capable of looking after himself. My uncle made an inventory of the contents of Colonel H.'s mansion. Putting items into storage before selling the place, he remarked on the strange disappearance of Saluting Man. 'The old bugger probably chopped it up for firewood.' But I remembered the story of how Saluting Man's hand had cracked at the same time the Colonel got rheumatism. No, the Colonel would never chop his alter ego into firewood.

Saluting Man had been on my mind as I carved a totem pole for 'Camp Manillan'. *Manillan* was Lundaiyo for 'python', literally 'swallower', and I had found a small tree strangled by a creeper, which, when I stripped off the creeper, had grown into a twisty snake shape. We were now inside Kalimantan, in an area Fowzi believed would be rich in snakes. We were off the main trail and had cleared an area of forest for the camp, all of us chopping away at the polelike trees needed to make the shelter. My own parang had developed an incurable bend from all the chopping, a sure sign of its inferior nature, and my soft hands developed

136

blisters, but I was happy we were at last getting down to real jungle living.

Fowzi had chosen the site. It was a place at the junction of two rivers called Long Tawen. I said to Fowzi: 'You Lundaiya don't like to stay anywhere except where there are two rivers, do you?'

Fowzi gave his shy assent to this observation.

'Why?' I persisted.

Fowzi turned the question on Baru, who thought for a while, breaking off from his habitual parang-sharpening in the stream. 'The reason,' said Baru, 'is that Lundaiya are river people. Only people like Fowzi are jungle people.'

I was beginning to realize that Fowzi was not an average Lundaiya tribesman. Most of them never went more than a day's journey from the village, except along major trails. By the third day we were no longer on paths that Baru had been along before; in fact, both of us had been lost when Fowzi left us to make our own way home after he deviated to pursue some game. The dreadful gnawing hunger of a few days previously had gone. Somehow we'd managed to shift off the civet-cat regimen and were now subsisting on *satoh* pheasant. The river next to which we had built the shelter was full of fish, quite small ones that were easy to catch using a pole with a hook and line attached. Like clever Boy Scouts, Baru and Fowzi had a hook and line in a pocket ready for such an eventuality. The hysterical good humour generated by the fishing served also to cheer our flagging spirits. We had been over a week in the jungle and still not caught even a glimpse of a snake, apart from the snake tracks in the mud.

I shouldn't have been surprised. Wiliam Hornaday, the great Borneo naturalist, had written more than seventy years before:

My imagination had pictured the forests of the East Indies as producing a big snake for every square mile, but they are almost as scarce as snakes in Ireland. In all my jungle wanderings in the east I did not encounter a snake four feet long, although I looked for them hopefully. It was disgusting after all the big snake stories I had heard. The only snake was eight inches – killed with a prayer book in Captain Douglas' drawing room while kneeling at prayers one Sunday evening – a vicious viperine affair.

But according to Fowzi it was just a matter of time before we would come across a big snake. I don't want to give the impression that he was a bullshitter; in fact, he was impressively pessimistic from time to time. This almost dour aspect to many Lundaiya made them seem curiously English. It was a marked contrast to the fulsome exaggerations of most Malays and all Indians I had met so far.

I wondered how Fowzi and Baru would react to the *manillan* totem, a small version of the totems found outside Python Man's hut. Since there was a strongly Christian bias to the Lundaiya, I was not sure if the totems would be torn down as false gods. But as we put days between us and the village, things began to loosen up and the Lundaiya seemed to regress. Fowzi even asked me if I had any 'whisky'. He never drank in the village, he said, but he liked to do it when he was in the jungle. He had a puff of one of my cigars, but he didn't like it. Sure enough, the totems went down quite well. They were quietly acknowledged by Fowzi and earned a backslapping bout of hilarity from Baru. We were in snake country – now all we had to do was catch a snake.

Baru, who now smelled strongly of garlic, thought we should hunt for a snake by night. The garlic smell was caused by his home cure for the caterpillar attack. Morning and night, as he squatted by the fire in his pink underpants, Baru rubbed cut garlic into his arms and legs to assuage the fearful itch caused by the caterpillars he'd encountered on the gibbon hunt. During the day he made do by scratching at his

138

inflamed crotch, an area too delicate for garlic treatment. Fowzi agreed that night would be good for the final assault, but thought that we should patrol the area by day first and get some idea of the lie of the land.

As Jung pointed out, the snake is always a chthonic being, a creature of the dark, primeval underworld. Chthonic, or earth-based religions have survived to this day as shark, crocodile and serpent cults, though evidence suggests the most widespread chthonic religions were always those that worshipped snakes.

Many of the chthonic snake religions include the serpent as a cosmic superbeing. In Norse myth, Midgard encircled the earth and did endless battle with Thor. When Thor killed Midgard, the world would come to an end. The Yarra Yarra tribe of Victoria, Australia, worshipped Mindi, a ten-mile-long serpent with a huge head and a three-pronged tongue. Mindi had a cavernous mouth which ejected poison. His job was to carry out the orders of Pund-jil, 'the god of things as they are'. Sesha was another cosmic serpent, a many-headed snake on which Vishnu slept during peaceful epochs.

The earliest cave paintings in southern France, older than those at Lascaux, are the snake carvings of the Avrignacian period, twenty to thirty thousand years ago. In the Dome of the Serpents at Rouffignac there are carvings of hundreds of intertwining snakes. The last vestige of this snake cult survives today in villages in the Black Forest where a 'house snake', ostensibly kept to keep down vermin, is considered a good-luck omen for the home. In certain regions snakes have been coopted into the new religions. At Cocullo in the Abruzzi Mountains it is said that St Domenico of Foliguo (AD 950–1031) was descended from a snake. On the first Thursday of May snakes are hung in coils on his shrine.

The question that was forming in my mind was: what brought about the demise of the old earthbound chthonic religions and the rise of the new religions of light of Apollo, Ra and Krishna? Why did heroes suddenly appear and strike down snakes and dragons and monsters the world over? This continued into our own era with the myth of St Clement of Metz, St George, and St Patrick driving the snakes out of Ireland. Before that, the true founding of Jahweh's supremacy had involved the casting-out of the brazen serpent, which had earlier been given to Moses to protect and heal those who repented for not believing in God. But when the brazen serpent became a cult object, Jahweh was not happy. It wasn't until Hezekiah of the eighth century BC that the brazen serpent was finally destroyed and the one God of the Hebrews firmly established.

The brazen serpent also highlights the connection of snakes with healing. Even today the chief symbol of the medical profession is a snake, an association that goes back to the healing priests of Aesculapius who used snakes as part of their diagnostic method.

We set off at dawn in single file, up the steep hill opposite Camp Manillan. Here the path could be detected by the churned mud underfoot. Soon this clue disappeared, but I was beginning to get the hang of Fowzi's seemingly miraculous skill of jungle navigation. For a start, path following wasn't so difficult once you learned to pick up the very slight signs. It was more like a snail trail, especially at dawn, where the early morning light caught the worn-down aspect of the foliage, indicating, just, that people had passed this way before. Because half the time we were clambering over fallen logs or having to go around them, the path was fluid, and because the undergrowth was often no more than ferns, it was easy to stray off course. Now I was beginning to see how the path system worked. The fundamental principle was that the main path followed the river's direction, but because the river snaked so much, it did not follow its actual course. Knowing the direction of the river, you knew the basic direction of the path, and the sudden confusing sections when we had to wade across the same river again and again throughout the day now became clear – we were actually following that river by the shortest route. Again, in the jungle, progress up and down the interminable hills was helped by following, as often as possible, a path along a contour. ('It is like deer,' said Fowzi. 'Deer always walk along the hillside, neither up nor down.') At first it seemed extreme to me that we were roller-coasting up and down deeply muddy banks following direct routes rather than zigzagging. But I could see now that the direct route was best, since none of the hills we climbed was that high. As I plodded on, I formulated the laws for path following: (1) All paths follow the general direction of a river. (2) Always ascend directly. (3) Ascend until you're at a point when you can walk level along a contour, never scale a hill to its summit.

Some survival books teach you to follow a compass course through the jungle, but this is sheer lunacy. You face the doubly tiring tasks of cutting a new path and constantly ascending muddy hill after muddy hill. Off the general area of the path, thorns, rotting matter and concealed pits make progress very slow. You end up in this kind of terrain very quickly if you're not following the above rules. As this is the method used by most armies when they lack native guides and don't know the terrain, you can evade them by simply following the path that follows the river.

Of course there were many subpaths that followed the courses of smaller rivers, some no more than a trickling stream in the bottom of a muddy ravine. Knowing the general lie of these smaller rivers, helped naturally by the fact that they all usually drained into the main river, was another aid to navigation.

Places in the forest that seemed very unremarkable always had a name. Seemingly by tradition, all rest stops had to be at certain prescribed places, the motorway service stations of the jungle. In fact, Fowzi used to announce, like those signs on the motorways, 'We can stop in five minutes' time or in twenty-five minutes' time.' We stopped for lunch one day at a place about the size of a cricket pitch which was devoid of trees. 'This place, the Place with No Trees,' Fowzi explained, 'has always been like this. No tree has ever grown here.' Folk explanations for bald patches in the foliage abound in England. Dragon's Hill (or maybe Knob, I can't remember exactly which), a hill close to where I grew up in Oxfordshire, has a chalk scar on its summit, devoid of grass since time immemorial because, local legend has it, the poisonous blood of the dragon slain by St George fell hereabouts. I asked Fowzi if there was a story explaining why the Place with No Trees was so named. He said there was no story.

You get the impression from reading anthropologists that tribes spend at least half their time amusing each other with stories. These stories are held to explain origins, natural phenomena, history and the hunting habits of bears. But I was beginning to wonder if it wasn't the other way round. Maybe it was the Western love of stories that led anthropologists to insist on milking every last drop of narrative out of the hapless tribe. Think of Claude Lévi-Strauss penetrating deep into the Amazonian jungle, wresting every last scrap of myth out of the bemused villagers. Stories are, after all, recordable. More than that, stories are of supreme importance to us in the West. Having outgrown the Bible in many cases, we have supplanted it with the stories of Darwin and Einstein. I thought back to Python Man. 'The Bible is our story now,' he had said. Maybe part of the attraction of the West was the superiority of its stories. Maybe it was our skill at stories that sent us off looking for them elsewhere. The Lundaiya weren't particularly great storytellers, but John, the

English anthropologist, had been there a year recording only stories. The Lundaiya were now heavily storified, in imitation of us in the West.

'This bald patch would have a better name in England,' I told Fowzi.

He seemed stung by the suggestion. 'What name?' he challenged. Despite his meek exterior, Fowzi was sure of himself, cocky even.

'Dragon's Knob,' I said, and left it at that.

As we made to leave the Place with No Trees, Fowzi pointed up into the blue sky. 'It is the Boeing making smoke,' he said. And high above – thirty thousand feet above, presumably – I made out the tiny glinting silver of a plane and the vapour trail across the sky.

'It's not smoke,' I said, 'it's steam, like the steam from your mouth on a cold morning. The engines heat up the air and make clouds of steam.'

Fowzi gravely explained this to Baru. Impressed, he said, 'All of Long Dao think it is smoke from the Boeing, but they are wrong.'

'Boeing' was the name given to any jet plane. Neither Fowzi nor Baru knew that it was actually a brand name. In the small segment of blue between the trees I watched the plane, a capsule of another world, far above and uncomprehending of our world down here in the jungle. I thought of that German girl whose jet plane crashed in the South American rainforest, who became riddled with the larvae of insects laid in the wounds of her body, and of *Lord of the Flies*, the plane making a huge scar in the island's jungle as it crashed to the ground. Though it sounds improbable, I think I even heard the noise of the jet as it went overhead, a far distant roar from another world, ending the isolation of the jungle tribe. Instead of being at the centre of our own universe of action, we were suddenly off the beaten track, in the margins of a no-account world defined by the jet's fast stream. There was something beautiful and unattainable about the jet passing overhead, but also intensely sad, because I knew that there are no places left in the world over which a jet plane cannot fly.

Day by day we crisscrossed the area Fowzi reckoned to be richest in snakes. I saw a lot of lizards, but not one snake. The only caves we came across were holes in the overhanging banks of rivers, or around the bases of fallen trees. Baru sniffed them and, after more scratching at his nether parts, pronounced whether it was a snake smell or not. One day we came across a fallen tree whose branches and dead leaves formed a rotting mound. Baru sniffed. Fowzi sniffed. They told me to sniff. It was the smell of snake, a distillate or variant of the smell of the reptile house, muggy, frowsty, a hint of bad breath, meaty, sweaty, not pungent but there, heavily there.

We chopped about with our parangs, clearing a way beneath the mound of foliage. It was then I had my first real fright in the jungle. A nasty stinging sensation made me look at my hand, whereupon I dropped my parang in shock. A huge spider, as big as my hand, seemed to be staring with pink eyes at me before it fled, almost coincident with the sting and my startled flick of my arm.

'Er, Fowzi,' I said, with an air of false calm, 'I've just been bitten by a spider.'

It was the look of concern in his eyes that really frightened me. Until then there had been an insouciance about everything in the jungle that made me feel the dangers of the place were vastly overstated. Suddenly Fowzi looked worried, and for such a cool jungle cat to be worried, it must be serious.

'What spider?' he asked, bringing up his parang, perhaps, I conjectured, for an instant amputation, the only way to stop

Ernie (*below*) and the author (*right*) grappling with 'Chain' at Howlett's zoo.

Snake-catching equipment, Kuala Lumpur style.

The Snake King and several scorpions.

(*Opposite*) Suleiman demonstrates on a reticulated python.

Long Dao from the Bamboo Hilton.

The python-jacketed goalkeeper.

Snake totems in Long Dao.

Long Dao villagers with reticulated python skins outside the longhouse.

Fowzi and Baru – the highly unsuccessful hunters.

The author in Lundaiya costume.

Baru makes camp and prepares a tiny pheasant.

Civet cat – not a tasty dish.

Chicken bait for a
hungry python.

Steerman peers warily
into Big Snake's lair.

Adam with Big Snake. Imran is on the left (*above*).

death by spider poison. I pointed at the disappearing pink-eyed monster. Then he laughed.

'That spider does not even have teeth,' he said.

'But it bit me,' I whimpered.

'It only has a hook under its body, it hooks on to you to change direction.'

'Is the hook . . . poisonous?'

Fowzi gave me a look which can only be described as scornful. I continued, in silence, to hack a way into the snake's hiding place.

There were suggestive-looking trails leading from the place, and that smell. Fowzi was convinced we were on to something. It was a bit of a long shot and I wanted to let it drop, especially when Fowzi suggested we come back at night, after having baited the place with some game. 'You mean a civet cat or a *satoh* bird, don't you?' I said. 'It'll have to be a pretty hungry python to be tempted by a dead civet cat.'

Fowzi was not to be put off. We resolved to bait the trap the next day and return the following night.

Taking a circuitous route back, we came across a *moomin*, a huge pile of round river boulders high on a steep hillside, on top of which was a formation of standing stones, one upright, the other leaning into it to make a T-shape when viewed from above. The standing stones were between six and ten feet high and five feet long. They were part of a chain, Fowzi said, of such mounds which lay in the hundred miles or so between Long Dao and the first village in Kalimantan.

The mound was some sixty-five feet in diameter and perhaps ten feet high in the middle. Baru wanted to show me the standing stones, but Fowzi wouldn't let me climb on the mound. Instead all three of us made a hands-together praying gesture facing the mound.

'This place built by spirits,' said Fowzi. 'We must respect.'

He explained that no man could have carried the stones from the river to the hilltop, it was simply too difficult. And, as I had observed, there were no rocks in the area large enough to make the standing stones on the top. 'These stones are from another place,' said Fowzi darkly, 'brought here by the flying tiger spirit.'

I must have looked puzzled or sceptical because he added with sincerity, 'This is the truth.'

He wouldn't let me photograph the *moomin* mound, though I was convinced, and later verified, that I was the first outsider to have 'discovered' it. When Fowzi told me that John the anthropologist had not seen the *moomin*, I felt very pleased with myself and suddenly understood the absurd desire to grub about in obscure places that grips archaeologists. It only takes being first on the scene to bring out the latent Indiana Jones in everyone.

But the implacable certainty of Fowzi's beliefs was both interesting and unnerving. It didn't seem at all out of place to pray at the mound, and though I didn't believe the flying tiger swooped in with a load of masonry, it felt right that flying tigers were involved. The *moomin* mound was a mysterious place (but no more mysterious than Avebury stone circle in England), and to try to reduce it to something that makes sense in our flying-tigerless world, well, 'such reasoning has the smell of fear about it', as the Colonel would say. I didn't want to indulge in New Age fantasizing, combining wishful thinking and a sense of drama with extravagant thoughts about the age of Aquarius. On the other hand I didn't want to be the old explorer type, noting Johnny native's nutty religious ideas and laughing at them.

What interested me was the way Baru completely accepted Fowzi's explanations. Christianity had not supplanted the old superstitions, it merely coexisted alongside them. And the beliefs weren't 'heavy', in the way I imagined Satanic cult beliefs in the West were, they were workaday superstitions. I too had plenty of those, but labelled them obsessions rather than superstitions: touching wood, always parking my car with the front wheels pointing straight, always running up stairs, always labelling my 'important' computer files with capital letters. I couldn't be high-handed with Fowzi and Baru, considering all these examples of my own nonrational behaviour.

It was almost evening when we came back to Camp Manillan. The last rays of the sun made the wide, shallow river twinkle, and in the distance, where it was deeper, it reflected a broad sweep of yellow. We stood on the bank in the trees watching for a while. Fowzi, with the gun resting like a yoke on his shoulders, said, 'Do you ever feel sad at sunset?'

'Why, because the day is ending?'

'No, sometimes I think about a long time ago, that's all. I see the sunset and I feel a sad feeling.' Then he smiled his boyish, almost apologetic smile.

While Baru prepared a meal, Fowzi went off to catch something as bait for the snake. We heard the gun go off far in the distance. Somehow I knew it wouldn't be deer, and when he returned and dropped another civet cat, *do takar* in Lundaiyo, down next to the fire, I was hardly surprised. It was a beautiful, sad thing, now dead, striped black and grey with a pointed nose. 'Snakes like civet cat,' he said optimistically. Baru insisted on arranging the dead cat in a number of semirealistic poses for me to photograph: civet cat sleeping, civet cat curled up, civet cat apparently drinking from a water bowl. Fortunately we wouldn't have to eat it, but I doubted whether a wild snake, unless extremely hungry, would be that interested in a dead feline either.

That night, very late, I was awoken by voices round the campfire. Baru and Fowzi seemed to be deep in discussion, the rekindled fire reflecting off serious faces. I glanced at my watch: 2 a.m. Perhaps they were going hunting again. For all our lack of success, they still had an undiminished fervour for tracking down and killing things. I made a mental note to complain about being woken up the next morning.

Making breakfast at dawn the next day, Baru and Fowzi were both oddly subdued and untalkative. I guessed they'd had no luck the night before.

'Went hunting again, did you?' I said in a jocular tone.

'No,' said Fowzi.

'So why were you up in the middle of the night?'

'I was praying with Baru,' he said.

I decided to leave it at that, but later in the day, as we prepared for our night hunt, he asked, 'Did you hear that stone being thrown at the camp last night?'

'No.'

'That's what woke me up. Normally I never wake up like that, but I was having a bad dream. Maybe it is the spirit of the civet cat saying, "Oh, no, Fowzi is hunting at night."'

'Is it bad luck to hunt at night?'

'Sometimes,' said Fowzi obscurely. 'But did you hear that stone? It was very loud.'

'No,' I said, 'but I heard you.'

'I told Baru and he made a fire and started to pray for me . . .' Perhaps he caught my expression, for he added hurriedly, 'But it was only a dream.'

Fowzi was definitely rattled because he announced after breakfast that we should move camp that day, before the night hunt: 'It is quicker that way, to get back after the hunt.'

Baru started to pack up our kit immediately.

'Is it that dream?' I asked.

'This is not a good place,' said Fowzi. 'I am a man not frightened of anything. But I am frightened by that dream because it won't go away. In the dream I wait to defend my younger sister. She is married now and has three children. I wait but I only have short knife. My friends want to kill me and they have long knives so they stab me and I die. I very

148

disturbed. I wake Baru. I say, "Did you hear that?" Baru said he heard the stone too. We pray together but I cannot sleep after that. You know in Borneo you can take a picture and kill that person?' He paused and, as if to quell any contradiction, said very matter-of-factly, 'This is true. I think maybe someone has my picture and wants to kill me. Maybe a friend.'

I didn't know what to say. In a moment I was taken back to when I was ten years old and my family were entertaining a family of Ugandan Asians, refugees recently resettled in England. Our house was at the end of a long, dark lane, but I played there even after nightfall without a jot of fear. The two young sons, Indian boys a little older than I, absolutely refused to take my go-cart up the lane after dark. 'There are ghosts,' they said, with the same absolute certainty that Fowzi had said, 'This is true.' I tried to persuade them that I knew this place. How could there be ghosts in a place I played every evening? It was no good, they would not be persuaded. And I could not see it from their point of view. To me they were entirely deluded.

Now, twenty years later, I had spent time among superstitious people in parts of the world that were not so familiar as the end of the lane. In Japan, most people take part in rituals as a way of warding off evil. It is a common sight to see a salaryman and his wife standing in front of their brand-new Mazda while a Shinto priest scatters salt over its bonnet and utters prayers that it should be spared collisions and other mishaps. On any building site, before work starts, you will see a small pyramid of salt; this is an offering to the *kami*, spirits, to make sure the work proceeds favourably.

Later, in Haiti, holed up in the Oloffson Hotel, I sat up drinking rum one night with a mad UNESCO filmmaker who claimed she could see ghosts passing behind me. In a still night, broken only by the odd gunshot in the distance, I suddenly heard a banging of doors and footsteps in a room

I could see was empty. Was it the booze, or my soft-headed suggestibility? I preferred to think the latter. The next morning we heard that the hotel guard had shot a cat dead. (I could see that cats were going to haunt me.) His reason had been simple, and was easily accepted in that place: he thought that the cat might have been a *loup garou*, a person intent on evil who had taken the form of a cat. 'I shot it, because I did not know who it was,' he explained.

So now that my snake-hunting expedition was altering course because of a bad dream, I wasn't quite so adamant as I had been at ten. Maybe Fowzi was right. Maybe someone did want to kill him and was hunched over a photo stabbing at his image with a long knife for that very reason. Maybe the civet-cat spirit was angry, having been killed, and had teamed up with the evil friend. I could tell that though Baru had great faith in Christian prayer, Fowzi thought it wise to hedge his bets by moving to a place unknown by the civet spirit, who perhaps was guiding the evil friend's intentions towards the camp.

What interested me most about the Aesculapian cult was the role snakes played in the healing process. The main diagnostic technique was to investigate dreams. These were believed to be issuing from the underworld. The snake, being the symbol of that vanquished region, became the symbol of the god that healed by dreams. It is not hard to see that for 'underworld' read 'unconscious'. Far from being vanquished by Apollo and Hercules, the snake had entered inside us.

And isn't the Garden of Eden about some kind of joining with snakes? Aren't Adam and Eve aligned with the snake after their fall, rather than with God? And, in a way, isn't the snake a keeper, a guide who encourages their 'growing up' out of the ignorant prelapsarian state?

I was beginning to see that the light religions, of which

150

the Middle Eastern monotheisms were the latest example, could never vanquish the snake, that in fact they needed the snake, and their apparent opposition to the snake was, on another level, a very necessary act of cooperation.

When I was making the totem I'd wanted to show the others that I too could do, or had sympathy with, jungle magic. It was like a return to childhood, building a den or going on afternoon 'expeditions' inspired by the Arthur Ransome stories. But like *Lord of the Flies* it had all gone sour. The silly totem was forgotten. We now had more serious things on our hands: the spirits were after us. I was prepared to make an allowance in logistics for this but I wasn't going to believe, or pray with Baru. What I didn't realize is that making a practical allowance for superstition is just the first step. When you're surrounded by believers you have to be right outside or you run the risk of being lost.

I tried to imagine what Colonel H. would have done. I'm sure he wouldn't have let himself be guided by the whims of dreamers. But things were different now. The hard certainties I had to offer were reduced to my Maglite torch and The Tool. There was no British Empire to back me up.

The plastic tarpaulin, the various big pots and pans, blankets and food, were very quickly stowed and we headed upriver to a place about halfway between the snake-hunting ground and Camp Manillan. While Baru made camp, Fowzi and I set off to the snake place to fix the civet cat as bait. We dripped its blood around the place to attract the snake and to cover our own scent. I suspected that the cat was already beginning to rot, but Fowzi proceeded with a glum authority, explaining that as we would be back in a few hours, once night had fallen, the cat would still be attractive as bait.

In the few hours before nightfall I dozed on the sleeping platform Baru had constructed. I did not dream. It was apposite, though, that a snake hunt should involve dreaming.

151

The light religions have supplanted the old snake, shark and crocodile cults, but they come to us at night, messengers from the underworld, the place where there is no light and the world is ruled by fear.

SEVEN

Night Hunt in the Jungle

Snakes haven't the brain to plan aggressive campaigns against creatures they've no use for.

C. J. Ionides

It rained heavily before we set off, and the greenery we walked through dripped wet all over us. The night was pitch dark. The trees above blocked out any starlight and there was no moon. For some reason I had had to surrender my powerful torch to Fowzi, who strode ahead in the lead, symbolically assuming leadership of the expedition. I came next, with Baru supposedly shining a way for me with his weak plastic torch. My hand brushed some leaves and I felt something slimy touching me. In the light of Baru's torch I saw a leech about three inches long sliming between my fingers. Yuk! I shook the thing off in a spastic flail. A few moments later I had another one on my other hand. I beat my hand against my trousers and after that constantly brushed one hand against another to try and keep them free of leeches.

In the complete dark of the jungle night, rustles and shuffles and far-off noises of sudden movement made stumbling along the path like a ride on a ghost train. I slipped while hauling myself up a muddy bank and cursed Fowzi for setting such a cracking pace. When we stopped in the pooled light of the torches to wade across the first river, I glanced off upstream, into the blackness. The sounds of the river and the insects made our whispering almost unnecessary, though we were, by that stage, whispering. Baru's feet were covered

153

with leeches when he took off his rubber shoes. Several had even managed to worm their way through the ripped eye-holes in my boots, though they were foiled by my double socks. Two more on my hands I pulled straight off. I now understood why the Lundaiya didn't mess with burning off leeches – in a full-blown leech attack there just isn't time.

The river was cold, and I made slow, crouching progress over the sharp stones. The water was shallow and fast running, but it was the unseen stones that made it difficult. My lily-white, soft feet were no good at fording rivers.

We then went up the steepest, muddiest slope we had yet climbed. I tried to remember it from the daytime but it seemed different, and if it was the slope I remembered, shouldn't we have reached it later on? I grabbed at roots, too needful of their help to worry now. Once I slipped down on top of Baru, allowed myself to be pushed up by him, and carried on. At the top Fowzi strode on, not waiting, and I relieved Baru of his torch. Especially when going uphill, it just didn't work, relying on beams from behind. But even with the torch I managed to get into difficulties. At one stage I found myself in the middle of a prickly rattan bush, a hundred or so thorns gripping my trousers in all directions.

We halted in a dark place on the other side of the snake ground. Fowzi whispered the plan. He would go in and check things out, then we would install ourselves in twos, watching for the snake. If the snake came, one person was supposed to hook it with the bamboo and rope-loop contraption we had made several days before.

Baru and I stood in the complete and absolute darkness. I knew he must be very near me because I could smell the garlic of the failed caterpillar cure. Then I heard a rustling and a familiar sound. Baru was taking a leak. But hold on . . . that's a bit strange . . . Then I realized: Baru was carelessly urinating on my foot.

154

'Baru!' I hissed. The spraying sound wavered and splashed elsewhere. 'You're pissing on my foot!'

He stopped, then started again, apologizing in intelligible grunts and other noises. There was another sound of clothing being adjusted and then there were only the night sounds of the jungle to hear; a lot less noisy, I decided, than the jungle soundtracks on most movies.

Fowzi and I took the first watch. Fowzi had rigged up a kind of early-warning system using a twig on which the cat balanced, tied via a piece of string to his finger. Anything disturbing the cat would alert him, at which point he'd switch on the light and the chase would be on. Fowzi told me he'd seen men in the village use this method of surprise, and when the snake went down a hole, several men grabbed it by the tail and hauled it out.

After an hour and a half of quietly sitting, I changed places with Baru. Now it was my turn to be on my own. I sat on a log Baru had found, remembering not to light a cigar since snakes avoid the scent of tobacco, just as they find snuff fatal. Feeling my pockets, I checked that I still had my tin of Irish High Toast.

I tried to isolate in my mind the number of different sounds around me, but my systematic approach was always foiled by some strange and unhealthy sound coming from the bushes and undergrowth. I peered into black nothingness until I was almost hypnotized or asleep, when I heard a sound I had not heard before: crunch, rustle, rustle, snap, rustle, all in slow, smooth progression. It was a snake.

I snapped on Baru's torch, shining it into the underbrush in a mad variety of places, lighthouse style. The noise stopped, or my frenzy overlaid it. I didn't want to walk away from where I was so I stayed in place, shining the torch about, but I could see nothing. It was very nearly the time to relieve Fowzi, so I decided to go over and tell them about my potential snake sighting, or rather hearing.

I made my way carefully, brushing my hands continually to detect any leeches. I knew I was going in the right direction so I was not too nervous and I was using the torch. It was a distance of about fifty yards, through forest with very little undergrowth.

I started to think about something, and I thought about that thing for quite a long time before I realized I should have arrived at the snake ground. I kept on walking out of a weak-minded belief that it must be just a little further on. Then I walked even further, thinking that somehow, because I'd been thinking, I hadn't actually gone as far as I thought I had. I began to doubt my own experience and walked a little further just to be on the safe side.

I was lost.

In the jungle.

At night.

It was not a good feeling.

I turned this way and that, hesitant, squinting for a familiar tree or bush. A familiar *tree*? What was I thinking of? All trees looked the same in this place. You'd have to be a psychotic arboreal fetishist to notice the difference between one tree and another. But I did not cry out.

I turned about and started to retrace my steps. I decided it would not be so difficult to go back to the log I had been happily sitting on and wait for Fowzi and Baru to come and get me.

This was a good theory. But since I had left no real trail through the forest, it was not clear which way I had come. I cursed myself for not counting footsteps, which is the only surefire way to avoid making the situation worse when you're lost. I walked back about as far as I thought the fallen tree was, but it wasn't there. Then some more, and some more, repeating what I had done at the other end. This time, though, the terrain looked unfamiliar. Now I was starting to panic.

Just then I heard the snake again. Quite distinct from all the other crashes and inexplicable night noises of the jungle, I heard the slow crunch of foliage, the suppressed snap of a dry leaf or twig, just as Uncle Izham had explained. The panic evaporated as something more primeval than panic took over. Rigid snake fear.

I tried to get technical as a way to quell the rising panic. I thought about the labial pits, infrared sensors on the first four upper lip scales of the reticulated python. When breathing they have been observed to exhale backwards over the head, so as not to interfere with the heat image of their prey. In my mind's eye I saw a quivering heat image of myself, warm and invitingly nourishing to the snake about to strike. Perhaps I should move?

But if I moved I would give the snake a sound to track me by. Although snakes lack external ears, eardrums and Eustachian tubes, they can still hear through the connection of the rudimentary earbone to the jaw hinge bone. It was scant solace to know that when the snake started to swallow me it would be, for the reptile, a deafening experience.

The slow crunching came closer. I twisted my head all around but I could not convince myself I knew what direction it was coming from. The crunching grew louder. I became convinced the snake was about to strike. Animals freeze as a normal reaction to seeing a snake; they wait for a cue to move. This has been mistaken for hypnosis but it isn't. The snake moves very slowly and this isn't registered as a sufficiently threatening cue. Then it strikes and it's too late.

I jumped, for every good reason, high into the air. Tore my shirt cuff on a thorn bush, tore free. Banged my head on a branch, fell over and carried on running.

And running, until I was out of breath and more lost than ever. My only consolation was, if Big Snake was on to me, that snakes have low endurance for intense activity. Their heart and circulation prevent long periods of such strenuous exertion as chasing after a frightened human animal.

Hold on. Get a grip. You're off the path, but you're still within about four hundred yards, probably less, of Baru and Fowzi. Forget pride. Yell! I opened my mouth but only a squeak came out, the kind of noise made by punctured rubber ducks when accidentally trodden on. I knew a real yell would call for real commitment to the idea of being lost, and I didn't want to feel I was really lost, not yet.

Probably if you could interview beyond the grave, quite a lot of tragedies occurred because the person was too embarrassed to ask for help before it was too late. Flashing through my mind was the macabre story of a second cousin who, in order to get into the USA illegally from Canada, had been let out into some woods on the border. The road doubled across the border. All that was required was to walk, in early autumn, through about four hundred yards of forest. She never appeared on the other side. A search party was eventually called out, but they never found her body. 'They never found his body!' The words rang through me like a death knell. And anyhow, how could they? What kind of a search could be mustered here, where we were illegally in Indonesia? It was a mess, a big mess.

The sage advice of Clifford Pope, the giant-snake expert, was being reversed: 'Man's ability to learn about snakes allows him not only to avoid them but to turn the tables by becoming the aggressor.' What else did he write? 'Alertness, incessant activity, and social habits make man anything but an easy victim.'

'Remember *you* are the alpha predator,' I said to calm myself. 'I am an alpha predator,' I whispered through gritted teeth.

The place where Baru rested on the tree trunk was just off the path. If I found the path, I could find the tree trunk.

The best way to find the path? I thought furiously through all the survival books I'd read as a kid. But finding your way when lost is kind of dull compared with how to drive through a mud slide, so I must have skipped those bits. I found I had a very poor information base to draw upon.

The best way . . . would be to walk in an ever-widening circle. Instead of walking in circles as I undoubtedly was, walk in a circle intentionally. Brilliant. I could have hugged myself. I was a genius without doubt. I set off on my circle walking.

I walked and walked and walked and began to try and figure if there were any flaws in my theory. Any gaping holes that would make a crucial difference, making it impossible, in fact, to find my way back with any degree of certainty. I very nearly cried out. The only flaw in the plan, as far as I could work out, was that I might not recognize the path when I came upon it. In any case I kept making my way with the weakening beam of Baru's torch through the hostile forest. It was not a place I wanted to be. I wanted out. Now. Then I snagged myself for at least three or four minutes on a bush of palms edged with razor thorns. Now I knew what I was looking for: footprints. When I crossed the path, as long as it was lower down than the place where the resting log was, then . . . I tried to orient myself. Where was the hillside, that small ravine I tripped into, that crunchy-sounding bracken stuff? I didn't know where I was. Time to stop, and take a breather. And I really was out of breath, because I had started to run, without knowing it, or sanctioning it, and I thought, for the second time that evening, This is how people get lost in the wilderness. They start running and they don't even know they're running.

My cigars were back at the camp but I still had the snuff. I took a huge pinch of the stuff, putting it on the base of my thumb. A few seconds later I sneezed heartily and felt the better for it. OK, start in . . . that direction. I meandered slowly, looking for signs of having been that way before. Somehow I knew it was hopeless.

But I kept on. Then I saw the light of the torch in the distance and at the same time I found myself by the greatest of miracles back at the place where I had started. When Fowzi and Baru turned up, without the snake, they did not even ask why I was out of breath, and I, of course, did not tell them. I had been scared, but much braver men than I have suffered from snake fear. The great game hunter Jim Corbett thought nothing of tracking a man-eating tiger, but when asked to hunt a seventeen-foot Indian python he refused, admitting, as an excuse, his strange horror of big snakes.

Fowzi and Baru would have continued watching the useless piece of dead civet all night, but I wanted to go home. I'd had enough. Fowzi was right, the spirits were against us. Besides, the stone in my pocket was as cold as ever. We could spend months in the jungle just flailing around. Getting lost had put the seal on it. I needed to be more organized, more in control. This was jungle recon, a learning experience, nothing more. It was time to move on.

My companions were happy to return to base. Their one request was to do a little more hunting on the way back, following a route on the other side of the river. The downside of the new route was that we would have to cross the wide river once, quite soon, and then a second time, just in front of the camp. I was reluctant but could think of no very good reason not to.

We were soon down at the river, taking off our footwear yet again, my feet the whitest white in the all-surrounding dark. At this stage I started to become a little difficult. I crossed the river even more haltingly than usual, and because I'd decided it was a pain, it was, doubly so. The two hunters waited for me on the bank and said nothing about my silent protest. Perhaps they were so keen to have another go at the deer that they did not pay attention to me. Baru, I noticed, had a handful of leaves ready to blow and attract an animal.

It was Baru's turn to lead the hunt, probably part of a deal about the gun. In previous hunts Baru had been, in Fowzi's words, 'too quick to aim and too quick to fire'. Behind Baru's back he even made a joke about Baru's wayward eye straying from the target. Whatever the cause, Baru missed everything he shot at apart from birds at virtually point-blank range.

With unerring incompetence Baru led us deep into thickets and jungle dead ends. Several times we ended up down on the beach of the river, but at a place where the river was deep and fast and would have entailed swimming rather than wading. Fowzi and Baru both tried charming deer with the leaf decoy trick. Nothing doing. In the end I said that it was time to go home.

I knew now that there wasn't a path on the side of the river we were walking along, which was why we kept running into such natural obstacles as gullies and thorn patches. Finally Baru decided we should work along the bank as close to the river as possible. Yet, interestingly, not within sound of the water; you had to be very close to hear that.

The next barrier was a wide, deep gully carrying a stream into the main river. There were broken branches lodged in the gully, but it was too deep to climb down. There was nothing for it but to jump across. It was no more than six or seven feet across the gully, but a slip would have meant a nasty fall on the uneven wood and rocks in the gully. Baru and I shone torches so that Fowzi could leap. Then Baru gave me both torches and leaped himself, which was very sprightly of him. I was stuck with the torches but no one to shine them. I decided against throwing a torch across the gully on the grounds that the two intrepid hunters were just as likely to shine the torch in my face as in the place where I wanted to land.

I memorized where I had to land, took a run up and,

giving myself a yell of encouragement, took off into the dark. In the few microseconds of midair darkness I knew something was going to go wrong. My feet connected with nothing; in fact, the only thing that touched the far bank was my nose, ploughing a deep furrow in the mud as I tumbled backwards. I visualized my descent into the deep ravine when an iron-sure hand gripped my shirt. All the buttons ripped off but I was saved. I smelled Baru's garlic smell and was, for a few minutes, so grateful I almost hugged him.

We got down to where we were going to cross and I knew immediately it was going to be a problem. I was particularly nervous because I had a notebook full of information gleaned on the trip, in the side patch pocket of my trousers. If I didn't catch the snake, and if I lost my notes as well, the whole trip would be a disaster.

Fowzi went first, wading from the security of one dark boulder to another until he got almost to the far bank, where I guessed the water was deeper. He moved downstream and was out of sight in the darkness. Then Baru went. I followed Baru.

Halfway across I knew the whole thing was a bad idea. My sense of humour deserted me and the notebook, which I could feel next to my thigh, assumed an overwhelming importance. I stopped on a rock and transferred it to my shirt pocket. But my shirt pocket no longer had a button and I knew if I leaned forward it could easily fall out into the fast-flowing stream. Feeling hideously constrained, trapped even, I put the book back in my trouser pocket. At this stage, I had lost all nervousness about being in a river at midnight in the jungle, or rather, the nervousness had re-formed as anxiety about the little black book. Fortunately the snuff was in a waterproof container.

We were all lined up on or near boulders along the far bank. Fowzi was up to his waist and just about to climb on to the bank. Baru had made it from my rock to his but now stared with trepidation at the deep section between his rock and the one Fowzi had just left.

On my rock I completely lost it. The rock was very small and though the river wasn't rising, it felt as if it was, and I had to maintain a permanent scrabble to keep out of the water. The notebook cried out in all its papery vulnerability. Save me from death by water, screamed the notebook.

'Fowzi!' I shouted, in a tone both demanding and imperious, but also ragged and nervous, the tone of the aggrieved shopper or man slighted by a restaurant waiter.

He looked round from where he was on the bank, drying his legs with the tracksuit trousers he had taken off to cross the river. He had a startled look as if caught by a flash camera.

'I'm not moving off this rock!' I shouted.

He said something back, but I wasn't in the mood for listening. With an admirable sense of duty Baru turned, stepped off his rock and plunged up to his chest in the raging torrent. As I prepared room for him on my rock, I dropped his feeble-beamed torch into the depths. Like a duck or wading bird he plunged underwater and retrieved the thing, which still shone underwater, sending a weird beam out from the depths.

'There's no room here, Baru!' I commanded. 'Here, take this!' I handed him the precious notebook. 'If this is lost, then everything is lost!'

Baru nodded like a trooper.

I had little faith in my ability to navigate the fast, deep water without falling in, but I believed that Baru, with his prehensile, work-toughened feet, would make it while keeping still some part of himself dry. Fowzi had finished skulking and now shouted encouragement at Baru, who prepared himself for his big mission. He nodded and smiled, holding the book clamped by one hand to the top of his head. Just as he stepped, Fowzi called, but it was too late. Baru stepped directly into a pothole in the riverbed and sank like a stone beneath the water. But as in a scene out of ancient mythology, his hand rose, holding the still-dry book above the swirling waters. Then slowly more of the arm emerged from the river until Baru's head broke the surface, wet as a seal but still grinning.

He plunged on, now holding the book like a trophy above his head. I followed tentatively and never sank below my waist, but it was still annoying to get that wet. I knew Baru and Fowzi had spare trousers in camp, but I didn't. And sleeping without trousers would mean a colder than usual night among nights that were noted for their coldness.

Some of this anticipated coldness entered my relations with Fowzi. I did not blame Baru. He was not the leader, and when the chips were down, he had proved himself a worthy man indeed – the important thing was never to let him take the lead. But perhaps I was missing the point. Perhaps Fowzi had to relinquish the lead from time to time, as part of the inherent democracy of the tribe. There was no standard of 'professionalism' to judge their exploits by. The idea of one leader all the time is a Western obsession, overcome with difficulty by groups that set out to explore the outback or climb mountains. It would be hard, actually impossible, imagining a Lundaiya as a control freak. The closest they got was Nelius, and even he had to give in to the footballers' drinking demands. The control freak can exist only when he has a constant unchanging background to control against, people willing to be controlled, or things that can be controlled. None of this was present in the jungle.

Fowzi lit a piece of resin firelighter and rekindled the fire. He took my trousers and started to dry them out for me. It was his way of saying sorry.

Meanwhile Baru stood in his underpants, which I had thought were a pale pink. Now, in the firelight, the front

164

seemed almost blood red. Baru noticed this at the same time as I did. His pants *were* blood red. Reaching inside with the kind of delicacy reserved for defusing a bomb, Baru, a look now of stern disgust on his face, detached a huge leech from his penis.

The leech went into the fire, blood and all. It was one of those airless moments of hilarity, where laughter, bottled up or restrained, has to escape until you're in severe pain. Baru was pleased we found it funny. He kept re-enacting the discovery to make us laugh more. All the cold wretchedness of the night hunt was forgotten. After laughing for a while, I'd apologize and then laugh again.

Fowzi said there was a Lundaiya children's story about the leech. A man went fishing and he caught a headless ghost. This ghost was angry and he stuck the man to a rock in the river. The man said that if he unglued him from the rock, he would give the ghost his wife. When the man's wife came down to the river to look for her husband, he called her over to the rock. Then he said to the ghost, who was hiding in the water, 'Here is my wife, let me go free!' The moment he was unstuck, he took the knife which he knew that his wife always carried in her basket and cut the ghost into small pieces.

A few months later the woman became pregnant. But instead of giving birth to a baby, she gave birth to an insect the size of a baby. At first the wife didn't want to let the insect baby feed at her breast, but her husband said that she must not starve their first baby. The baby gripped its mandibles around her tender nipple and wouldn't let go. It fed and fed and the woman got thinner and thinner. After a year the baby had grown as big as a four-year-old and knew the names of all the trees and animals in the forest. The man said to the baby, 'I bet I know one tree you don't know the name of.'

The insect baby replied, still sucking at its mother's breast,

165

'I know all the names of everything in the forest and nothing knows my name.' Which was true because the man and his wife had been so shocked by the baby that they hadn't given it a name.

So the man took the baby and his wife through the forest and when they passed a tree the man said, 'Name that!' and the insect baby always did. At last they came to the tree he had planned to test the insect baby on. 'This is the tree you do not know!'

'That's easy,' said the baby, 'that's a pa'ang tree.' As it spoke the word, it had to let go of the nipple for just a second, and in that fraction of a moment the man cut the baby into a thousand pieces – which all became leeches and squirmed away.

EIGHT

Murder in the Forest

From the time I first started living this kind of life
I've always assumed the probability of a violent
death, and it still seems to me the natural and
sensible one.

C. J. Ionides

When we came out of the jungle into the cleared fields of
the first hamlet near to Long Dao, the sudden light was so
bright I had to squint. After two weeks of jungle half-light it
took time to readjust to the sun. And the heat rising off the
ploughed field was intense compared to the cool of the forest.

The man with thick specs came out to meet us. 'My son
caught a snake!' he said.

We wearily climbed the ladder into the hut where the
bundled baby was still asleep in its sprung cradle. The fat
woman laughed at our lack of success and ladled out pieces
of charred meat. Not as chewy as deer or monkey, a texture
of tuna but not fishy, I realized I was eating snake.

'Better than civet cat,' I said to Fowzi.

'My son caught the snake by the stream. It was as long as
a man. He cut its head off like this,' and the old man made a
sudden chopping motion.

'Was it a python?' I asked.

'Yes,' said Fowzi and the old man together.

Despite our failure in the forest, I didn't feel downhearted.
The trip had nurtured my snake fever and increased my
confidence. I was keen to move on. In fact, I was feeling
pretty good ever since recovering my hat from the 'hunting

lodge'. It had been there, just as Fowzi said it would, undisturbed for days.

As we hiked up the narrow path, I smelled what I thought was a strong whiff of snake. I tugged at Fowzi's sleeve, but he laughed. 'That is *bohukan* – pangolin – smell, not snake.' The pangolin, a scaly anteater, is sometimes mistaken for an armadillo, which is a South American creature and not at all related. The pangolin's pong is strong and sour, with more than a hint of unwashed armpit. Now that it was pointed out I could tell the difference easily.

'Pangolin catch ants under their scales,' said Fowzi. 'Then they swim in the river and eat the swimming ants.'

The bamboo-pole bridge, which I had been dreading for some days as we returned home, was not as bad as I had anticipated. It creaked and bounced but I did not freeze in the middle as I had in the river the night of the great hunt. As we rounded a curve we could see the main village up ahead. It meant fording the river, but this time I didn't waste time undoing my boots, knowing that I'd have some time to dry them out. I forged ahead through the stream and, laughing, the other two followed. Baru shouldered his gun proudly. 'We are like soldiers!' said Fowzi, though I knew this wasn't entirely a compliment. A few years before he had guided a British paratrooper unit on jungle exercises. 'The sergeant is strong man. The captain is good man. He tell the men not to laugh at my English. But the private soldier is no good – too big for the jungle and some of them frightened of the night. They come back to camp because they are frightened on their own!' I know that feeling, I thought. Being like a soldier meant not taking your boots off, according to Fowzi. He was right – now I had wet, steaming boots I really felt as if I'd just come off advance recon in the Nam, with my Montagnard companions.

As we passed the villagers working in their fields in conical straw coolie hats, Baru gave yelping whoops at every group that came into view. Exactly the kind of noise teenagers make at bus stops waiting for the school bus, except Baru was about fifty. He was pleased to be home and glad to show it. Fowzi whooped once, but it had none of the vim of Baru's cry.

I asked Fowzi if I should pay Baru directly. Without hesitation he said, 'Pay me and then I pay to him, this way there is more respect to me.'

We passed an old couple digging out roots in a field they had just burned. The man spoke to Baru, who, judging by his gestures, was explaining just how big the one that got away had been. We went to the village 'shop', which had opened a year or two before. It was unlocked, unmanned and self-service, a wooden hut with a poor selection of soap, cans of soft drink, brushes and packets of biscuits. I bought the entire stock of Coke, which we had to drink warm, there being no fridges or ice in Long Dao. Two or three cans disappeared mysteriously with Fowzi's rather sullen kids. Baru's two young daughters had sweeter tempers. Their names, which I recorded phonetically, were suitably odd; the elder was called Phoney Dorcas and the younger was called Fitchit.

I went back to the Bamboo Hilton, took my boots off and slept.

The next day I told Fowzi that I definitely wanted to give the football to the headman. And finally I got to the bottom of why the headman was so little about. He was, it seemed, a puppet headman, appointed by Nelius and his cronies, who had staged a coup against the last encumbent, Laban. Laban, though he shared a longhouse with Nelius's uncle, was not in favour. He had allowed people from the village to sell off their 'custom rights' to the logging companies on the other side of Long Siau. The government had given this land in perpetuity to the villagers, but once a few had sold, it gave

169

the logging company a foothold. Some of those who had sold land no longer even lived in the village; they lived in Sipitang or Kota Kinabalu. The stooge that Nelius and his friends had put in was in favour of tourism and against the selling of land for logging, but he had little real power. Nelius, for example, was also the government representative responsible for reporting from the headman to the government. It didn't take much imagination to see that this job, combined with his various policing roles and managership of the football team, constituted greater real power than the nominal headman had. 'Actually,' said Fowzi, 'the headman is quite poor. Each day he has to work in his fields.'

Fowzi suggested I donate the football to the church, but first I had to sign it, adding my signature alongside the eleven players of Manchester United already on the ball.

I still hadn't given the photo to Mr Balan, the old man with whom Roy Goh's father had stayed some years before. I found his house, wooden and on stilts like all the others, and called through the door. A younger man, one of Balan's sons, I guessed, came out. He spoke English but did not seem very pleased to see me.

Me: Mr Balan?

Him: Yes?

Me: I've come from Raymond Goh to deliver this picture.

Him: Ah. Raymond Goh.

Me: Yes, I'm a friend of his son, Roy Goh. I've come from England.

Silence.

Me: Nice and quiet around here.

Him: (smiles) Where are you staying?

Me: Up there, the Bamboo Hilton.

Him: Have you seen Fowzi?

Me: Yes, I've seen Fowzi all right.

Silence.

Me: Well, nice to meet you.

170

We shook hands and I left. What had I been expecting?

I had better luck at the church service on Sunday. The daily service was about an hour and a half, but the Sunday service was three hours long. I sat with Fowzi and his family and braced myself for three hours of Lundaiya religion. As the Bible had been translated into Lundaiyo, that was the language of the service.

Before the service Fowzi introduced me to all the village bigwigs. Baru was there, with his hair slicked back and wearing a jacket and tie; I almost didn't recognize him. He was very happy to see me, genuinely happy, and it had nothing to do with my football, which was heartening. News of the football, which I had in a plastic bag like an illicit party donation of loose cash, became a real talking point. The pastor, who was a young man, the only one in a suit, said that he was sorry he could not speak English, but that the football was a wonderful gift.

Inside the church, which was a clean, white building with a tin roof, the service dragged on in a relaxed fashion. There was a drum kit next to the altar and at various intervals Lite, on guitar, and his friend on drums, and two girls with tambourines played cheerful Christian rock music, and the congregation joined in singing rousing Lundaiyo hymns. Many of the men had small notebooks, and as the pastor spoke they made little notes in their books. I thought of Fowzi and his endless writing about his 'ideas'.

The big old man sitting next to me, who had been a sergeant major in the Malay army, wrote in a little blue book, and when he got tired of this he clipped his toenails, brushing the clippings neatly under the pew. We had talked earlier and he had told me he'd served in Kuala Lumpur during the Malay Emergency of 1948–60. When I mentioned Colonel H.'s name and the pillarbox-red jeep, he thought, yes, perhaps, he did remember such a man.

When the time came for the blessing and dedication of the

football, I stood up and found myself mouthing the usual ambassadorial platitudes: 'The people of England are most happy to donate this football, all the way from Manchester United [lie] to Long Dao. Long may it be kicked!' Everyone clapped and the pastor said nice things about me. Lite took up his guitar again and we all sang some more rousing hymns. For a three-hour service, it all went surprisingly swiftly.

After the service I went back to Fowzi's to discuss some more of his 'ideas'. 'I have a plan in three stages,' he told me. 'I do stage one and move to stage two. I do stage two but when I want to move to stage three, Long Dao people all stop me. All my stages fall down, foof!'

'It's very difficult to get things done, even in England,' I said.

'But it is harder in Long Dao. The people have no vision. I tell them my vision 2000. They say yes. But a week later they have forgotten.'

'You'll have to work on your own. At first, I mean.'

'But I am just one man. How much can one man do?'

'A lot,' I said.

What exactly was Fowzi's problem? There was something a little too earnest and grasping and ambitious about him. Though he did have fun, I felt he didn't enjoy life enough. He could learn a thing or two from Baru. I felt that the dissatisfied Fowzi was very much a product of the modern world. He glimpsed the immense possibilities of modernity, tantalizingly close to his grasp. But he lacked the charisma to be able to persuade others. He was still locked in the traditional pecking order of the village. As a man with children and a house, he was dismissive of feckless youngsters like Lite, but that didn't help him to get employees. And the Lites of the village just didn't want to work that hard. They liked the easy life, supplanted by a little cash from the outside world. Fowzi had vision all right, but I got the impression that he didn't like people enough. In this twilight time of the tribe, that was important. I'm sure in the West he would have become a millionaire; he was a bank manager's dream. But by the standards of the tribe, he desired too much for himself, he was too much of an individual in the wrong way.

Now that I had my football-donating celebrity, we were duty bound to make several Sunday-afternoon house calls. Peter, a young Malay teacher sent to Long Dao to teach English and maths, lived alone in a hut next to the school. In his kitchen he had the rusty back axle of a four-wheel drive, which he used for weightlifting. 'It's so boring here,' he told me. 'Only my axle to lift! And the prop shaft for one-handed curls! I live alone, I eat alone. The best thing is going to get my eggs from Sipitang.' Next to the sink were three cardboard trays, each designed to hold thirty-six eggs. He was halfway through the first tray. 'When I feel really bored I eat eggs all day. I'm so full of eggs sometimes I can't shit! But when the eggs are finished, I can go to Sipitang for more.'

'How long will you have to stay in Long Dao?' I asked.

'Until the government decides to send me somewhere else.'

'You could get sent somewhere worse.'

He looked at me with incredulity and then his smooth young face broke into laughter. 'You're right – I could get sent somewhere with a longhouse for the whole village and that would be really shitty.'

Peter and Fowzi explained that only poor people lived in large communal longhouses, noisy, dirty places where nothing was done. 'And it's hard to look after children in a traditional longhouse,' Peter added, though he was single and had no children of his own. They talked of the long-house, which I had romantically assumed to be a cornerstone of tribal life, in the same way that people in England talk about inner-city council estates.

Crossing the village we bumped into Nelius, who was ostentatiously strimming his lawn, or rather the closely pruned ground vegetation that grew in profusion around his house. He held up the strimmer for my inspection. 'It is the first in Long Dao,' he said proudly.

Inside, Nelius's subdued wife, who came from Indonesia, served tea and biscuits while Nelius showed me his certificates. After he had boasted himself dry, he explained, more cogently than Fowzi, why Long Dao was at risk from logging. 'It is the agathis trees, a kind of softwood, very valuable, and it is growing all around Long Dao.' And even though the new, tame headman refused to let any of the villagers sell their 'custom rights' land to the logging company, there had been enough sales in the past for the logging company to be pressing all the time.

'Perhaps the WWF can help us,' said Nelius. 'But as half of the village have worked already in the timber business, it is hard for us. Some of the young men here only know logging. It is easy money for them. Why should they then go back to their farms?'

'But when all the trees go, they'll have to,' I said.

He smiled smugly. 'Kampong people do not think like that. They have a deficiency in the planning sense!'

'They have no vision,' said Fowzi gloomily. Then he perked up and suggested I stay and become 'a real Bruno Manser'. For a few vain minutes I considered the idea. But fighting against the logging companies when only half the village was on your side sounded like a losing battle.

Fowzi believed that they would save the agathis trees of Long Dao. Nelius was more circumspect. When I asked him outright if they could stop the company logging right up to the edge of the village, he said quietly, 'Probably not.'

I brought the subject back to snakes. Nelius told us of a snake he'd seen killed as a boy that had eaten a 44-pound deer. This was far from a record feed. A twenty-five-foot python was found to have eaten a 71-pound ibex, two days after consuming two goats weighing 28 and 39 pounds. Gustav Lederer measured one snake that first ate a 120-pound pig and then had a 105-pound donkey for afters. Long Dao, I suspected, was not the land of the really big eaters. It was time to move on.

My overall strategy of covering as much ground as possible made it sensible to leave on the first Hi-Luxe out of Long Dao. Besides, I had convinced myself I needed experienced snake hunters, not willing amateurs like Fowzi and Baru.

I was preparing to leave when the headman of Long Siau arrived. He was a thin old man in ragged clothes with a deeply lined face and hardly any teeth. But he was full of life, stood very straight in his odd Wellington boots and shouted up to us on the porch the latest news he had run all the way from Long Siau to tell us. There had been a killing, perhaps it was a murder, he didn't know. Three men had gone out on a hunting trip and only two had come back. It had taken six days to find the third man, lying by the river, dead from a gunshot wound.

As head of security for the area, Nelius had to investigate, make a report and take photographs of the scene of the crime. My own camera was on the blink after the excessive humidity of the jungle, but I still had a lot of film sealed in plastic tubs. I told Nelius that if he was to take photographs in the dim jungle light he would need faster film than the 100ASA stock he had. I generously handed him a roll of 1000ASA film and then asked if I could come with him. He wasn't too keen on the idea, but as this was the first crime he'd ever had to make a report on (chicken theft in the village didn't count), there was no precedent for him to fall back on. I told him, truthfully, that I'd worked with the police in Japan. 'I'll be an expert witness,' I said.

The sheer power of the term overwhelmed him. 'We go at

seven tomorrow morning,' he said. Then he turned to Fowzi, who looked expectant, and snapped in Malay, 'But don't think you can come as well.'

I was willing to put off my return because of one thing. The old headman in Wellingtons had known something bad had happened, long before the man had failed to return, because he had seen a sign. 'I saw a sign!' he shouted up to Nelius's veranda. Flying high over the muddy village of Long Siau, an eagle had passed with a snake in its claws.

It is in Homer's *Iliad* a most potent image and a terrifying omen, signifying victory of the Achaeans over the old earth ways of the Asians. I felt a need for the symbolic, was hungry for it. Eagles catch young snakes all the time, but that one had flown, just at that time, over the old head in that village – surely it meant something, something terrible indeed.

Next morning, as we drove in the Hi-Luxe to Long Siau, Nelius explained excitedly what he had learned. The man who had been shot had been asked three times to come on a hunting trip. That was significant. If he didn't want to come, why? And why did the others insist so much on his coming? It had taken six days to find him, and that too was suspicious, since the river was an obvious place to look.

'Maybe they just got scared and ran away,' I suggested.

'Hmm,' said Nelius in a very knowing way. 'There are too many loose ends.'

In the back of the Hi-Luxe, clinging on to the roll bar, was Nelius's father, Mr Daud. He was a wizened old man in his seventies and had been the first headmaster in Long Dao before Nelius took over. Mr Daud was the dead man's second cousin, making Nelius his second cousin once removed, but Mr Daud was the only person Nelius trusted who could recognize the dead man.

When we got to Long Siau, a cluster of poorly dressed villagers gathered round the open windows of the Hi-Luxe.

Nelius stayed in the car and heard their testimony through the window, noting things down in a small exercise book.

'The dead man is in a place two days' walking from here,' said Nelius, 'but these people will take us there in a boat, which will take about three hours. They believe the killing is an accident. The family of the dead man say that he was forced to go hunting but they are not saying it is murder. Those men are the friends of the hunter who was killed.'

They didn't look like murderers, not my idea of murderers. One I took to be in his late twenties, he was of medium build, clean-shaven, with friendly, untroubled eyes. He nodded his head with a faint smile when I looked at him, as if he was above all this. The other was older, perhaps in his forties, with long hair and a Zapata moustache. He wore a shabby waistcoat, was taller than I, but thin with wiry arms. He smoked a Gudam Garam cigarette, but seemed relaxed enough. They would guide us, the headman, and another middle-aged man who just seemed to be tagging along, to the dead man's body.

We travelled in two boats, built-up dugouts longer than Lite's, with Yamaha outboard engines on the back. The middle-aged man steered one boat, and the younger of the suspects steered ours. It was quite noisy in the boat, but before everyone lapsed into silence, Nelius kept up his interrogation of the two men. They answered casually, sometimes one answering for the other. 'Shouldn't you keep them separate?' I asked Nelius. Instead of answering, he just made notes in his exercise book, which he crouched over to keep it from being splashed.

The river was wider than at Long Dao, a humming expanse of green water overhung by trees, not too dissimilar, apart from the boulders, from stretches of the River Cherwell in Oxfordshire. I couldn't resist dangling my fingers in the water as we powered along, feeling the sun on my face and wondering what it would be like to see a man killed by a shotgun wound. Apart from motorbike and car-crash victims, I had never seen a dead body before. When I went to Haiti, a human-rights lawyer who lived there told me, 'No trip to Haiti is complete without seeing at least one dead body.' I had been lucky and seen none. But I had to admit to a kind of sick fascination, now that I was on my way to view my first murder victim – well, possible murder. As a child I had been very keen to see a 'real skull', not just a life-sized plastic one you could make from a model kit. The first one I saw was in the Pitt-Rivers Museum in Oxford, which is, to my mind, the finest museum of its kind in the world. But the first skull I handled was actually in Haiti, owned by a voodoo *houngan*, who charged me a fortune to take photographs and offered me a cure for AIDS.

After two hours' boating we stopped on a gravel curve of the river for an early lunch. From a flat woven basket, the younger of the murder suspects brought two Milo tins of meat and several palm-wrapped slabs of rice. Because no salt was used to cook the rice, it was always tasteless to me, edible only when rolled around a piece of wild boar or deer meat. The murder suspects chatted quietly to each other and to the headman. Nelius walked a slight way upstream and urinated in the river. True to Lundaiya form, our group left the meat tins as the first unsightly rubbish on the gravel beach.

Nelius updated me on his thinking. He believed that the young man, the one piloting our boat and the one who claimed to have accidentally shot the man dead, each had a story that we could check. All three had been hunting separately, at night, though they had been keeping close together. Each had a torch, though they did not need to use them all the time as there was plenty of moonlight. Somehow they came to the river and the young man saw what he was sure was a deer drinking. When he fired, his friend suddenly stood up from behind a rock further on, where he had been resting or pissing. It was sheer bad luck that the deer was missed and the man was killed.

'What was the range?' I asked.

'He tells me twenty metres or more.'

'It's easy to miss a deer from closer than that in daylight,' I said with feeling. 'Maybe they really did accidentally shoot the man.'

'We will play the murder again,' said Nelius, and though I knew he'd been on a week-long course in Sipitang, his current methodology owed more to Astra Satellite reruns of *Columbo*.

We were closing in on the scene of the crime now and my appointment with the dead. Brought up in an environment where dead relatives were hustled as quickly as possible from hospital to the crematorium, and having experienced neither war nor natural disaster, I expected it to be something of a landmark experience. I hoped it would provide me with clues into the one certainty of life. In my mind I held two responses to dead and decomposing bodies: that of Glubb Pasha, founder of the Arab Legion, and that of an American lieutenant from the Vietnam War. Glubb, on seeing a rotting corpse in the trenches of the First World War, felt an absolute certainty about the holiness of life, how it draws its life breath from the divine. The corpse is so utterly a thing and not a man that what has been subtracted stands in high relief as majestic and unfathomable. The Vietnam veteran saw the opposite. He claimed he lost all religious faith on seeing his first dead body. 'I knew then that it was all a lie, that man was just a bag of meat and pus and nothing else.' Like all experiences, it depends for its significance on what you bring to it. The experience itself is not enough; there has to be preparation and reflection or it will have little value.

My father and his brother had played among corpses as children in northeast India. Living in Kohima shortly after the bloody battle – which had its centre point in the tennis court of the district commissioner, where, shortly before, my grandmother had played tennis – the children were free to roam in the margins of the forest, scene of fierce fighting between British and Japanese. They crawled into Japanese foxholes to retrieve bayonets and gas masks from dead soldiers. One of their favourite adventure playgrounds was a burned-out Japanese tank. My grandmother drew the line at my uncle's collection of Japanese jawbones, which he had threaded on a string to make his own fearsome warrior's necklace.

They dug their own foxholes and played at war in a place where the real thing provided an easy model to copy. Neither my father nor my uncle appeared disturbed by such childhood experiences and neither of them ever joined the armed forces. My father's childhood ambition was to join the Indian Civil Service and become a district commissioner like Sir Charles Pawsey, whose tennis court had been wrecked in the battle.

Most children like skull necklaces. I had a friend when I was eleven who had a necklace of cat skulls. My own collection included a bottle containing the skeletons of one large vole and eleven baby voles, a mummified cat from the attic of a thatched cottage, a fox skull and a ram's skull with horns, which hung over my bedside and never frightened me once. There is something almost homely about a skull. Corpses, I knew, would be different.

There were other dangers involved in living on a recent battlefield. When the Naga tribesmen burned the forest to clear new land, the sound of exploding ammunition was like a firework display. At an evening party with bonfires for warmth, my grandmother was suddenly, for no reason she knew, taken with an urge to leave her chair by the fire and move to the table nearby. As she did so, there was a great explosion in the fire and a piece of shrapnel the size of an egg tore through the back of the chair where she had been sitting. But my grandmother had always been known to have second sight and had, perhaps as result of having been born and brought up in India, seen ghosts all her life.

Bringing your children up in a battlefield would probably today count as irresponsible parenting. Colonel H., who had run away from home at sixteen, thought boys learned more quickly and more easily by being allowed to run wild. And the advantage of India was having an ayah to run around after the kids to pull them out of any real danger at the last minute.

We rounded a bend and veered across to a beach of small stones and the bedraggled roots of driftwood. I went forward and got out without wetting my feet. Nelius, rather than risk this, took off his neat lace-ups and rolled his khaki cotton trousers around his white ankles. City feet, I noticed, not like Fowzi's and Baru's. Ashore, Nelius dried his feet with a clean handkerchief and we followed at a short distance the two men who must, by now, have known they were suspected of murder.

At the edge of the river, behind a soft, rotten log, lay the bloodstained bundle of clothes, the body.

He lay face down. There was a bad smell already, a smell I knew before as rotting meat. Because it was human, I searched the odour for different notes, for that putrid sweetness I'd heard was the smell of human death, but it was not there. In this jungle place the dead man smelled of meat gone off in the fridge and dead roses. That was the closest I could get. But unlike a fridge smell it wouldn't go away. It was a smell you could never get used to.

Nelius took photographs with his camera. In one shot, macabrely, the two hunters asked to pose with their dead friend.

'This is the exit of the buckshot,' one of the men explained, pointing at the blood-soaked plaid shirt that adhered to a lumpy, broken-up surface beneath.

When the body was rolled over, the shock was too great for me not to flinch. The man's face was almost entirely eaten away. Eyes, nose and mouth were now a pulsating raw mass writhing with larvae. The tip of his nose cartilage showed white. Rats or beetles had torn lumps away from the flesh of his face and then insect larvae had completed the job. Strangely, the rest of his body, though puffy, was unaffected.

In spontaneous reverence, Nelius's father bowed his head and started to say a long prayer. Everyone joined in. The hole in the man's chest was covered by the bloodstained remains of shirt. I could see that he had also been shot in the stomach and, Nelius pointed out, the arm. These were lesser wounds; it was the gaping crater in his chest that must have done for him.

There now followed the most fantastic excuse I had ever heard. Nelius heard it out without snorting in disbelief, merely nodding curtly from time to time and noting details in his book. Yes, the younger man knew that he'd shot the man. They saw that he had died straight away, but then they became very scared. The guy with the moustache kept nodding agreement, his eyes now full of tears. The young man spoke quickly, in bursts, and gestured to where they had been standing. They had run to the shot man from over there. But he was dead and they felt this was a very bad place to die. They thought they might be killed themselves by the badness of this place. They ran away into the jungle and even got lost from each other. But they were too frightened, couldn't we see that, to come back to the dead man. They feared the spirit of this place had caused them to take his life and would kill them somehow too. That was why it took days to find the body. They could not even properly remember this place. It was a bad place, didn't we agree?

We walked over to the place where the shot had been fired. It was about fifty feet away. The tearful older man pointed out the log to us, how the other man must have been crouching behind it, having his piss, hidden from view. It wasn't that big a log. To be totally hidden he'd have had to lie down. I thought then that he might have been hiding from the hunters; perhaps they were hunting him, not the deer that they claimed. We examined the place where the deer was supposed to have stood, but the ground was covered in pebbles and there were no traces.

'Where is the shotgun cartridge?' Nelius asked.

'It stayed in the gun. Then we threw it away in the jungle because it was bad luck.'

Nelius noted this down.

We went back to the body. 'There are no signs of a struggle,' said Nelius.

'Maybe they moved the body,' I said, feeling like Dr Watson. I remembered a detail from Agatha Christie and checked to see if his *adidas kampongs* were on the wrong feet, but they weren't. Then Nelius took the rubber shoes off and leaves and pieces of dirt fell out.

'I think the body has been moved,' said Nelius.

He had to be right. No one would walk around with earth and leaves in his shoes. They must have dragged the body and jammed the shoes on later.

As the man had no face, it was hard for Mr Daud to identify him. The Lundaiya have no medical or dental records so in the end it was down to the shape of his ears. Mr Daud claimed he recognized the ears.

From the boat we brought a canvas tarpaulin and rolled the man into it. Under the body was a flattened pack of Gudam Garam cigarettes. Nelius picked the pack up between finger and thumb, just like a real detective. We both stared at the cigarettes as if they were evidence, as if we'd find a telephone number written on them which would locate the

183

murderer. Then Nelius threw the packet a long way into the jungle.

When it came to lifting the body I was squeezed out. Everyone wanted to help, keeping the feet level at the end and stopping the tarpaulin from hanging down. I followed the jerky, curtailed walk of the men. It was a heavy body.

The boat journey home was a sombre affair. I kept glancing at the light-green tarpaulin, bulging up just above the sides of the other boat. The others in the boat were all looking straight ahead. Then the man with the Zapata moustache looked across at me. His expression was blank, zero. For some reason I nodded at him, but it was too late after staring into his blank expression and he did not nod back.

I had seen my body and now I did not know what to think. The most I could say was that dead bodies look very dead. But they also look human. A man sleeping might be confused with a man dead, but not when his face has been eaten away. It did not make me doubt or believe but I agreed with Glubb Pasha that what animates the body does not seem to be of the body, it is of another order. There is life and no amount of chemical equations can ever be more than the faintest shadow of an explanation. And the dead man, whom I did not know – where had his life force gone? In the face of the full force of mystery I registered only the subdued thunder of engines, the fizzing rush of water along the sides of the boat and the incredible beauty of sunlit leaves on branches bending from the river to white cloud-covered skies above. I searched the skies for more signs, but there were none.

There is a mundane explanation for the appearance of heroes. It is tied to the rise in agriculture. A farmer needs to know his seasons and is dependent on good weather, or at least the right weather. A hunter is closer to the earth, but a farmer is always scanning the sky for clues. A farmer clears land which allows for a good view of the heavens. The hunter lives in the woods and knows that it is raining only from the continuous dripping of the trees. The hunter's friend and enemy are wild animals, not the weather. To a farmer, wild animals are just pests to be destroyed.

In the mythomanic lying history of humanity, Hercules was a peasant farmer who speared a viper with a pitchfork on his threshing floor.

We returned the body to the bedraggled Long Siau villagers. It had been raining and they looked as though they'd been out in it. In the boat we had sheltered under plastic sacks. The tarpaulin was taken carefully up the steps of the longhouse. Nobody was crying.

Back in the Hi-Luxe, I asked Nelius what he planned to do next.

'I must make a report. I will report the facts.'

'But they killed him, didn't they?'

'It is a difficult case. We still have the custom right in this place. It is law that if the family of the man killed receive eight cows, a Chinese vase and a coffin, then there will be no need for the police. It is their custom right to choose, and by this right I give them three weeks to sort things out. If there is still a complaint, then we must go to Sipitang.'

I had thought that thoroughly modern Nelius would have leaped at the chance of involving the government. But he wasn't a fool. In some ways he seemed like an old-style district commissioner, bridging two worlds, perhaps more effectively than they did in those days, but with an understanding lacking in the urban world and its easy resort to institutions. Let the villagers sort it out for themselves. At least give them a chance to govern their own lives, to take responsibility.

I heard later that the case never went to court.

NINE

Magick River

The human animal must have moral courage if it
wants to go on living. It's a natural weapon, after
all, like venom to the cobra. Indispensable.

C. J. Ionides

I was back in Kuala Lumpur and the haze was worse than
ever. As we drove at twilight into town, the tallest building
in the world appeared out of the smog like a science-fiction
rocket and launch tower in front of a blue screen matte. The
telecom tower was invisible; only the disc at the top of the
tower hovered like a flying saucer with its lights on. The
stock market was crashing daily but Harun had achieved a
fatalistic calm. 'If we're fucked, we're fucked,' he said. 'And I
always wanted to be a movie director anyway.'

My plan was to spend a few days recuperating at Harun's
luxury home before heading off for Indonesia. Surprisingly,
it was cheaper to get there via KL than direct from Borneo.
And as soon as I touched down, the hot and humid nonstop
socializing sucked me in.

We were in the Daimler heading towards a rooftop rave
that coincided with the fortieth-anniversary celebrations of
Malaysian independence. 'Lawyers are vultures and parasites,'
said Harun, weaving through taxis bedecked with Malaysian
flags. 'At least movies leave something behind. All laywers
leave behind is wills – other people's wills.'

'I never knew you wanted to direct movies,' I said.

'Didn't you? Haven't you seen those books on screenwrit-
ing I've got at the house? I've got this idea for a movie about

186

a lawyer who sells his soul to a logging company, kind of John Grisham with . . . logs.' He smiled at his own joke and we sped on through the traffic.

Prime Minister Mahathir had recently accused George Soros of deliberately sabotaging the Malaysian economy. Those in the know knew better. The Japanese had over-extended themselves for the second time in the century. Tiger economies had just prolonged the inherent weaknesses of the Japanese economy, the real money behind the Far Eastern boom. Now the ever-expanding bubble of the new Far Eastern co-prosperity sphere had finally burst. The currency was plummeting, which was good news for me but bad news for everyone else. Harun lamented not having gone into currency speculation, and now it was too late. He hit the steering wheel with both hands in mock frustration. 'Even the Bakun dam is looking uncertain!'

'Good,' I said.

On my last day in Long Dao a flashy red crew-cab Hi-Luxe had arrived at the village. It was from the logging company, 'just looking around', said the two men in their phoney safari suits and penny loafers. I hoped the collapse of the economy would delay the exploitation of Long Dao.

In Kota Kinabalu, my standing with Wallace Wong had increased dramatically when he discovered I'd been living off civet cat. 'Civet cat!' He gestured round the crowded res-taurant. 'There can't be a hundred people in KK who've eaten civet cat!' He told me about Kong Taishi soup – a chicken, civet cat and snake soup known as dragon, phoenix and tiger soup. The snake is the dragon, the civet cat the tiger, and the chicken the phoenix. 'It's supposed to be delicious,' he said.

Roy Goh had found a Chinese dealer in snakeskins who had a roadside sign offering to buy any snake offered to him. Roy explained that the man mostly dealt with transportable snake sizes, those you could easily take on a bus in a large carrier bag, certainly no more than six or seven feet. The man professed no knowledge of any giant snakes in Borneo.

After two days in Kuala Lumpur I was sorely missing the jungle. Like Martin Sheen, I took to lying on my bed and watching the fan rotate like a helicopter blade. Whenever I made sorties alone into the city, things went sour. On one occasion it was very hot and fumy, and I was desperate to get a taxi home. The few taxis I saw were deeply embedded in four lanes of unmoving traffic. In my hopelessness I got into a futile conversation with an Indian, a middle-aged man with a grey moustache who was sitting on a wall chewing *pan*. He told me he had once been a rubber tapper and he was in KL to 'see some friends'. He said he 'had no definite plan', but pretty soon I realized he'd formed a rather definite plan to rope me into his aimless life. I tried to escape along the broken gutter of the jam-packed highway, but he limped after me as the traffic honked and fumed, calling, 'We must have tea! We must have tea! What is your rush, my friend? Where are you going?'

I relented and we sat at a tea stall behind a high-rise building. As the man talked, it began to dawn on me just what a hopeless case he was. His limp was caused by some vague industrial accident; it wasn't his fault but now he was out of a job. He was forty-eight, unmarried, and his aim was to 'stay free' all his life.

At the open-air tea stall, a bald-headed Chinese man sat down, opened his briefcase and took out some pills. He grinned all over his face at me and my companion, who, I could tell, was pleased to have someone new to show off at the tea stand. But the Chinese man had his own agenda. He fired off a question at the limping Indian man. 'How many years you work?'

'Thirty-five. I work thirty-five years,' said the Indian,

sitting a little straighter as if thirty-five years' service demanded a respectful posture.

'You work thirty-five years,' said the Chinese, fiddling with a pillbox, ''s a long time. You must be very rich man!' The Chinese man laughed and the Indian man smiled gamely, for he was obviously a poor man; maybe this gibe even hurt him.

Taking a red and white capsule out of his pillbox, the Chinese held it up and pronounced, 'Antibiotics.' The Indian looked at this pill as if it might be a cure for his bad leg. The Chinese man didn't look ill at all. 'Against cocksackie virus,' he explained.

'What is that medicine?' asked my poor Indian companion.

The Chinese man seemed to be on the verge of telling us a secret formula. After a theatrical pause he said, 'Penicillin!'

I paid for the tea as a way to speed up my escape. The Indian man said, 'You have paid for the tea and that proves you are my friend. I cannot let such a friend as you leave now.'

'I have to go now,' I said.

'One more tea,' said the Indian.

'I'm leaving.'

'I will accompany you!'

'Stay here,' I suggested.

'I will come with my friend!'

In the end I had to say it. 'I'm not your friend!' I shouted as I lumbered away in the midafternoon heat. I could hear him coming after me, calling to his 'friend' to wait, but I had some distance on him and mercifully he was slowed up by his limp.

When I was with Harun in the Daimler, I felt safe again. KL was making me nervous and I needed a barricade of luxury to keep me from sliding downhill psychologically. The rave was supposed to cheer us both up, to allow Harun to forget that he would be poorer at the end of the evening simply because of the swift and ever-downward movement of the currency, and allow me to forget my quest, which did not appear to be going anywhere.

It was easy to be, or fancy yourself to be, a hero out in the leafy jungle. In the concrete variety, urban anomie sets in fast. The alpha predators of the city inhabit banks and brokerage houses, using money as their weapon. At least my money wasn't in the local currency – that raised my status considerably, say from an epsilon to a delta predator, still way off the scale, the urban equivalent of a tree vole or a slow loris.

I could not connect to the heroes of the city; I needed something older, more elemental to inspire me. I wondered if the dawning of the religions of light had caused similar reflections. The farmer, controlling and despising his former forest foes, talks up their strength to reassure himself in his sedentary life. The need to hunt is transformed into a quest mythology, the killing of the snake into the ultimate hunting yarn.

I remembered something I had read about ancient cave paintings: the anthropologist P. A. Leasen has shown that the pictures of animals are not there to inspire good hunting. Rather they have been painted in anatomically accurate positions of death. The pictures are records of beasts killed, remembered on the cave walls to placate the animals' spirits.

The farmer, and even more the town dweller, gives no thought for the spirit of the slain beast. Only hunters do that, dependent as they are on the good will of the hunting grounds. And if the spirits are not placated, they come back to haunt us. The heroes of the new religions killed serpents with abandon. And then the snakes came back to haunt us in our dreams.

Nani's rave was on the top of the Hong Kong and Shanghai Bank. It felt very good to be so high up and looking out over the smoggy city. There were many people there, most of them clustered together on the dance floor, which was a kind of terrace garden on a higher level than the main roof.

Nani was an architect who had studied in the UK. On her card it said '(UK)' after the initials that told you she was a qualified architect. You got the feeling she was proud of having been educated in England, and yet at the same time it gave her the hump. Her rave was to show that KL could be just as hip as London, but no one was convinced.

Many of the people at the rave were Europeans. Nani told us she had 'handed out invites to all the best-looking models in Bangsa'. It looked as if most of them had turned up. Harun shielded his eyes as a phalanx of blonde stormtrooping beauties clumped by in their stacked platforms. I watched for a long time an ambiguous lad wearing a flowery batik T-shirt and white hipster jeans dance with a similarly ambisexual girl. Clutching a mobile phone in one hand and a leather-covered address book, or so it seemed, in the other hand, he danced, transfixed by the trance-inducing techno music.

'Do you think many people are on E?' Harun whispered.

'Anyone who looks far happier than they should probably is.' I walked around squinting into people's faces, trying to check if they were happier than they ought to be. Not many people seemed overhappy, though Harun and I, having both read about the E culture of the tiger economies in Asian *Business Week*, were determined to observe the widespread use of this drug.

Nani wandered around in what looked like a set of pyjamas. She told us she had made them herself. She also had an ID card in a plastic wallet around her neck, like a backstage pass at a gig. Nani looked pleased with herself but no happier than she ought to look. It was her party, after all, and quite a coup to get a bank roof on the fortieth anniversary of Malay independence. 'But they should have had traditional Malay music,' I said to Harun, risking his ridicule,

191

which he had last showered on me when I suggested Malays should not speak English.

'Malay music would be really hokey,' he said. 'At least this is global culture.'

Despite Nani's efforts (big PA, screen with old movies and cartoons projected, beautiful people), the whole effect was like being at a party at a sixth-form college. Nani herself looked like the head girl. It wasn't the lack of drugs or the lack of violence or the good weather, it was rather, I think, the degree of self-consciousness of the affair. A little too well thought out, a little too middle-class. It wasn't 'grown-up', whatever that meant. We were being tolerated on the roof of a massive financial institution which deep down most of the happy people were committed to. No one was a full-time raver. Raving after hours on the bank roof said it all: We may pretend to reject you but we need the global economy so that we can have enough money for our IKEA shelves and our new Mitsubishis. When we left the rave I was glad.

Snake trails were drying up all around me. The King of the Snakes had left to do another show on the east coast of Malaysia. The Jabatan boys had caught no big pythons for months. Harun suggested that we pay a visit to Magick River for some inspiration. 'The local people, the *orang asli*, say this river is a snake river, at least that's what Kit Lee says.'

'Who's Kit Lee?'

'Well, actually that isn't his name any more. What's his new name, dear?' Harun called up the stairs to his wife.

She called down, 'Antares * Noumion.' She pronounced the asterisk as 'star'. The asterisk was part of his name, like the ! of a click language.

'Yeah, Antares,' said Harun. 'He is one weird dude. The name thing is just the tip of the iceberg. He lives in a native hut with an *orang asli* wife and kid. Most people just protest that the *orang asli* have been marginalized and ill treated. Antares went further – he married one.'

'So is he originally Chinese, assuming Lee was his first surname?'

'Chinese, educated in the USA in the sixties, became an ad copywriter, then one of Malaysia's best-known journalists and cartoonists, before publishing his poetry and dropping right out. Magick, spelled with a 'k', River is where his hut is.'

The first thing Antares said to me as I got out of the car, grinning, to shake his hand, was, 'Hmm, you don't look like much of a snake hunter. Well, at least you haven't got contact lenses.'

He was a small, thin, wizened, hyperactive hippie with long hair and a few strands from his chin, and he swam into your face when you talked to him, or rather, he talked to you. He had a beaten-up Datsun and we followed him along the track to the top of Magick River. There was a bungalow of which Antares had, until two years before, been the caretaker. 'That was just after my spectacular ego death in 1992,' he explained. 'I let all the grass grow long and the owners didn't like that, so in the end they kind of fired me.'

He took Harun and me down to the river. It was a wide mountain stream with a twenty-foot waterfall, rapids and large, calm pools for bathing. 'Notice the sediment,' he said. 'Illegal logging.'

We stripped off to go swimming. Antares was deeply sunburned and very gung ho. He jumped off the high, rocky banks into the stream, then persuaded us to stand under the pounding force of the waterfall and 'imbibe the magic'. 'One time,' he said, 'I was standing midstream and seven water snakes came up to me. These were the snake guardians of the river. They checked me out. It was cool.'

'Is this guy for real?' I asked Harun, as Antares did several more stunts off the waterfall, gambolling like a teenager, not the fifty-year-old former advertising executive he was.

'I don't know,' said Harun. But before he could elaborate, Antares was at our side lecturing us on the Mayan revelations that indicated we were all in for a paradigm shift of cosmic dimensions. 'Things will just disappear,' he said confidently. 'Whole corporations will just find themselves space-time-shifted into another dimension. A very cold, lonely dimension, I might add. Can you imagine that? You wake up one morning and Microsoft or McDonald's will no longer be there.'

'Hold on,' said Harun, who had more experience of Antares than I (Antares had acted in a play with Harun's wife). 'How do you know this stuff?'

'It's all there if you care to look hard enough,' said Antares breezily. 'Hey, do you want to come up to the hut?'

Antares lived in a hut on another, smaller river. The hut was on a piece of ground Antares had claimed for himself, about a mile past the *orang asli* village his wife came from. Before we left, we met his wife and child. Alat, his wife, had a crippled ankle, and spoke a fast and furious proto-Malay that Harun could only just make out.

The village we drove through was a shanty town of tin-roofed shacks. Skinny kids and old people looked on with little interest as we drove by. I noticed piles of bamboo stacked by the roadside.

'Their only source of currency,' explained Antares. 'They collect the bamboo, which they make into incense sticks to sell for ten ringgit a thousand to a Chinese businessman. It's a pretty lousy business but it's all they've got.'

The track, which now wound through jungle, got bumpier and bumpier. Antares lectured me on the necessity of connecting with my kundalini force. 'Like, this snake-hunting thing is very male, very external, whereas the kundalini force is female, coiled up inside you, waiting to be awakened.'

'Kundalini force?' said Harun.

'It's a basic tenet of tantric yoga: the serpentlike kundalini

194

force has to rise up through the five centres, chakras, in order to be united with Siva, the male force. That's when you're supposed to get an incredible rush, as the thousand-petalled lotus explodes into bloom at the top of your head. Supreme nonduality, or that's the theory.'

'I think I've got the opposite – supreme duality,' said Harun.

'Hey, man, we all need a good lay!'

'How do you awaken your kundalini force?' I said.

'Apart from sex? I would guess that, in the snake metaphor, you have to catch the giant snake and know at the same time it's unimportant.'

We parked the Daimler and all piled into the Datsun. We drove past an old Esso tank left behind by the logging company. 'My private gas supply,' Antares quipped.

The hut stood in a beautiful triangle of open ground. At the far end water gushed from the hillside. A second spring, not far away, was the 'natural mineral-water supply', as Antares put it.

'How did you get this land?' I asked him.

'Well, over there, maybe you can just see that cave entrance?' I couldn't. 'That's the entrance to an old tin mine that was operated here about sixty years ago. There was a cave-in and thirty miners were killed. The local *orang asli* think this place has bad juju' (he really said this) 'so when I decided to build a place here, nobody objected.'

The hut was some nine feet off the ground, traditionally made from bamboo and woven rattan with a palm-thatch roof. 'I got Alat's uncle to do the roof. He was one of the few villagers who still had the skills.' There was a second hut, like a summer house, nearer to the stream. 'That's my sky chamber,' said Antares. 'The place where I slip, momentarily, into other dimensions.'

'Right,' said Harun.

We climbed the rickety ladder to the open-air platform at

195

one end of the hut. It was like being in a tree house, but very neat with piles of books and sumptuous cushions to rest on. On top of a wicker basket I saw a photograph of two young women. 'My first experiment in breeding,' Antares explained.

Before his spectacular ego death, Antares had been married with two daughters. 'What do they think of you now?' I asked.

'They probably think it would be nicer if I could provide them with an inheritance, but hey, don't all kids go through a mercenary phase?'

It started to get dark and Antares lit some candles. The night air was so still that the candles burned straight up without guttering. I was surprised at how few mosquitoes there were. 'Because there's nothing to feed on,' said Antares. 'Parasites are attracted to the lower dimensions, hence this recent dengue-fever thing in KL. The more we take from the earth, the more it lets us know we're not wanted. Ever wondered why the rat population exactly equals the human population at any given time in history?'

'No,' said Harun, but I wasn't really listening. I was too caught up in Antares's rap. The man was really living what he preached – a genuine Malay hippie.

Antares was about to give us both copies of his poems, which had recently been published in collected form. Harun and I just managed to force him to accept payment instead. It was the right thing because, as he pocketed the money, Antares said, 'Time to get another bag of rice.'

He told us about his 'lodger', who wasn't there right now but had been living with Antares and his wife for the last year. 'I figured this guy had failed a lot recently – lost his job, lost his wife – so if I told him to shape up, he'd just go and dump his misery on some person else. So I just let him hang out here and heal himself. But months, and I mean months, went by and he was spending most of his time just bedded down in the spare room. So recently I've started fixing him up with job interviews. In fact that's where he's gone now. I think he could be on his way.'

'Was he a good friend of yours?' I asked.

'Nah, he just kind of turned up and stayed,' said Antares.

'But how do you live without money?' asked Harun, the question we'd both been wanting to ask.

'The thing about money is that to understand it in its full dimensionality you have to learn to love it.'

'I do love money.' Harun smirked.

Antares was suddenly stern. 'You don't love it, man, you fear it.' Then he said more gently, 'Which is at least better than being greedy for it.

'By love I mean a certain relationship, a functional relationship, not a sentimental one. Maybe saying you have to love money is a bit strong. What I mean is that when you're in this special relationship with money, it's like being in a relationship with a person. You don't possess them, they don't possess you. You're free to let them go whenever you want. You know what's good and bad for them. You know what effect you have on them and they on you. Maybe what I'm saying is that you have to know money for what it is.

'Take the idea that money is the root of all evil – obviously that doesn't apply to a starving man who can be saved by a little well-spent money. Or the reverse, someone wins the state lottery and they're destroyed by having so much money. What this comes down to is that you have to hold all these different ideas in your head at the same time. People don't like to do that. They want things to be either this or that. With money, when you know what it can and cannot do, you're free of it. And it always turns up just when you need it, because it receives a communication from another dimension.'

'How do you mean?'

'Like now. I needed forty bucks to get some rice and some gas. You guys come along and give me forty bucks. But you guys wanted to come here in a different dimension from the money thing. Everything works in parallel.'

Light from the candle played over his now serious, now humorous face. The insects in the dark jungle sounded their continuous raucous chorus. We smoked some cigars I'd brought, drank coffee and talked on, oblivious to the time of night.

'You see,' said Antares, 'we've made some serious miscalculations about the stars.'

'Uh-huh,' said Harun.

'The star Sirius, for example. You know all these end-of-the-world cults, they have this thing about Sirius?'

'I didn't know that, actually,' I said. I wondered if Antares was going to get really mad about astrology. It wasn't totally off my path, since snakes and astrology go well together. Great serpents were thought in India to be the cause of solar eclipses. To attract their attention it was necessary to bathe in a sacred stream. The Milky Way, too, was known in early Sanskrit as 'the path of the serpent'.

'The Sirius thing has been miscalculated. What really is the situation is that stars function like a high-level computer language. It's like dowsing over a map, reading off the coordinates and actually finding water where the pendulum or whatever says it is. From a scientific-causal point of view that's impossible, but if you subscribe to the holographic paradigm . . .'

'The holographic paradigm?' I had a feeling I was about to lose Antares but I really wanted to keep up with him.

'In a hologram every pixel contains the totality of pictorial information, like a cell containing the entire DNA programme for a lifeform. More pixels just result in greater intensity, not greater information. Greater visibility. In the holographic paradigm the information content of the universe is present in each moment, but very faintly. Hence a

198

star has a connection to a mental state, the secret is to be open enough to very subtle indicators. When people talk about men from outer space, they are using the current mythological language for establishing the cosmic influence on events. And like the pendulum swinging over the map, if it works for you, it works.'

'Does that mean everyone should try and establish their own personal mythology?' asked Harun's voice, which came out of the dark beyond the light of the flickering candle.

'They do anyway,' said Antares. 'We can't help it. Our human programming language is the language of myths and stories. But there are a lot of good off-the-shelf myths that have been around a long time, as well as some exciting new ones. But people get too literal. They confuse a scientific myth like UFOs with scientific facts as produced in MIT laboratories.'

'Where do snake myths fit in?'

'Snakes, as you probably know, can be symbols of knowledge and healing as well as monsters to be vanquished. Whatever, you can be sure a snake is never just a snake. A snake is the symbol *par excellence*. Snakes are woven into the system like an Internet browser or something, a universally useful program without which you can't make contact. Snakes appear in dreams sometimes as portents; in other words, they are urging you to make contact with something or some part of yourself. Like in biblical stories: the snake knows and it offers man the chance to know too, but at a price. The snake offers freedom from the beneficial tedium of the Garden of Eden. The snake promises total freedom. But the price is: you have to take responsibility for yourself and your actions. You have to accept cosmic comebacks, God's little slaps in the face, or worse. That's why the medical profession has a snake symbol, which seems weird at first, since the snake kind of infected the human race with dissatisfaction, which is another form of the freedom feeling; but at the same time it says if you accept the flipside of freedom, which is responsibility, then you have knowledge, healing knowledge.'

'Wow,' said Harun.

Antares gave me a copy of an article he'd written about a cosmic guru who'd held a workshop in Kuala Lumpur. A magazine had commissioned Antares to write the article, but, as he put it, 'I kind of overstepped the "my mind has been blown" factor,' and the article was spiked. When I read it later I was surprised at how humorous it was.

Rooting through papers, Antares found an envelope sent to him by an air hostess. As well as a long letter, it contained hundreds of pictures of herself, many just tiny head shots cut from larger photos. 'Guess that means she's all in pieces,' he said.

'Sometimes you can never put the pieces back together again,' I said in a tone of voice I wasn't entirely happy with.

'Sometimes,' said Antares.

Antares didn't style himself as a guru, but he didn't shy away from giving answers. He was definitely in the 'seeker' mould, though I knew from past experiences that seekers can often become finders, and it's not so difficult to move from being a finder to a guru.

In Malay, *guru* just means 'teacher'. An English teacher is a *guru bahasa ingris*. Only people who know English have the other meaning of 'guru' as a know-all who exploits the disciple to make him dependent on the teacher. All the people I'd met who had guruish tendencies were autodidacts. Antares was no exception, and though Fowzi was hardly in the same mould, I remembered how he had taught himself the secrets of the jungle, just as Ionides had taught himself the secrets of snake catching.

Some people learn early that they have to be their own teacher. Perhaps this was what General Gordon meant when he said, 'All men are either fools or their own physician by the time they are thirty.' Autodidacts like to give answers, that's why they sometimes seem like gurus. In reality they're offering an example lesson in how to be your own teacher. I was looking for someone to teach me how to catch snakes, but maybe this was just an analogy for the way I approached life. It was up to me to become the snake catcher, symbolically the catcher of knowledge, to become my own teacher. And anyone who helped me to teach myself was a kind of guru, worth looking out for.

Colonel H. was skilled at many things (though he never learned to dance). But any skill was always acquired in secret. He'd hide away and practise and practise and suddenly emerge a fully competent practitioner. He taught himself gymnastics and was selected for the 1936 army Olympics team; he boxed and shot for the army, again after hours of secret mastering of the art. It was hard to know whether he just hated making a fool of himself in public, or whether he was on to something, some secret of self-education.

Antares's weird ideas were a catalyst for drawing together what I'd experienced so far, confirming what I'd expected at the beginning, that there was more to hunting the snake than hunting the snake. If Antares was right, I was putting together my own mythology, and the snake was just cover. It was beginning to dawn on me that the hunt was for bigger game, a worldview in which ways of learning were very important.

In an age when people were slightly embarrassed to talk about personal heroes (called personal icons at London dinner parties), Colonel H. was never shy to mention men he considered personal heroes. The explorer Richard Burton was one, and Wynwood Reade, author of the 1920s bestseller *The Martyrdom of Man*, was another. He was fond of talking of those he greatly admired: the anthropologist administrators Hutton and Mills; Kipling, of course; Ayub Khan, the

Pakistani general; and, perhaps bizarrely, Muhammad Ali, the boxer.

Heroes and gurus, if I can use those words, have something in common. They point the way, provide clues. Why should we fear them? Why have they lost their currency? Because something has spread with the spread of machines, a feeling of redundancy, of uselessness, fuelling the culture's thinkers to promote ideas about the meaninglessness of life. 'Learned meaninglessness' I'd heard it called. In the code of the cynical I was just distracting myself by hunting for snakes. The real business was eat, drink and be merry for tomorrow you will be no more. Such is the existential vacuum that ever threatens to develop. Heroes and gurus, passing quickly over those words, offer an alternative vision, throw down the gauntlet to go and seek meaning, to find out what makes you more than a bundle of possibilities, more than a number.

It was pitch dark now. My mind was reeling with Antares's discourse, literally out of this world. Harun was getting restless. I had remembered to bring the Maglite with me and it was useful for finding our way back to the battered Datsun.

Antares talked about the time he and some friends had explored the gaping wet mouth of the mine.

'Yuk!' said Harun. 'I don't know how you could go down there.'

'It was one of those things,' Antares explained without a shade of aggrandizement in his voice. 'I knew I'd never forgive myself if I didn't explore that mine. Or rather it would continue to really bug me. So we put on our rubber boots. It goes back about three hundred yards before you get to the rockfall that sealed it off.'

'Was there anything living down there?'

'A lot of bats and lizards – no snakes, though. I wouldn't do it again, some things you only have to do once, I guess.'

I thought about that dark hole in the side of the jungle hillside. I had to agree with Harun, it was a deeply unpleasant prospect. But as Antares said, there are some things you have to do, those things that bug you, do them as soon as you can, because they can pile up all too fast.

The parked Daimler showed up in the headlights of the Datsun. 'Well, at least it hasn't been transported to another dimension,' said Antares.

As we said goodbye, Antares quipped, 'Remember, the secret of kundalini force is not to resist it.' Then we drove away into the night, past the *orang asli* settlement and on to the superhighway that carried us bullet-fast back to the city.

'I never know whether he's for real or not,' said Harun. 'I mean, all that stuff about Sirius and Mayan cosmology.'

'It's just his personal mythology,' I said.

'But you have to admit one thing, he lives what he preaches all right.'

'And he doesn't even preach, really.'

Silence enclosed the cockpitlike interior of the Daimler. As we approached the toll exit, cars swung in front of us, causing Harun to brake sharply. 'I hate that when it happens,' he said. 'You know, I'm getting to be more and more nervous driving on the highway as I get older. Why's that, do you think?' Then he electrically depressed the window and paid the toll.

Suddenly the hazy glow of the city was in front of us. The car picked up speed down the off ramp. 'But I'm still OK town driving,' Harun carried on, almost talking to himself. 'It's only the highway that freaks me out.'

TEN

Black Magic Riot

Never complain of bad luck; at least not
consistently. *C. J. Ionides*

The first shop with all its windows smashed could conceivably have been a freak accident or the result of a protection racket intent on showing muscle. The second shop, a stove-in mess of metal and jagged glass, could also just about be explained away, perhaps by a ram-raid or a typhoon-strength wind funnelled between narrow streets. But then we drove past cars still burning and a whole street of shattered glass on the empty pavement and I knew things weren't quite right in Sulawesi.

'What's going on?' I asked the taxi driver, a big, nervous man with a fleshy nose.

'It is trouble,' he said, glancing back at me in his mirror. 'But it is finished now.'

'What kind of trouble?'

'There are always troublemakers,' he said. 'They have a revenge . . . on Chinese people.'

I saw soldiers on the streets now, lounging and smoking with red rattan riot shields, guns and long sticks. They stared back at me as I hung out of the taxi window trying to take it all in. The weather was hot and parched and the streets were deserted and dusty. Joseph Conrad had called this 'the prettiest, and perhaps the cleanest looking of all the towns in the islands' but it didn't look that way any more. I was in Ujung Pandang, formerly Macassar, the capital of the Indonesian island of Sulawesi, and it was the first day of what would prove to be a long season of rioting. It made me nervous to see so many burned-out and burning cars and I hoped that European tourists weren't lumped together with Chinese as unwelcome visitors.

Every now and then we'd pass a shop that hadn't been wrecked and houses that didn't show signs of recent fortification. They had chalked messages on their doors or large painted signs, hastily made and stuck in the fence. The signs all read: '*Bumi Pribumi*' which meant 'Muslim-owned house'.

I'd had a bad feeling about Sulawesi; though I knew I had to go there, I felt a strange reluctance to do so. It had a theoretical importance on my itinerary as the site of the capture of the longest snake in the world, according to Guinness Publishing. That was back in 1912, when a thirty-two-foot reticulated python had been shot at a mine not far from Macassar. I knew that area would probably no longer be rife with giant serpents, but Sulawesi was a big island and it had many less well-explored areas of jungle and highland.

The taxi pulled up at my hotel, the Golden Macassar, which came highly recommended and was right on the waterfront. 'It's not that one, is it?' I said, as we drove slowly up to what looked like a building midway through construction. Soldiers were sitting in a line on a low wall at the front. Massive sheets of hardboard blocked off the entire frontage except for a hole cut for an entrance.

'This is the Golden Macassar!' said the taxi driver, with a flourish that was distinctly out of place.

'Are you sure?'

'It is one of the finest hotels!'

'Is it Chinese?'

'I think so,' said the driver, who was undoubtedly a Muslim and knew very well that it was a Chinese hotel. But he was nervous and anxious to be off.

I got out, dusting my trousers off under the uninterested

205

gaze of the soldiers, and carted my bag through the cardboard hole. The harassed-looking manager wasn't Chinese, and he looked as if he wished he weren't working at a Chinese-owned hotel. My first, disturbingly mercenary, thought, as I glanced round the large, empty lobby, was, just how big a discount could I get for staying in the most unpopular hotel in town?

At the desk I bargained hard with a miserable-looking young man and a girl I took to be a receptionist. The harassed manager came over. In the end, after I'd made pointed references to the boarded-up frontage, he offered me a waterfront chalet suite for half the normal price of a single room. I'm usually very bad at negotiating discounts, and this sudden success made me nervous. Maybe things really were bad. I mean bad in a bad sense, the kind of bad that is really rather dangerous. Greed prevailed. The discount drew me to my suite, but at the back of my mind, as I took in its marvellous view of the whole bay, I hoped the Muslim looters and burners didn't have an amphibious attack squadron, lying low in their dhows ready for sundown and defenceless foreigners.

After I'd relished the suite for a while, watching a TV movie about a man who receives the transplanted arm of a mass murderer, I decided it was time to scope out the town. If I was nervous I didn't show it, tipping room service with a fat bunch of currency and casually enquiring where the post office was; riot or no riot, it wouldn't do to skulk.

I had, scribbled by a friend in my notebook, the name and address of a man who specialized in animal collecting. His name, Mr Wang, told me he was Chinese, which was not propitious. I guessed he might have other things on his mind right now. He was known, notoriously, for his collection of cockroaches. It numbered thousands, from the microscopic

and endangered Hissing cockroach to the huge and ubiquitous American brown. But roaches were just a cover. He also
collected butterflies, beetles, bees, scorpions and snakes. He
could supply the article dead and nicely mounted, or alive
and crawling. He operated, after the Chinese fashion, with a
complete disregard for international treaties and protocols
on the collection, sale and export of endangered species, but
he did not buy and sell rhino horn and tiger's penis, so he
escaped the most intensive attentions of the environmental
lobby.

Although I was importuned by many *bechas*, bicycle-rickshaw
drivers, who were suffering from the lack of people on the
streets, I decided to walk at least for a while to get a feeling
for where I was. Ujung Pandang was not a huge city, and
after some hours of sweaty walking I had a mental picture of
the central district. In the airline offices of another hotel, I
enquired about flights and asked for the latest news on the
riots.

A helpful young man with frizzy black hair explained,
'Two days ago a Chinese man, who was crazy, went amok.
He killed a young Muslim girl with a long knife.'

'A parang?'

'Yes. This was as some people were leaving the mosque.
They chased this man. He attacked another woman. But the
crowd killed him.'

'So how did the riot start?'

'I am a Muslim,' he said, smiling apologetically and touching his chest briefly with his hand. 'And I do not support this
firing of cars and breaking into shops. These people are
always looking for an excuse to make violence against the
Chinese. I am actually ashamed.'

'Will they attack the Golden Macassar Hotel?'

'Oh, no, sir, that will be a secure place. I think that the
worst trouble is over now. These groups should be ashamed

207

of themselves.' Then the man looked around as if he had said too much. 'You're not from the newspapers, are you?' he asked.

'No,' I said, 'I'm a defenceless tourist.'

'Good,' he said.

Usually it was Indonesians who went amok and not Chinese. According to Alfred Russel Wallace:

Macassar is the most celebrated place in the east for 'running a muck'. There are said to be one or two a month on the average, and five, ten, or twenty persons are sometimes killed or wounded at one of them. It is the national and therefore the honourable mode of committing suicide among the natives of Celebes, and is the fashionable way of escaping from their difficulties. A Roman fell upon his sword, a Japanese rips up his stomach, and an Englishman blows out his brains with a pistol. The Bugis mode has many advantages to one suicidally inclined. A man thinks himself wronged by society – he is in debt and cannot pay – he is taken for a slave or has gambled away his wife or child into slavery – he sees no way of recovering what he has lost, and becomes desperate. He will not put up with such cruel wrongs, but will be revenged on mankind and die like a hero. He grasps his kris-handle, and the next moment draws out the weapon and stabs a man to the heart. He runs on, with the bloody kris in his hand, stabbing at everyone he meets. 'Amok! Amok!' then resounds through the streets. Spears, krisses, knives and guns are brought out against him. He rushes madly forward, kills all he can – men, women, and children – and dies overwhelmed by numbers amid all the excitement of a battle. And what that excitement is those who have been in one best know, but all who have ever given way to violent passions, or even indulged in violent and exciting exercises, may form a very good idea. It is a delirious intoxication, a temporary madness that absorbs every thought and every energy. And can we wonder at the kris-bearing, untaught, brooding Malay preferring such a death, looked upon as almost honourable, to the cold-blooded details of suicide, if he wishes to escape from overwhelming troubles, or the merciless clutches of the hangman and the disgrace of a public execution, when he has taken the law into his own hands, and too hastily revenged himself upon his enemy? In either case he chooses rather to 'amok'.

Psychiatry has never really been able to pin down the cause of running amok. It has been labelled a 'culture-bound rage reaction', which of course gets us nowhere. The term first appeared in the West in the Portuguese form *amouco*. Barbosa, writing in 1514, noted, 'There are some of them [the Javanese] who go out into the streets and kill as many as they meet, these are called Amuco.'

It is only in Indonesia and Malaysia that running amok appears as a cultural concept with a recognized name and defined type of behaviour. A man who goes amok almost always hacks down his nearest and dearest as well as any passer-by foolish enough to get involved. In some cases there is some reason for going amok: evidence of adultery, loss of a job, some form of in-family bullying. Colonel H. believed that the tendency to go amok was a genetic fault in the Malay racial stock: 'Bulldogs wheeze, racehorses get colic and Malays and sometimes Japs run amuck – genetic weaknesses, all of them.' There is considerable evidence that the Japanese at early stages in their history have had connection with this Malay stock. The almost Semitic Roman nose, which is not uncommon in Japan, does not come from China, but rather from the Malay seafarers who reached Japan centuries ago. This, for the Colonel, explained the Japanese propensity for murderous mood changes when under extreme stress.

But in this case the perpetrator was Chinese, which had provided an excuse for revenge against the always more prosperous Chinese community. In Malaysia and Indonesia, the Chinese are the ubiquitous traders. They are wealthier and more successful and they keep themselves apart, a combination not guaranteed to endear you in the community. In Malaysia, riots in the late sixties had resulted in the *bumiputra* laws, where native Malays were favoured in education and the business world. The Chinese were kept in check by this discrimination, and somehow this provided an outlet for anti-Chinese feeling.

Using my street map I found, with difficulty, the address of Mr Wang. It was a back street with no shops, except one on the corner which had its main window broken. Mr Wang's house was behind a white-painted sheet-metal fence, which in the circumstances seemed wise. There was a letterbox and no bell. I banged on the gate in a way that I hoped did not sound moblike or threatening. There was no response from the house, which was only just behind the fence. I rattled the letterbox. Up and down the street nothing stirred. The front of my shirt was pricked with the first signs of a sweat blotch. Everything seemed hopeless. I left a note with my hotel room number and trudged back to the main road. This time I allowed a *becha* driver, who performed a U-turn and homed in on me like a bicycle shark, to ride me bumpily back to the hotel. I wished I'd taken a ride earlier as it was a fine and imperial way to travel in the high heat of summer. As we passed a burned-out car, the *becha* driver raised his finger to his forehead in the universal sign of madness.

I stayed in my hotel room and read the memoirs of an Indonesian general called Soegih Arto. At one stage, when he is asked to become an ambassador in Singapore, he writes, 'I said to myself I could become a good diplomat, because I was used to lying much of the time and besides, I considered myself a good actor.' It was a curious book, refreshingly honest about his own vices, but obscure and mendacious about the actions he had taken part in. Arto had been involved in turning Buru Island into a vast prison camp, but in the book he only briefly refers to it, and then as a 'rehabilitation centre'.

After reading for a while, I watched some more TV movies, but none was as gripping as the one involving the murderous transplanted arm. I opened my balcony windows and watched the sun set in a long golden line directly across the water from the hotel. Dhow-rigged outriggers cut across the golden bar, black shimmering outlines with a huge sun behind them. The situation, if you could forget the rioting, was absolutely idyllic.

But I could not forget the rioting. After nightfall I heard shots in the streets and saw the glow of cars burning in the distance. I became increasingly nervous and ordered a forget-table meal from room service. I was getting to the stage where I didn't even want to leave the room.

I called Harun and told him about the situation. He told me about the falling Malay currency. Big deal, I felt like saying. The haze was worsening too, he said. 'And get this – Princess Di has been killed in a car crash!' I thought he was joking, but when I switched to a news channel it was true.

'But hey,' he added, 'don't do anything too Chinesey. Stay out of trouble.'

The next day I ate a timid breakfast in a restaurant near the hotel. Truckloads of soldiers drove by, stirring up the dust on the road. The owner of the restaurant, an Indonesian man busy frying up fresh fish, told me the Chinese man who had started the riot was called Benny, and was thought to be a mentally disturbed youth. He had run amok and killed Rasunah, a nine-year-old girl on her way back from a Koranic recital class. The owner looked at me meaningfully through the steam of the fish as he added this detail. Benny had been captured by the police, but a little later he was murdered by the mob. That sounded suspicious: it seemed that the police had allowed him to be lynched. The owner didn't care about Benny. He thought he got better than he deserved. But whatever way you looked at it, getting rid of Benny would have been a problem.

Having finished the Indonesian general's memoirs, I moved back to my snake notes. Once the chthonic symbolism of the snake is understood, lots of things become clear. Even the innocuous game of snakes and ladders is, in effect, a play version of the deadly serious duel between the sky and the earth. You go down a snake, into the underworld, as a penalty for failing to elevate yourself, rise up through the chakras, achieve self-perfection before the next journey into the great light of the heavens; climbing, if you like, Jacob's ladder.

Snake cults, like snakes themselves, are bloody hard to stamp out. Because snakes resemble penises, rivers and rainbows, there are thousands of footholds for the mythological imagination to cling to. But these symbolic interpretations are just signposts, reminders that the snake cannot, will not be driven away. In medieval times an unpropitiated snake was said to cause barrenness. In modern Bombay barrenness is commonly ascribed to the killing of a snake in a former existence. The snake here is clearly a stand-in for the male member, but it runs deeper than that. When the Brassmen of Nigeria insisted in the diplomatic treaty of the Bight of Biafra in 1856 that a clause be inserted protecting the sacred cobra, they were not just thinking of female fertility. They were applying a very advanced form of ecology: an ecology of the unconscious, acknowledging that we are not just the outward form of hard facts, Western clothes, a few neuroses and a decrepit old age to look forward to. Underneath all that lurks something far stranger than we imagine, a noumenal world where nothing is what it seems.

More movies, more looking across the bay. Eventually the phone rang. It was a hurried, insistent voice – Mr Wang. He told me to come round to his house that afternoon, if I really had to. Normally such unwelcoming invitations are meant to be turned down, but Mr Wang made it sound as if I must, without question, have important business, otherwise why would I be so foolish as to be in Sulawesi at that time?

I took a *becha* to the end of Mr Wang's road. He had told me that for security reasons I mustn't take one to his front door. The *becha* driver circled the end of the road, eyeing me as if he was intent on picking me up whenever I'd finished whatever my business was. I lit a cigarette and he continued to circle. I tapped my watch theatrically and waved him away. He made one more circle and rode off.

I approached Mr Wang's with a caution worthy of a trained spy. I checked the street was empty before knocking softly on the metal gate. Unfortunately this elaborate cover was broken when a truck roared up the street just as the door opened a crack. An elderly Chinese man with a grey crew cut and thick glasses stuck his head around the door and hustled me in. We went down a corridor and into a room with the walls covered with glassed-over collections of cockroaches and butterflies. There were grey metal cabinets with thin drawers arranged in a central aisle. On top of the cabinets was a work surface littered with more glass frames, killing jars and a beetle pegged on a white piece of plasterboard. There were shelves and several glass cabinets standing against the walls. In one I noticed several tightly rolled-up snake-skins, python skins.

Mr Wang was pleased to see me but he had something on his mind. As I talked generalities, he looked about the room

213

in a distracted fashion. As if to shut me up, he beckoned me with a rapid gesture to come and stand next to a wooden desk, the kind where the desktop locks up to make it like a cupboard. Producing a key from a chain which dangled down into his grey singlet, he unlocked the desktop and inside was a wooden box the size of a cigar box topped with glass. He laid it on the now flat desktop for me to admire. His grinning face kept going from mine to the display case and back again. Inside the case was a beetle, a small, brown, nondescript beetle.

'Very nice,' I said.

'You are very surprised,' he said.

'Sort of,' was all I could manage.

'It is the first one, as you know,' he said.

'Really?'

'The price has to be very high.'

'I'm sure it does.'

'Very, very high!' He looked at me inquisitorially.

'The higher, the better,' I said.

In a fluster of activity he wrote down a number on the back of a brown envelope and slid it across to me with a poker face. I looked at the number: $2000. I didn't know anything about beetles but that seemed an awful lot for such a feeble-looking specimen.

'It's a nice beetle,' I said, 'but I don't want to buy.'

'No offers!' he screeched, and crumpled up the manila envelope. I was beginning to think Mr Wang had more in common with Benny than just being Chinese. 'This is what we agreed,' he said.

'No, we didn't.'

Mr Wang now looked at me with suspicion. 'You don't like beetle?'

'Not really, no.'

'So why you come?'

'As I tried to explain, I'm interested in snakes, pythons. Big pythons.'

214

'Ah, python?' Mr Wang looked nonplussed. Then he hurried me round to the glass cabinet with the snakeskins. He tapped the glass. 'Python skin!'

'I know. But I want a live python. A very big live python.'

'Animal collector?'

'Yes,' I said.

'You like Chinese tea?' he asked. He shouted in Chinese through a door hung with plastic strips, and motioned me to sit down on a wooden stool. 'Very big python live near village. I only catch for skin.'

'How do you catch a python?'

'Sometimes village people kill with knife. Sometimes I put duck or chicken on rope. After python eat, I put rope around head and also tail. Pythons try to' – he made a throwing-up gesture – 'but rope on tail pulls rope around head. Python become circle! You can roll him away! But soon he die from this.'

'What about a live python?'

'Not so difficult. But only if big python not hungry. A hungry *ula sawa batik* is dangerous. Men can be bitten and bite does not heal.' This reminded him of something and he rolled up his dark-blue trouser leg to reveal a bandage wrapped tightly around his lower calf. 'That is bite, but not snake, spider!'

'A poisonous spider?'

'Of course poisonous.'

'What kind of spider?'

'It is a kind of black widow spider. But you know, biology textbook is wrong! Black widow only become dangerous in last fifty years. Before that, no problem. I know this from my uncle who studied this thing. Textbook say that these things do not change. But for example I can tell you flowers that have smell now but a few years ago had no smell at all.'

'Fascinating,' I said.

'In fact, man can stand most kind of bite from snake and

215

spider. But only if his mind is strong.' He peered at me through his thick lenses, as if checking my mental strength. 'Weak people die because they do not have a reason for living. The snake takes their reason away.'

'Are there many long snakes in Sulawesi?'

'Many. But now is not good time for look! I come with you to this village, that village. You cannot go alone.'

'Why not?'

'Because you want snake so much, snake will hear you coming!'

'Are there any other good places for long snakes?'

'Yes.'

'Where?'

'Ceram, Halmahera . . . Buru, but Buru maybe you cannot go. It is *transmigrasi* prison. You need place where there is village, or hole in ground, but far from roads. If there is a big road, animals do not grow so big. I do not know why.'

'Where do you collect beetles?'

'Everywhere. In the forest. You are English. Darwin and Wallace collect beetles in the forest.'

'Wallace collected many beetles here in Sulawesi.'

'Of course. He was a great collector. Collect number one, biology number two.' He counted them off on his fingers, and then grew serious. 'Collecting means you have active mind, hunting mind. Just looking and writing down is not hunting mind. It is a mind that makes up stories. That is why textbook lie! Hunter has to find. He does not lie. You cannot know animal except by hunting. Conservation! Greenies!' He laughed and rapidly beckoned a boy, also in singlet and thick glasses, to hand us some tea.

I felt obliged to stick up at least a little for ecology. 'But what about extinction? When too many people hunt one thing, like whales, or even the bird of paradise?'

'Ah, the bird of paradise. Well, there is no paradise left for the bird of paradise!'

I must have looked disgruntled because he hastened to explain. 'Extinction is three things, not just one thing. One, there is the killing. Two, there is the destruction of habitat. Three, there is breaking of animal's mind. That is why I talk about roads. A big road with truck and car break animal's mind. Animal will not eat, will not breed. Animal is sensitive to many thing. Textbook lie!'

'But what about overfishing? Seal culls? The clouded leopard? Endangered species?'

'The problem is road.'

'In the sea?'

'That is ship road!'

I sipped my tea and Mr Wang sipped his. I wanted to ask him about the riots, but I didn't want to appear over-inquisitive. To my general enquiry, he replied, 'Trouble on street is fault of many thing. Bugis people like fight, but they have no chance to fight, day to day. Chinese like business, not fight. In peaceful time, make money. But this trouble cost me money! Also KFC shop is broken first.'

I had seen the pulverized shopfront of Kentucky Fried Chicken. 'Why's that?'

'Because this big business, big Chinese and foreign business. Connection to dollar rise.'

'Is it safe for me to travel in Sulawesi?'

'Maybe safe, but difficult, I think. This trouble will get more and more bad. Remember, snake like peaceful place – like Garden of Eden!'

As I left, Mr Wang presented me with a small piece of reticulated python skin 'from small snake'. He told me that it would give me more luck because the picture in my head of the snake would be stronger. That is how he learned collecting as a boy. The bigger the collection, the more successful you become, because your idea of what you want is stronger. Mr Wang had never been to university. For several years he had owned a motorcycle shop before he had become a full-time collector. 'Textbook lie!' was the last thing he said before I left him.

Back at the hotel the manager pleaded with me to stay a few more nights. 'The trouble is finished,' he said.

'So why are there soldiers outside?'

'It is an exercise for them,' he said.

'What about the boarded-up front?'

'That is to protect the new glass. Very expensive.'

I had made other plans for Sulawesi, tracking the most beautiful women in the world, who were said to come from Manado in the north. But what if I ran into another riot there? And anyway, hadn't I already met the most beautiful woman, Miss Revlon Asia? Wouldn't she do?

Snakes and beautiful women are inevitably intertwined. Their relationship extends from Eve and the serpent to the modern nightclub stripper and her pet python. The obvious symbolism is not the whole story. In the chthonic interpretation Eve is the Mother Earth, the serpent her guardian. The snake is dangerous and it cannot be ignored. A rich dynasty in the Upper Volta ascribed its wealth to the yearly sacrifice of a young maiden dressed as a bride who was thrown down a well which contained a giant python. Failure to appease the python brought drought and sickness. This is a pure form of a chthonic cult. When the cult is disbanded or 'beaten' by a more powerful religion, the same players re-emerge as symbols. Metaphorically we must achieve union with the earth, our unconscious. We must acknowledge our duality (the danger of the snake, the beauty of the woman) but somehow seek a reconciliation. This is the promise of knowledge brought by the snake. 'Be ye therefore wise as serpents, and harmless as doves.' Matthew i:16. The uneasy alliance between the chthonic and the light religions is to give the serpent a role in knowledge and healing. It is as if the old king had managed to slink back to court and got the plum job of king's physician. A most powerful position indeed.

Mythologically, knowledge is often represented as buried treasure. In Grimm's *Teutonic Mythology* King Guntham's soul achieves serpent form to visit a mountain full of gold. Urcaguay, the Inca snake god, was also said to guard treasure, in a way very similar to the Norse myths of dragon's hoards.

Snake charmers in Tamil Nadu prick the finger of a first-born child. This blood is supposed to attract snakes, which are the guardians of treasure and can be then tracked back to their treasure hoard. Connected to this is the belief that a wealthy man who dies without an heir returns as a snake to guard his loot.

Sometimes the snake's wisdom is stated openly. The Greek Ophites identified the serpent with Sophia, wisdom. The sage Garga, father of Indian astronomy, owed his learning to the serpent god Sesha Naga.

Sulawesi was looking increasingly unpropitious. Beautiful women were a distraction, and besides, having just written a postcard to Samia, I felt uncomfortable even contemplating research into stunning women. The stone was, predictably, cold. At least I was sure it wasn't hot as the old *tamu* trader had said it would be. Time was ticking by and instinctively I knew that Buru Island was my ultimate goal.

I opened the map in the front of my facsimile edition of Wallace. The islands of Ceram, Halmahera and Buru were all to be reached from Ambon, a trading port famous since Portuguese times, and capital of the Spice Islands. There was very little information about Buru in any guidebook, but I found one fact that intrigued me: there were only twenty-five miles of paved roads in Buru, an island a third of the size of the Netherlands. I thought about Mr Wang and his warning about roads. All signs seemed to be pointing me towards Buru.

But first I would have to fly to Ambon. As the last guest I got a royal send-off from the Golden Macassar, but it felt good to be driving away from the wreckage on the streets and the promise of more to follow.

The difference when I landed on Ambon Island was palpable. The streets were packed with children, many of them apparently marching though they had no teacher to order them. The taxi driver said that South Moluccans liked marching.

The place where Wallace had been attacked by a twelve-foot python was now a busy little suburb; the hut where he had made his base long gone. Ambon town was bustling but relaxed. I took *bechas* everywhere.

The people were mainly Christian and I spent most days at the Bishop Rumphius convent library, a marvellous building in one corner of a secluded cloister. Sometimes I sat in the cloister on one of the chairs, which thoughtfully had a standing ashtray next to it, and read from books fetched for me by the stern-faced nuns. My favourite was Sister Terseytulle, fluent in Dutch, German and English, whose only departure from a fearsome reserve had been to ask my name and shake my hand.

One day I ordered some books in manuscript form, including a comparative grammar of Burunese. I had to read my manuscripts in a dusty room full of cardboard files and shelves of books. The door was a little open and I could hear Sister Terseytulle dictating to a younger nun in perfect German. Behind me, between files, I noticed a bottle inside a large manila envelope. I took the bottle out; it was green glass and unlabelled. I glanced at the door. I could just see the sharply creased headpiece (a wimple?) of the dictating nun. There was a continuous drone of flat German. It seemed like a marvellous dare as I uncorked the bottle and sniffed. Undoubtedly wine; it must be the communion wine, kept in the manuscript room for safety.

I put the bottle back and tried to go on reading about Burunese grammar. There were some excellent words in the glossary:

Abo: to feel one's way in the dark.
Ahak: to cry like an eagle in flight.
Beak: to move ahead, out of sight.
Bofel: the water upwelling from a snake rising in a river.
Boso: to wash the anus.
Epkasiak: in a dispute, favouring the side in the wrong.

It was no good. I'd flunked some kind of courage test in Sulawesi. Now I was in the Moluccas, I had to be of sterner stuff. I checked that the German dictation continued, turned on my chair, uncorked the wine and took a long, sweet sip, expecting at any moment to be caught. It was sweet-tasting wine, made doubly so by its illicit nature. I drank to success and I drank to the future and then I recorked the bottle, replaced my manuscripts and hastened out of the convent feeling joyous and naughty.

ELEVEN

Johnny's Got a Gun

Hunting is a stage in a man's evolution if he is
absorbed in wildlife.   *C. J. Ionides*

Two people were sick in the steerage class, which was
surprising because the sea was almost a flat calm. I sat up all
night on a plastic chair welded to the deck floor, surrounded
by snoring Burunese with their bundles and crates, the faint
whiff of vomit sometimes replaced by the pleasanter aroma
of clove cigarettes. I was the only foreigner on the ferry to
Buru, and though I usually avoid backpackers, I was sad there
were none on board. I was feeling mightily alone and it
would have been nice to have swapped yarns with an Aussie
in a surf singlet, carrying a tattered rucksack and a wallet
with five locks on it. Backpackers are always tight, but the
tightest are always Aussies. I would have gladly shelled out a
quarter of a dollar to buy one a delicious glass of sweet
coffee, to hear the latest Lonely Planet-style gossip that
backpackers cherish as insider information. Though Buru is
only twelve hours by leaky ferryboat from Ambon, no tourists
ever go there. This was thrilling. The downside was the
gnawing uncertainty.

I had decided to put into practice a theory of travel. The
theory was: the further you go off the beaten track, and the
further you are from cities with McDonald's outlets and a
soaring crime rate, the more likely you are to fall on your
feet. Cities are actually very lonesome places to visit on your
own, but you are made welcome in a superficial way by hotels

222

and restaurants and such. The back of beyond has none of this, but people are therefore much more likely to be really welcoming. I knew no one in Buru; indeed, I was surprised I was able to get there without a special permit. (I later discovered I needed one.) I didn't even know if there was a hotel in Namlea, the main town. All I knew was that Wallace had written, nearly 150 years earlier, that Buru had 'a great many snakes'.

Before we landed at the small concrete jetty on Buru, I had been taken in hand. A quick young man, who could understand my botched Malay, agreed to take me to Namlea and find me a hotel. The town was about a mile from the jetty, through fields of high *kusu kusu* grass and low, scrubby plantations. There were communal taxis, the odd truck, very few cars, but motorcycles and lots of bicycles. My new friend took me to the hotel, the second best in town, and I gratefully crashed out in the foetid concrete box of a room I was offered. The price was six pounds a night, half the weekly salary of an Indonesian high-school teacher.

In the foetid box, on the foetid bed, I started to dream. Daytime naps are usually more dream-laden than night-time sleeping, for me at least, but this time I was shocked at the seeming veracity and gratuitous sex and violence in my dreams. They were definitely X-rated dreams, verging on nightmares.

The worst dream, and the most memorable, started with a beautiful woman. She was tremendously alluring, with raven-black hair in wild curls. She pouted and flirted like a soft-porn actress, raising up her negligible skirt a fraction to lure a figure, a man, further on. Like a foolish, panting dog he advanced, eager for this easy seduction. The skirt went up, inch by tantalizing inch, and the brazen hussy formed her ravishing lips as if demanding to be kissed in passion. By this time, such is the fast-forward jump-cut nature of dreams, the half-naked man was poised and ready, trousers out of shot

223

but presumably around his ankles, the hot fires of sex stoked to unbearable heat. When the skirt at last was jerked fully up, it revaled no underwear, but advancing from the place of her pudenda was the writhing head of a snake, jaws and teeth dripping, tongue flicking. In panic I checked her laughing face and found instead a kind of knowing, yet still sexy, sneer. And I knew then that the hapless victim was like a sailor clutching at wreckage after his ship has sunk in a storm, at the mercy of the fates. Knowing all that, he still advanced and entered the snake's gaping voracious mouth, he thrust in his tool like a boy intent on losing his virginity and fearing, like the boy, for what wrath the gods will surely bring down on him for this unholy act.

And when I awoke I could not forget this dream. I swung my legs down, sat on the foetid bed and wrote the dream down and wondered what the devil it all meant.

I needed to walk around to clear my head. I hoped I could 'make contact', the first stage in advancing my latest snake-hunting tactic. On Buru I intended to do the sensible thing. I would make contact with as many villages as possible, spreading the word across the whole island. It would be no good, unless I was sure I was on to a winner, to spend too long in one village. Instead I should base myself in Namlea and make sorties into the hinterland.

Namlea is a small town composed of shacks, single-storey houses, a large tin-roofed, concrete-floored fish market right by the small harbour and yellow bicycle *bechas* that kept reminding me of stop-me-and-buy-one bicycle ice-cream salesmen. The main concentration of shops is around the market entrance. This is also the place where communal minibus taxis start their journeys.

I wandered in what I hoped was the direction of the market area. Some distance from the hotel I crossed a kind of village green surrounded by small white huts with front gardens. In front of one stood a white-haired man with glasses. He wore a white singlet and disreputable green shorts and he stared at me in the way that people stare at the sun, cautiously, eyes squinting, ready to look away. Suddenly he ran forward and seized my hand in a grip surprisingly firm and pincerlike for such an old man. He was eager to talk and eager to help. His name was Peter, he was a Christian, of Chinese descent. I was the first foreigner he'd seen in Namlea for a year, though he had been on the lookout. Peter believed it was the duty of Christians to be on the lookout to help people.

In Malay, he asked me to come to his house. I instantly agreed, and we walked hand in hand, me a little self-conscious at this, along the edge of the green to Peter's house. I checked the expressions of passers-by for that wry smile that would tell me, 'old Peter's done it again, snared another dumb foreigner'. But Peter engaged all passers-by in conversation and people were impressed by him, amused but interested and not cynical.

His house was one of the hut-bungalows. We sat in the front room and drank coffee grown in Buru. Peter's wife, son, daughter-in-law and several kids were all keen to talk to me, but Peter shut them up with a wave of his hand, and then asked gravely, 'And how can I help you?'

There was silence in the room as they awaited my reply. 'I'm looking for a snake,' I stammered. There were murmurs and nods. 'A big snake, *ula sawa besar*.'

Ah, yes, they understood. 'There are many snakes in Buru,' said Peter.

Peter's next task was to take me to the other hotel in Namlea, the Nu Santara. The owner was the ex-headmaster of the school, and spoke English. He in turn decided to ring a former colleague, a teacher at the high school called Mr Ferdinandus. I waited in the lobby of the Nu Santara with the owner's family watching TV. Children tried to watch

225

through the open door, but if they crossed the threshold they were shooed away.

Mr Ferdinandus arrived on his Honda moped. He was a clean-cut, dark-complexioned, moustached and serious man, who seemed at first sight somewhat weighed down by the responsibilities implicit in dealing with me. He didn't bat an eyelid when I told him I was looking for a very long snake.

'I see,' he said. Then he looked out of the window for a few seconds. He was thinking hard. 'I will get my friend Imran,' he said eventually. 'I will come in one half-hour as I am teaching a lesson right now.' It was a measure of Mr Ferdinandus's dedication to helping that he had left his classroom to ride across town (actually a very short distance) to deal with the snake-hunting foreigner.

More waiting, more telly. Then the loud pop-pop of an ancient motorcycle and, grinning all over his face, with Mr Ferdinandus on the back, the irrepressible Imran arrived. With his motorcycle and his grin he reminded me of the boy with the motorbike in *Emil and the Detectives*.

Imran was a Muslim, Mr Ferdinandus was a Christian. They assured me they were still the best of friends. Imran was more relaxed and confident than Ferdinandus, spoke more fluent English with more mistakes, seemed less burdened by the world. He had a light-brown, smooth face, and a moustache. Whereas my first impression of Ferdinandus was of someone eminently trustworthy, Imran seemed rather dodgy. But I'd learned in the past that it is sometimes the dodgy people who come up trumps – sometimes.

Imran had a plan. It was necessary to hire a minibus for the day and drive ten or twenty miles up the coast to a place known to be rich in snakes. I explained that I wanted to show people I was serious about catching the snake. Imran nodded. The cost of hiring the bus was only ten pounds, though I realized that by Buru standards it was a lot of money.

The minibus came complete with driver, driver's mate and

226

a boy to shut the side door. It pulled up in front of the Nu Santara. We got in, lurched off, drove about seventy feet and then stopped. We had arrived at Johnny's roadblock.

'Johnny is my cousin,' said Imran. 'He is a soldier.' But he said it with a certain amount of hesitation in his voice.

We got out of the van and I was paraded in front of Johnny, who was bursting out of his paratrooper's camouflage uniform, sitting with two friends on wooden chairs arranged at the side of the road. Johnny had a sergeant's stripes, a cigarette in his scowling mouth and a bottle of clear spirits in his hand. 'That is *sopi*,' said Imran in a newly respectful tone of voice, 'fermented coconut.'

Johnny scowled at me with his small bloodshot eyes in his fierce, almost Papuan face. He handed me the bottle without smiling, thrusting it under my nose. I knew what I had to do. Seen the movie a hundred times. Without wiping the neck, I took a manly swig of the vicious firewater. Wiped my mouth with the back of my hand. Johnny nodded slowly and then burst into hilarious laughter, showing all his white teeth. He grabbed part of his uniform shirt and held it in front of my eyes. 'This, same uniform as your country, yes?'

I now made a mistake: I disagreed with Johnny. I told him, presuming somewhat on our recent firewater-bonding experience, that no, noncommissioned officers in the British army didn't wear skin-tight camo shirts and trousers with a huge buckled side arm.

Johnny's bloodshot eyes narrowed. He waved away my disagreement, like a gorilla tormented by a mosquito, and took another swig of 70-proof *sopi*.

'Uniform is similar, though?' said Imran.

Then I understood. Johnny was his cousin, but Johnny had a gun, and everyone agreed with Johnny. 'Yes, it's similar,' I said.

'You see,' said Imran to Johnny, 'it is the same.'

Johnny seemed to have changed tack. On our trip up the

227

coast we would pass through villages that were part of Johnny's administrative area. Suddenly Johnny, and his *sopi*, and one of his drinking companions were coming with us.

I had thought it excessive to hire a whole bus but I now saw a bus was hardly enough. The driver, who was forced by Johnny to swig from the *sopi* bottle, stopped to pick up a few passengers for good measure. Imran immediately started talking to the passengers, finding out whom they had in common. Imran was one of those people who just have to make contact wherever they go.

Johnny was in the front, next to the embarrassed driver's mate, next to the fired-up driver. The *sopi* bottle did the rounds of the van. Imran and Ferdinandus respectfully declined. When the bottle was handed back, Johnny would hand it to me and reward me with a manic grin when I took it. He lit new cigarettes from the glowing butt of one he had just finished smoking. He may have bulged in his uniform, been a drinking and smoking machine, but he looked as tough as old boots and no one was going to tell him what to do.

After a lot of *sopi* Johnny got thoroughly warmed up and had the whole van in sycophantic stitches of laughter. His party trick was to talk to me in Burunese and make smart replies which I couldn't understand. Imran always translated and we all laughed dutifully. There was a narrow section in the road and we met a truck head on. No one wanted to give way. Johnny, leaning out of the window, waved the bottle at the truck to make it back up. It backed up and Johnny forced a swig on the normally aggressive, now cowed truck driver.

Johnny gripped his uniform again. '*Ingris, Indonesia, sama, sama*,' he said.

'*Sama, sama*, the same,' I said, now I'd learned how to play.

'Indonesian soldier drink – bad soldier!' shouted Johnny. Everyone tittered, it wasn't something that anyone wanted to agree too strongly with. 'Indonesian soldier smoke! Indonesian soldier—' and here a sly look came over Johnny's face and he made the universally obvious gesture of fucking, a thumb protruding from between the first and second fingers of a fist. We all laughed, though Mr Ferdinandus was looking out of the window. The *sopi* bottle did another round. Johnny lit two cigarettes from his butt, one for me and one for himself. He held the *sopi* bottle up, swigged, shook it again, and there was half an inch of liquor still left in the bottom. It was almost as if I could see him deciding not to show he was a niggardly drunkard, for in a move of deliberate bravado he threw the bottle with great force straight through the window to smash on the road. It was a moment of terrific and rather uncomfortable violence and unfortunately the back wheel went over the broken glass. The driver looked for the first time worried. Johnny laughed uproariously but there seemed to be no puncture.

Now that we were out of *sopi*, Johnny became a little subdued. Then he announced he was going to make me a present of my own bottle of *sopi*. The snake hunt now turned into a hunt-the-bottle expedition. We pulled off the road at a village and Johnny took us to a house where, he explained loudly, they made their own liquor. 'It's against the law!' he shouted. 'I'll take it off them!' As he blundered out of the van I saw that he was a lot drunker than he looked sitting down.

After a while he came out of the house empty-handed. 'I know another place,' he said. We went to another place. Before going in, Johnny turned to us on the bus, undid the release on his holster and grinned. 'I'll show them who's boss!' he bellowed. But despite shouting coming from inside the house, there was no joy there either.

Johnny was now definitely getting grumpy. He turned to me. 'Indonesia soldier, *Ingris* soldier uniform *sama sama*?'

'*Sama sama*,' I parroted.

229

'Indonesia, *Ingris*, drinking?'

'*Sama, sama,*' I piped. He liked that.

'Smoking?'

'*Sama, sama!*' I said. Johnny started to grin. I knew what had to come next. 'Indonesia soldier, *Ingris* soldier,' and I made the thumb fucking sign.

'*Sama, sama!*' shouted a delighted Johnny.

We stopped at yet another small shack. A man came out and Johnny bellowed at the man, who bellowed back. Then Johnny reached for his gun belt, but instead of drawing his weapon he undid the belt and it fell heavily to the ground. Johnny then relieved himself on the man's fence. Forgetting the gun belt, he went into the shack and the man came out with him holding an empty plastic soda bottle. Johnny shouted some more at the man and grabbed his hair, pulling the man to the ground. The poor fellow tried to get up but couldn't. Johnny landed a kick in the man's ribs and let go of his hair at the same time. Chastened, the man slunk next door. Johnny picked up his gun belt.

In a few minutes the man came back with the bottle full of *sopi*. In place of a cork was a tightly rolled plastic bag. Johnny took the bottle and gave the man a playful swipe, which he ducked.

Johnny came to the van with an eager look on his face. He gave me first swig. 'Thank you,' I said. He waved this aside and took a swig himself. He then rode, hanging out of the door and standing on the inner step, until we reached another tin-roofed dwelling.

'Johnny has some business here,' said Imran.

Johnny shook my hand, laughed like a madman and turned to go into the hut.

After we had driven on in a rather subdued mood for a while, Mr Ferdinandus said, 'Johnny is a very naughty soldier.'

*

230

I had gathered from Imran that the place famous for snakes was also the village where his mother-in-law lived. 'That is how I know it is good for snakes – sometimes after rain they come out from the rocks on the beach and into the garden.'

Mr Ferdinandus, Imran and I sat outside the front of the house, which was a small cement-covered building with a roof of palm leaves. We drank tea and Imran sent a boy to fetch someone in the village who knew about snakes. Several old men walked by and Imran greeted them. We saw other old men and I noticed they were all wearing orthopaedic back supports around their waists. I asked Imran why. 'I don't know, maybe a fashion,' he said breezily. Then I noticed that all the small boys had hundreds of coloured elastic bands around their wrists, and every woman we saw had a mud pack on. Every single one. Imran explained, 'These people, my wife's relatives, originally come from Sulawesi. That is why they have white skin. They are so proud of their skin they do not want it to be burned, so they wear white mud on their faces.'

By now we had quite a crowd of men interested in snake hunting. Imran explained that I wanted to go up the hill above the village to the caves where the snakes lived. Ionides wrote, 'You sometimes find pythons in trees, ant bear holes, under bushes and by the side of water.' Rolf Blomberg, who caught a twenty-three-foot anaconda in Colombia, asserted that catching a big snake while it was in the water was exceedingly difficult. Better to lure them out of their hidey-holes. Blomberg's method of capture was to use five men, 'forks, lassos and a grim determination'. All that could come later; what I needed to do now was to find out whether there were actually snakes lurking up the hillside.

· We talked and explained and drank tea and one by one the men melted away. Then Imran also excused himself. Mr Ferdinandus turned to me. 'All these villagers are frightened to go up to the caves. They say only one man goes up there.

His name is Steerman. But he is working. Imran has gone to look for him.'

It began to get very hot sitting in the dusty road in front of the house. We went around the back and sat in the shade of the palm trees on the beach. It was an idyllic village, occupying a curve of white sand with a few boats moored in the bay and many outriggers drawn up on the beach. 'They are fishermen,' said Mr Ferdinandus, 'but they also collect parrots from the forest. That is how they make their money.'

At long last Imran came back with a short, wiry, middle-aged man in Wellington boots. This was Steerman. 'He is called Steerman because his father was a steerman on a big ship,' said Imran.

It now fell to me to set a day's wages for Steerman. 'How much?' I asked Imran. He was evasive. Rather shyly Steerman asked for five thousand rupiah, which was about a pound sterling.

'Is that all right?' asked Imran.

'Fine,' I said.

It was agreed that Mr Ferdinandus would stay behind in the village and find out more snake information while Imran, Steerman and I headed up the large, bare hill that rose up from the sea behind the village.

Steerman set off in his Wellingtons at a cracking pace. I did my best to keep up and Imran wheezed along behind. He was a plump man, and I got the impression that as an English teacher with a motorcycle he considered exercise a little beneath him. But he soldiered on manfully, begging for rests from time to time. Halfway up the hill he said, 'This is the first time I've ever been up this hill, though I have been to my wife's village many times.'

At the top of the hill Steerman stopped for the first time. He rolled himself a cigarette and sat smoking. A few minutes later Imran puffed into sight. He collapsed on the ground and said mournfully, 'My heart is not so strong!'

'Nonsense,' I said. 'You're just out of condition.'

He got heavily to his feet and we entered the forest. 'My heart is not so strong,' he whimpered, but the path through the forest, while still uphill, was not as steep as the bare hillside.

There were huge boulders and rocks overgrown with trees. We had to step over gaps between rocks and wade through piles of leaf mould and dry, snapping branches. It was all right for Steerman in his wellies, but I only wore desert boots. Imran was even worse off in his dusty trainers. Every boulder was imprinted with fossilized coral, still sharp, despite, no doubt, millions of years and the considerable eructations needed to push the coral bed about a thousand feet above sea level. It was the first time I had come face to face with bona fide physical evidence that either the sea level has dropped very considerably over the millennia, or the earth moves in such a way as to lift the seabed high up into the air.

We left Imran wheezing in the shade, fearful of snakes but shouting through the trees to us from time to time, partly for reassurance and partly to spur us on in our quest.

Scratched by brambles, fingernails loaded with dirt, sweat soaking my entire upper body, I began to experience the supreme happiness of such backwoods exertion. Meanwhile Steerman climbed ever upwards, towards the cave of caves.

The cave entrance was a hole in the overhanging rock face, the line of scarp that topped the hillside. I stood aside as the nimble Steerman sent down small boulders in his scramble upwards. The path I was standing on was very narrow, too narrow for comfort, and below me was a long and troubling drop.

When it was my turn to climb, I hauled on a slender tree root and it came away in my hands. I felt like giving up but a great surge of curiosity had come upon me. With sufficient curiosity almost all fears can be overcome. I reached higher, for a nub end of rock, and began my inelegant climb.

To be climbing, unprotected but without fear, was something of a triumph for me. Years before, I had been a keen rock climber and had fallen forty feet while solo climbing on a Ben Nevis crag. A narrow ledge had saved me from falling another forty feet, but the severe impact of landing on my backside resulted in two months lying flat on my back in Fort William hospital with fractures in two vertebrae. Many climbers recover from much worse to go on to much greater feats of courage and enterprise. I wasn't one of them. My nerve was shot and I retired gratefully. I kept my ropes and climbing gear for a few more years but every time I got them out I felt that sick old feeling of fear – 'bad juju' – and hid them away again.

For a few years I felt as if I'd 'proved myself' by getting busted up, like Hemingway getting injured as an ambulance-man on the Italian front in the First World War, and bearing my scars as a badge of courage. But I came to realize that my scars did not indicate courage but rather folly, youthful bravado, a belief that I was indestructible that was rudely shattered by the back-breaking bum landing. Courage is what may develop after such an accident. As I lay on my back in the hospital and watched the leaves outside my window turn from green to red and then be torn off by the approaching winter wind, I read philosophy and poetry and tried to be a 'good patient' for the friendly Highland nurses.

The first time I walked, after two months of inactivity, the pain in the soles of my feet was almost unbearable. It took a week to get used to the pressure on my feet again. When I returned to university, I gave up midnight climbs across the college rooftops and settled for the more usual student distractions of excessive drinking and partying. A tutor befriended me because he was also interested in rock climbing and my absence from classes had gained my accident notoriety. But the person he wanted to know wasn't interested in danger any more. When I came back to college, the first fellow student I met said, 'Aren't you supposed to be dead or something?' I had been confused with another undergraduate who had died that summer in the Alps.

But man cannot live without adventure. If he tries, the body, or the mind, invents a new adventure for him called illness. 'We cannot abolish adrenalin,' Bruce Chatwin wrote.

With adventure comes fear. Orde Wingate, the eccentric genius of long-range penetration warfare, used to defend his love of riding to hounds on the grounds that it frightened him and so kept his courage in trim. I had long neglected mine. My fears had become the fears of the sedentary man: bills, failing health, failure. Climbing up to the cave with Steerman I felt again the life charge of adventure that is all too easily lost with boyhood. I was again concentrating on this foothold or that handhold, focusing on the details that would mean the difference between falling and climbing higher, living and dying.

At the cave mouth Steerman grinned. We were in it together. Imran called from the woods below but we did not shout back. Our situation was too precarious; I stood on a shoe-sized slab of rock and Steerman was wedged into the mouth of the cave.

Shining my torch revealed that the cave rapidly dwindled into a narrow crack big enough for a man's leg, or a big python, but impossible to explore further. Steerman and I exchanged places in an awkward shuffle, made worse by looking down. With considerable agility Steerman then retraced our way down the face and then further along under the scarp and out of sight.

I was in trouble from my first tentative move away from the cave mouth. Downclimbing is a particular art. It is often more difficult than upclimbing even though you have gravity on your side. One problem is not being able to see where to put your feet; another that it just seems to make more sense to climb upwards and the counterintuitive aspect of down-climbing blocks abilities used easily on the journey up. There's a climbing rule of thumb that says that if you can climb down something you can also climb up it, but the reverse is not true. After a few slip-sliding moves I began to realize I was stuck.

The drop to the path was only about twenty-five feet, but the path was narrow and I doubted that dropping that distance, which could still be dangerous, would leave me safe on the path. More likely I would bounce off it and down the cliffside. Could I reach that slender bush sprouting from between two loose pieces of the face? I lunged and held on, but my feet could find only tiny ripples in the rock for footholds.

It was the same position I'd been in years before, just before my fall in Scotland. Hands in position, feet scrabbling away, strength running out. Then I'd given up and peeled off. This time, when I looked up for air, or inspiration, I saw a black butterfly with three yellow dots on each wing.

This butterfly, the Opalescent Birdwing, is found only on Buru. Almost forgetting my predicament, I shouted down to Imran in excitement that I had seen the famous black butterfly of Buru. He shouted something vaguely back. Thinking now with my feet and not my worried mind, I found that at my lowest extent I could just get my toes on to a tiny ledge. The predicament was miraculously over. Back on the path, I followed the by no means easy track of Steerman down to the boulder caves below.

There was a smell of snake everywhere. Though textbooks will tell you snakes, like pigs, are odourless, they aren't, or at least their immediate surroundings aren't. Apart from cloacal scent glands which serve to attract a mate, snake faeces and the very fact that snakes are carnivores causes them to have their own peculiar odour, a meaty, musty, pungent odour.

Some writers have exaggerated the smell of snakes, perhaps encouraged by the mythological Midgard, whose bad breath was notorious. It was in a final dying spurt of halitosis that Midgard's slayer, Thor, was overcome and asphyxiated. A more recent offender is Major Percy Fawcett, the Brazilian adventurer who disappeared in the South American jungle in the 1920s. In 1907 he claimed to have shot a sixty-two-foot snake, presumably an anaconda. He noted, 'A foetid odour emanated from the snake, probably its breath which is believed to have a stupefying effect, first attacking and then paralysing the prey.'

I knew now how to act the expert. Being a man of action involved the ability to convince others that you were the business. My sniffs were knowledgeable, sure of themselves. Unfortunately I blew some of my credibility when I suggested to Steerman that we set fire to a newspaper and shove it in one of the holes we had found beneath a boulder. He looked at me with horror. I was glad that he rejected the notion as I did not know what I would do when a smoked-out python emerged, no doubt a little peeved at being so disturbed. I was also pleased that Steerman had shown at least some fear. Now we were in it together. In one pyschological study I read, children of two, three and four were tested for instinctive snake fear. Children of two showed no fear; three-year-olds showed caution; and four-year-olds and above showed fear, which increased as they got older. Snake fear, it seems, is learned, from others or perhaps from dreams – the appearance of snake fear coincides with the earliest age at which infants can recall dreams.

We bent and sniffed for snakes and I wondered, if I saw a snake, would I have the courage of Frank 'Bring 'em back alive' Buck, the American game hunter? He once caught a twenty-two-foot python by the tail and distracted it from taking a chunk out of him by getting it to bite on a rolled-up cloth. The herpetologist Malcolm Smith also recommended something similar: 'Take a bath towel and wrap it several times around the left hand so as to protect it completely.

Push this into the snake's face. It will at once be seized and before the creature can free its teeth for a second bite it can be gripped round the neck and carried off.' It was fortunate that no snake appeared since the nearest thing we had to a towel was Steerman's patched cap.

Steerman explained that until the rainy season the snakes would remain hidden. I told him to contact Imran if he came across a big snake while walking on the clifftop.

Imran was perched on a boulder, making brave bird noises at the trees but keeping his toes well out of harm's way. He was uninterested in the butterfly and was glad to hear we would now descend. I handed out a round of cigarettes and stripped off my sopping shirt. The moment after the adventure, however small the adventure, is the finest of all pleasures. I smiled at the trees and the sun filtering through the canopy and at Steerman and Imran and myself. I had come a long way to feel that feeling, which is its own reward; better than success, which always drives you on to further questions and adventures. A small and self-contained adventure is the pinnacle of satisfaction, and I was relearning all that on this prison island just south of the equator.

On top of the hill overlooking the sea and the beautiful curve of the beachside village, Imran recovered some of his bravado. 'If we had a mortar,' he said with enthusiasm, 'we could mortar the whole village from here.' He made his characteristic bird sounds as we descended to the village.

I paid off Steerman at a house whose front window was open to sell a poor selection of biscuits, tobacco and soda drinks. I insisted we drink a warm Coke together but, as the Coke cost half Steerman's day's wages, he not surprisingly hugged it close to him and disappeared to drink it somewhere more congenial.

The bus was a long time coming, and the villagers were keen to question me. Imran told them about snow, which he had seen on television. There was no television in the village, but many had seen it in Namlea. Imran said that if there was snow in Indonesia, everyone would die before the winter was out. The villagers agreed that snow proved the superior ruggedness of the British over the Indonesian.

When they discovered I lived some forty-five miles from the sea, there was great consternation. They were concerned that I would not have hygienic toilet facilities. On Buru, only the wild men of the interior can exist far from the sea. They are animists and are looked down upon by the fair-skinned immigrants from Sulawesi who cling to the coastline. In the village, just as in Namlea, all the houses had access to the beach, which served as a communal sewer outlet. The more ingenious had rickety wooden walkways extending out over the water with a rudely made cubicle at the end.

When the bus arrived, it was full of men with black and green parrots on bamboo perches. 'In this village they all collect parrots,' Imran explained. He made his generic bird noise, but the parrots ignored him. A parrot sold in Namlea for less than a pound sterling, so it did not seem to be such a good business to be in. The perches were clever, made from a strip of bamboo bent down to a crosspiece of bambo. Remaining on each end of the strip were cylindrical sections of bamboo that served as food and water containers. 'People come from Ambon for the black and green parrot,' said Imran. 'Buru is the only place where they live.'

The bus motored along the coastal road. I looked out of the window and saw, in the middle of nowhere, a small boy walking along with his head in a see-through steamed-up plastic bag. He was grinning through the bag, happily walking in the late afternoon sun and breathing in his own carbon dioxide. 'Why's he doing that?' I asked.

Imran shrugged. 'Perhaps it is his hobby,' he said.

TWELVE

The Three Pas

Never discourage anybody – life will do that soon
enough.   *C. J. Ionides*

It became obvious that there was a price for Imran and
Ferdinandus's hospitality: I was to be a star attraction at the
school where they both taught. At first I was just dragged in
during their lessons and asked questions by the more competent children. The standard of English was extremely poor.
Once I made the mistake of correcting one of Imran's
spellings on the blackboard during the class. Later I realized
it was better to let the children imbibe falsehoods than
damage the social status of my host. But after ignoring 'Aisa
is as nice girl as Hetty' and 'Lombok is more beautiful island'
even I could not allow the class to blindly copy down 'Ridwan
is taller than Ridwan'. As Imran created a cloud of chalk dust
wiping clean his error he remarked, 'The chalk! Every day
the teacher must meet with it. It is a danger for us.'

I was introduced to all the other teachers, who sat in one
room in a horseshoe-shaped arrangement of metal desks.
Ferdinandus gave up his desk for me to sit at while he stood
respectfully against the wall. At the top of the horseshoe sat
the fat wife of the headmaster, who for the next month was
on a visit to Jakarta. The wife presided over the school,
which was for boys and girls aged eleven to fifteen. Because
of a lack of teachers, the children came in two shifts. The
younger children came from seven thirty to one, and the

older children from one thirty to six. 'That way,' said Imran brightly, 'a school for four hundred can teach eight hundred!'

One teacher who was very pleased to meet me was Mr Rasey. He came round specially to meet me at Ferdinandus's house. 'Call me Hans,' he said, which I did for a while until I realized he had made the name up for himself and no one else called him that. In my diary I called him Hans for a page or two and then it was plain 'Rasey', and later 'Rasey' plus some expletive. As he rose to meet me from the wooden settle in Ferdinandus's front parlour, he was grinning with a kind of knowing excitement, and immediately launched into a long speech on internationalism. He was as intrigued as everyone by my small cigars and readily took one. He then lit the cigar while it was still encased in its plastic wrapper. His expression as he drew on the molten plastic, after his long and lofty speech, was somewhat stunned. He tried and almost succeeded in recovering by turning to Ferdinandus and saying breezily, 'We must go to Holland.'

'That's you speaking,' said Ferdinandus. 'Go if you want to.'

Rasey was a small man, very dark-skinned, keen to talk and tell me about all the foreign people he had met in Ambon. He was only half qualified as a teacher, though he was thirty years old, and served on the staff without the guarantees of full-time employment. His teaching style was less boring than Imran's, though his English was worse. I liked the way he casually smoked in class, flicking the ash unconcernedly on the floor as he explained some point in animated detail.

At first I was quite happy talking to Rasey. In a way he fascinated me. It was as if he had consulted a book on how to create a bad impression. After the international speech and the wrapped-cigar incident, he proceeded to tell a joke about a crippled boy at the school and then, when that raised no laugh, to criticize Imran behind his back. I had to admit he

241

had done well to rise to being a schoolteacher from his early life as a carpenter. Imran told me this. Rasey had lost both his parents early on and had been brought up by distant relatives. He came from Kai Island, which is far to the south of Buru. He had learned his English as a tour guide in Ambon and because Buru was something of a hardship posting he had been able to find work there despite his lack of qualifications. As well as teaching at the school, he taught students privately.

Giving private lessons was the main scam open to the teachers. Because the school was operating on double time with large classes, it was generally felt that the kids were not getting enough tuition. Three nights a week the school was opened for further lessons which had to be paid for by the parents. The teachers shared the burden and the booty of this task, but on one of the days I was due to help Ferdinandus, Rasey did not turn up. His class was already running at seventy-plus because of another teacher being ill. Generously Imran assigned me to teach this class.

It was not a success. I had taught English in Japan and felt quite confident that I could control most classes, even one that was packed to bursting with three or four kids to a desk. But Indonesian children are not like Japanese children. They are much more excitable. Waves of excitement would sweep across the class from back to front and from side to side. Sometimes it was just the sheer fact of being alone with a foreigner in a room. Other times it was something seen through the window, or something called out from the back of the class.

Pretty quickly I knew that it was less a question of teaching than of getting through the two hours of the lesson. I cursed Rasey – why hadn't he turned up? His chirpy, monkeyish face, the fact that he always called Ferdinandus Mr Ferdy, his bogus name, Hans, all his irritating qualities were called to mind by his absence at this crucial hour.

I tried various 'tricks' used by teachers to quell unruly classes. Keep the pace up, draw funny pictures on the blackboard, ask them their names or other simple tasks. Some students were very shy and refused to speak, some were garrulous, but all were highly excitable. In the end I opted for 'the freeze', which is touted by most teaching manuals as a sure-fire success in controlling the class. Mid-sentence you just stop talking and moving. Usually it takes a second or two for it to sink in, longer for a really rowdy class, but after a while everyone realizes there is an oppressively silent adult just standing and waiting. In Japan it *always* worked. I have a feeling it would work in England too. I think it would work anywhere where the kids felt the slightest guilt about their behaviour. In Buru they didn't. Just when a modicum of silence was attained, a new wave of excitement swept from one side of the room to the other. The kids found my behaviour so strange that they had to talk about it. 'Why isn't he teaching?' 'Why has he stopped moving?' Perhaps they thought I'd had a mild seizure. I did not restrain the three or four children who just upped and left, but it was the final straw. Teaching manuals need to be rewritten – 'the freeze' had failed. As a final, final resort I got them all chanting – numbers, months, colours, dates, anything. At least time was passing.

Imran and the four escapees appeared in the classroom. Perhaps for my benefit, Imran berated them in English, which no one understood. I then realized that the kids had gone to fetch Imran. They had asked him, 'What is wrong with Mr Twigger?' Imran went back to his class and I soldiered on. After an hour and a half I thought, Hold on, I'm in Indonesia, teaching someone else's class because he's too lazy to turn up – why should I sweat it? I told the kids the class was finishing half an hour early and they greeted the news with perfect comprehension and ecstatic hoots and catcalls. Now I really was a popular teacher. They clustered around me as I walked around to the front of the school. A chair was brought for me and I smoked contentedly until the other classes finished.

Ferdinandus appeared looking harassed. He had trailed my appearance in *his* class and by not showing up I had made him look foolish. I explained that I had been sidelined by Imran's last-minute decision that I teach Rasey's class.

'Why is Rasey not here?' he demanded.

'It is far for him to walk,' Imran suggested.

Later, in private, Mr Ferdy (I was beginning to catch Rasey's habits) told me, 'Rasey is a naughty man.'

At Ferdinandus's house I was treated with the utmost courtesy. Imran, after first suggesting I stay with him, suddenly rescinded his offer and suggested I would be more comfortable at Ferdinandus's. Imran dropped me off on the back of 'old grandad', his loud, ancient motorbike, after a night ride along the beach road to where they lived. Imran lived in a house with a palm-thatch roof; Ferdinandus had green tin. I wondered if that was why I was staying with Mr F.

He was also a Christian, which made things easier, they felt. The house was a stone-floored bungalow with a walkway on shaky pilings out over the sea. The bathroom was a tin shack, for which Ferdinandus apologized. There were two water butts and water drained away through the crushed coral on the floor. They prepared hot water for me, which was very kind, but did not tell me about the loo at the end of the walkway. In the end I got desperate and realized that there were no other toilet facilities, that Mr F. did not maintain the jetty as a quaint reminder, like an outdoor loo in an old country house. This was the business, or rather, this was where the business should be done. Using the Maglite I managed at night to find my way out along the wooden walkway. The shed at the end was made private by

244

fixing a piece of sack in front of the door. Down through the hole in the floor I could see the crabs massing, revealed now and then by the retreating waves and foamy phosphorescence. Though I was at least eight feet above the water, I became strangely paranoid about being attacked from underneath as I performed my squatting business. I searched for any rogue crabs that might have sequestered themselves beneath the sacking. In the end I let fall with a troubled conscience, quieted by the finality of the bowels' demands and the ever same sound of the sea.

Out across the bay there were a few lights to be seen: night fishermen and, further up, the lights of the small town. It was all very peaceful.

My room had a huge double bed. Ferdinandus, his large wife, mother-in-law, young daughter and baby son all slept in the adjoining room. There was definitely something inequitable about the sleeping arrangements but no other combination would have been decent and I consoled myself with knowing that I would not be there long and with that old lie of the scrounging backpacker: that I was somehow doing them a favour by letting them expend hospitality on me.

The family rose at six in the morning. It was a bad time for the dog, which was kicked by everyone, even Archie, Ferdy's twelve-year-old daughter. After a few days the household suddenly included a young lad of about ten who slept in the kitchen. No one introduced him, though he quickly made himself useful by cleaning and fetching drinks. When I enquired, Ferdinandus explained in an offhand way that he was the son of a relative who had come to Namlea to study and would now be living with the family.

I wanted to visit more villages to spread the word about Big Snake. It was time to take seriously the advice of Ionides: 'Until there is news of the quarry, I will not stir.' Actively promoting my search would, I hoped, result in news of the quarry. Wallace too had relied heavily on local information, using cash as an incentive to get help.

After some discussion, Ferdy decided it would be a good idea to visit Pa Boah. 'He is Hindu,' Ferdy explained.

'You mean an Indian?' I said.

'No, we call Hindu the uncivilized men who worship trees and stones.' Ferdy advised me to bring a hundred Gudam Garam cigarettes as sweeteners for Pa Boah and his tribe. He was a jungle man, said Ferdy, and would know about pythons.

Pa Boah lived across the bay in a swamp some miles from Kayeli, the site of the old Portuguese fort, and the place where Wallace stayed when he came to Buru. Ferdy and I, suitably provisioned, went down to the small muddy beach where the motorized long canoes ferried people across the bay. As we waited, one log canoe came in with a raised wooden armchair in the middle carrying a smiling fat man in a bright-red coolie hat. He disembarked daintily, carrying his thin leather slip-ons tucked one under each armpit.

We waited for an hour until one boat was full. It was carved from an enormous log, perhaps thirty-five feet long, with a forty-horsepower 'Johnson' on the back. Actually the engine was a Yamaha, but the generic name for an outboard in Buru was 'Johnson'.

The waves became higher as we cleared the protecting headland of Namlea. The sun was shining and the salt spray splashed just enough to create a fine feeling of excitement in a sea crossing. Two shark fins cut the water not a hundred feet from the boat and I grew very animated pointing them out to Ferdy. In my mind we were now crossing 'shark bay', where any mishap might result in certain death, and this added an even finer edge to the proceedings. But when we had landed and were out of the roar of the engine, Ferdy explained that they had been dolphins, not sharks. 'We have killed all the sharks around here,' he said. 'They are too frightened to enter the bay.'

246

Kayeli was a poor village, a series of mud roads with shacks dotted around. It did not seem to have changed since Wallace's day. We paid a visit to the headman, who arranged for a boy to guide us to Pa Bossing.

'Who's Pa Bossing?' I asked.

'He has recently converted to Christianity,' Ferdy explained gravely. 'He has turned his house into a church. We have to cross his land and the land of Pa Veruca to get to Pa Boah's.'

I questioned Ferdy closely on the pronunciation and spelling of Pa Veruca's name and it remained an enigma, though I have spelled it here as he instructed me.

The boy, whose pace quickened almost to a run when I gave him two cigarettes, set off along the sodden duckboards into the swamp. On either side was tall kusu kusu grass, sometimes so high that it curled over the duckboards, making a light-green tunnel for us to hurry along. There were many lizards and things just out of sight in the swamp, which made rapid noises of evasion as we approached. Sometimes we crossed streams through the swamp, and the duckboards became rotten or submerged. Bamboos and logs served as temporary bridges in such places.

Sometimes other duckboarded paths met ours. The swamp was crisscrossed with manmade walkways. We met people who greeted our guide and passed on news about Pa Bossing. It was now very hot and mosquitoes buzzed around my covered arms. I thought of King Hereward, who fought against William the Conqueror and lived secure in the marshes of Ely. His place must have been like this before it was drained. Knowing English wetlands, the biting insects were probably worse there than here, and in Hereward's day there was probably malaria in England too.

For three miles we raced on through the boggy land. When we finally broke through to the island of forested dry land that was Pa Bossing's territory, I felt as if I had been at sea for a long time. The trees curved over mysteriously as if something weighed down on them from above. We met an archetypal trio: a man with a *sopi* bottle, his wife laden down with cassavas and a small, completely naked boy. The man looked aged beyond the years I expected for someone to be the father of such a young child. Perhaps he had drunk too deeply of *sopi*. The wife had glum, heavily Papuan features. These were interior folk, noticeably different from the sea-loving immigrants who populated Namlea and the coastal villages.

Pa Bossing, being the headman, had the largest dwelling in the village. It was a rambling collection of sheds, though the interior was swept clean and tidy. We sat in the dark mud-floored 'church' which was the communal front room of the house. Ferdy had visited Pa Bossing on a church mission some time before, and the old man, who was grey-haired and dignified, received us with courtesy. My presence baffled him, but when it was explained I was after a snake he warmed up and ordered tea from the women tittering behind a blanket that hung over the door to the rest of the house.

On the walls of the church room were crude paintings of the fighting in Buru during the Second World War, done by Pa Bossing himself. They depicted Australians and Japanese shooting at each other, with bullet trajectories marked as dotted lines from the rifle barrels.

Pa Bossing agreed that Pa Boah was the man for snake hunting, though he had considerable reservations about his refusal to become a Christian. Since his own conversion some years before, Pa Bossing had been evangelizing in the swamps but had met with limited success. Pa Veruca, it seemed, was on the verge of baptism, but Pa Boah would have none of it. A coastal logging company had encroached on Pa Boah's land and though the company concerned was undoubtedly Indonesian Muslim, this had turned him against

248

the Christian religion. Pa Boah and Pa Bossing were not on the best of terms, and a Bible sent to Pa Boah had been returned, which was not so surprising as Pa Boah had never learned to read.

We were served a meal of chicken, *papeeda* and *swami*. Before eating, Pa Bossing impressed us with a ten-minute grace. During the lengthy prayers I kept eyeing the *papeeda*, made from sago, and the staple diet of the Moluccas. It bore a worrying resemblance to brown snot, with the same gluey consistency, and apart from the gravy added as seasoning it had little flavour and a quite horrible texture. I made the mistake of trying to chew a mouthful, much to everyone's mirth, and simply ended up gluing my mouth together. Pa Bossing's elderly wife demonstrated how to suck it down without chewing. I sucked my snot down, but I knew this was not a food I could get used to without the prospect of starvation to prompt me. *Swami* were cassava patties, bland also, but inoffensive.

I have always tried to subsist off the native food wherever I have found myself, attempting in a modest way to emulate the explorer Wilfred Thesiger, who never pampered himself with home comforts. I tried in Japan to live off Japanese food, and succeeded (I agree it's not that difficult), though I began to lose my ability to really *enjoy* food. Wallace, I think, struck the most sensible balance. He adapted native food with a few choice condiments which he had shipped from England – mustard, marmalade – and butter, which he probably obtained locally. If he had travelled in the twentieth century I'm sure he would have doused *papeeda* in brown sauce and smacked his lips with relish. For future trips to Buru I planned to bring marmalade and Lea and Perrins sauce. There is something unutterably English about Worcester sauce, and it is very economical too. A few drops in a mysterious Burunese stew would transform it into a very palatable dish. And as Wallace advised, marmalade and a little butter was the perfect accompaniment to sago cakes baked fresh in the morning.

Out of fear of upsetting my hosts, I just bolted anything offered me, and I did not try to adapt the food to my own particular taste. In England I commonly adapt foods – mango-chutney and cheese sandwiches being one of my favourites. Some spurious notion of relativism had entered my thinking, that all food was equal, and that to refuse or modify certain items was a kind of culinary racism. Well, I would pay the price later for this intellectual foible.

After the meal there was another, very long grace, with Pa Bossing half singing some of the parts. We had more tea and waited for Pa Bossing's son to come and guide us to Pa Boah. He had been out collecting cobwebs, which was an interesting enough fact, but also involved a certain controversy. It seemed that Pa Boah's village specialized in cobweb collecting and selling and Pa Bossing's village specialized in eucalyptus processing. Pa Veruca specialized in growing cassava. Cobwebs commanded fifty thousand rupiah (ten pounds) a kilo. They were collected and sold to a Chinese merchant who came to Namlea to buy them. No one knew or particularly cared what they were used for. By illicitly collecting cobwebs (to buy a cassette player) Pa Bossing's son risked upsetting the delicate economy of the swamp. Pa Bossing was vaguely disapproving, but now he was a Christian he felt a certain moral superiority to Pa Boah, and, after the Bible rejection, was not above messing him around a bit.

Pa Bossing's son eventually turned up. He was a thickset young man and wore only shorts. He disappeared for a long time and came back elegantly groomed in his Sunday best of pressed shirt, ironed trousers and a pair of shiny plastic loafers on his bare feet. He had wetted his springy hair and doused himself in perfume.

An hour later, his trousers spattered with mud, twigs in his hair and sweat stains burgeoning under each armpit, Pa

Bossing's son led us out of the swamp and into the forest. We followed a dusty dirt road that went from the coast to the edge of the swamp. This was the logging frontier and I could see why Pa Boah was not happy. For a hundred or so yards either side of the road, the only trees growing were short and thin. The place had been raped for wood and now the bush was growing back with difficulty because of the poor soil. We left the track and things became better the further we went. Crossing more patches of swamp, we entered the woodland abode of Pa Boah.

The village was the most rustic I had yet seen on my trip. In the centre was a wooden platform, like a square bandstand, roofed over with palm leaves. On the platform Pa Boah sat crosslegged with his friends. On a smaller platform, a few yards away, Pa Boah's womenfolk sat. No one seemed to be doing anything, not even the dogs, which were curled up in the dust. This was sensible as it was hot and the middle of the afternoon, and only a rabid Christian or an Englishman with snake fever would want to be active at that time.

Pa Boah was short, very dark and wiry, and was barely clad in torn old army shorts. He was not an old man, perhaps in his early forties, but his face was wrinkled and weather-beaten. His eyes were very much alive and there wasn't a hint of modernity or 'civilization' about him. When we spoke, he was both humble and forthright. I think he feared that I was a missionary, but when we told him about the hunt for Big Snake, he grew less wary.

'Of course there are snakes. I have seen a snake this wide' – here he encircled his arms to barrel width – 'only a day's walk from here. But I have never caught a snake alive. I have only killed snakes.'

I explained the plan I had evolved for catching a snake. I drew in the dust a chicken and a stake and a bamboo pole with a rope noose coming from it. Ferdy backed me up with enthusiasm. Pa Boah looked impassive and then asked if a thirteen-foot snake would be OK. He knew of a thirteen-foot snake in the nearby swamp. I said I wanted one thirty feet long. The womenfolk on the other platform all laughed, but Pa Boah didn't. 'If we catch a snake like that, we will be very strong,' he said.

The issue of money was sensitive. I'd blown a previous deal by being too stingy. But I knew if I said the snake was worth millions of rupiah, I ran the risk of being disbelieved. I settled for saying that the snake was worth the same as two Johnsons, about two thousand dollars. I wanted to show willing so I gave money to an older man, who seemed to be Pa Boah's financial manager, to pay for some chickens as bait. There were scrawny-looking chickens pecking near to the huts of the compound, which would do nicely. If people protested at the cruelty of live chicken bait, I agreed, but diluted their criticism by mentioning the experiment which showed, under lab conditions, that chickens show no fear of snakes.

It was time to hand round some packets of Gudam Garam cigarettes. Pa Boah accepted a cigarette and started to talk about the cobweb business. I noticed the perfumed bulk of Pa Bossing's son slink a little further into the background. He had already told me proudly that he didn't smoke so I did not have to bring him to attention by offering him a cigarette.

'The cobwebs are taken by the Chinese. Once they were used by us to make fishing nets! It is true, but to make the net you have to handle the webs with wet hands – this is important. The Chinese pay well for the webs. They use them for paper, for a special medicine and for a magic jacket that stops bullets.'

It is true that cobwebs have been researched as a Kevlar substitute for bulletproof jackets. Here on Buru I had found the source. 'How long does it take to collect a kilo of cobwebs?' I asked.

'Many mornings, or many hands!' Pa Boah replied.

'How long have you been collecting them?'

'All my life. This family has always been collecting them. It is because of these trees that there are many spiders.'

'Have the logging company cut down many trees?'

He looked at me but did not reply. When it became a little uncomfortable, he said, 'Many things die all the time. What is true will always survive. Perhaps we will have to learn another trade like eucalyptus processing.' Here he cast a sly glance at Pa Bossing's son, who was sitting with his back straight against one of the smooth log supports of the roof. I knew then that Pa Boah knew that Pa Bossing's son had been collecting cobwebs.

'Perhaps we will become snake hunters!' Everyone laughed a lot at this idea, though some of the women winced in mock fear and disgust.

'I can say that we are not happy to lose the forest. But we are not against these men. Nothing of real value can ever be stolen or lost. If there is a spirit in the tree, it will leave and become a spirit in the bulldozer, or a pair of man's boots.'

Pa Boah's face was serious. Then somebody made a comment and everyone laughed. I asked Mr Ferdy what had been said but all he replied was, 'They make a joke.'

Pa Boah showed us a cardboard box full of cobwebs. It felt like nothing but he said it weighed half a kilo. Wetting his fingers in his mouth, he lifted out a strand, offered it to Pa Bossing's son and roared with laughter when he declined to hold it.

I thought of the Chinese merchants, coming to collect their cobwebs, supplying some hazy foreign market. It was a modern version of the Roman emperor Elagabalus, who ordered slaves to bring him ten thousand pounds of spider's silk. On receiving them, he announced, 'From this one can understand how great a city is Rome.'

*

Just as we were leaving, having made all kinds of elaborate arrangements for runners to come to the school to tell us when a snake had been caught, Pa Boah signalled to his 'manager' to hand our money back.

'Why's that?' I asked Ferdy.

'He does not want to take your money for nothing. If there is a snake, he will use chickens and then you can pay him later.'

If there was a snake to be caught, I felt Pa Boah could do it. More importantly, I knew that he was an honourable man.

Pa Bossing's son, who was now rather sullen as well as sweat-stained, took us to the edge of Pa Veruca's land and then made his excuses. As we parted, his mood lightened and he made off at speed back along the duckboards through the swamp.

Pa Veruca also had an island in the swamp, which, unlike Pa Boah's, had no connection to the dry land of the coast. This ensured that his cassava trees were safe. His village was less run down than Pa Boah's but less affluent than Pa Bossing's (no one wearing shoes, home-made knives instead of factory parangs, not a tablecloth in sight).

We found Pa Veruca sitting on his porch on a worn wooden bench. He was an old man, older than Pa Bossing, tall and bent. For some reason he reminded me of William Burroughs. After some general chitchat as we were waiting for a boy to take us to the coast, he asked Ferdy if I was a Christian. Ferdy answered yes, which, in the approximate history I'd supplied, was correct. Pa Veruca went into his hut and came out with a worn Bible. I examined it with polite interest and handed it back. He nodded and took it back inside his hut.

'Has he converted yet?' I asked Ferdy.

'He is waiting for something special, I think,' said Ferdy.

Pa Veruca appeared with a bag full of runner beans, which he gave to me. 'I see,' I said. 'He's waiting for a sign. Maybe the snake will be the sign.' I urged Ferdy to translate this,

254

but Pa Veruca just grinned a toothless smile, so I don't think he did.

Back in Kayeli we were faced with either staying the night or chartering a logboat to ourselves. The cost was ten pounds, half a month's wages for the unlucky Rasey. Thinking about the damp mud floors of the village, I didn't want to stay the night. Wallace had searched high and low for a hut without a damp floor when he had stayed; I had less time and would probably be less lucky. 'Let's get a boat,' I said, and Ferdy heartily agreed.

The sun was low in the sky as we walked to the beach with the boatman. Suddenly the *papeeda* and *swami*, which I had anticipated bunging me up, began to demand release. '*Berak*,' I muttered to Ferdy. He nodded and gestured to a lone palm tree on the beach. With as much dignity as I could muster, I scarpered behind the tree and relieved myself. In my haste I had nothing to wipe my arse with. I thought about sand, but it didn't seem practical, and the tide was too far out to perform *boso*. All I had in my pockets was my precious notebook and a big bundle of Indonesian currency. Taking care not to soil a big denomination, I found that the smallest note I had was five thousand rupiah, a day's wages for Steerman or Rasey. I briefly considered the inequities of the capitalist system before using the note to the full and burying it in the sand. Feeling guilty, I rejoined Ferdy, the boatman and his naked boy, and set sail across the bay.

A sublime happiness came over me as we powered across the now rough sea, whipped up by the cool evening breeze. The sun had almost set and the lights of Namlea were just visible. Crossing the bay, the engine drowning out conversation, I felt all tension disappear. The snake in my belly, the anxious snake, brother of the one that had to be caught, uncoiled and slid away. Yes, for that moment I was truly happy.

255

THIRTEEN

Mr Greasy's Rep

Never allow yourself to be deterred by apparently
great difficulties from achieving something you
really wish to achieve. We are creatures of habit,
and persistence can be cultivated.   *C. J. Ionides*

Mr Greasy lived near to the fish market, a huge concrete
barn of a place, full by nine in the morning with boys and
women selling fresh fish dangling by the gills from a loop of
bamboo sliver. Mr Greasy came up to me as I wandered
around the place with Imran. He was overweight, with long,
black hair, and addressed me in excellent English, enquiring
politely after my health, my plans and the expected duration
of my stay. I could tell that Imran was uncomfortable and,
though Mr Greasy invited me to visit his house, I made an
excuse and quickly left with Imran.

'He is greasy man!' Imran hissed conspiratorially as we
walked off.

'Is he? Perhaps it's the heat. He didn't look that greasy to
me. Well, maybe his hair was a bit greasy . . .'

'He is greasy man. He live for ten years in Egypt, studying
at Al Azhar University. The people of Namlea pay for him
to study Islam there. He speak English, French, Arabic and
German. But everyone know he is greasy.'

It seemed unfair that a simple hair problem should cause
someone to be so vilified and ostracized. It surprised me. At
school, perhaps, it wasn't unusual to avoid those with a grease

problem – the hated acne and lank hair of lonely adolescence – but here on Buru it seemed very out of place.

I was now staying at Imran's, idling away each day waiting for word from Pa Boah. Imran and Ferdy had decided that I should move further up the beach to the cluster of palm-thatched huts where Imran lived, and I was quite happy to do so. Ferdy had to leave in a few days for Ambon, on a church mission. He was taking his wife and family and they would have the treat of being among the first Burunese to travel in the big passenger ship that was due any day. It was the first time a big ship had called at Buru within recent memory and everyone was excited. 'If I have to teach that day,' said Imran, 'no children will come. They all want to see the big ship.'

Imran's front room was dominated by his prize possession, a large television set, which was on during most of the day. On top of the TV was what at first I thought was a rotating disco light. Imran showed me with great pride how he had made this light. Inside a paper tube with holes in it were several coloured lights. At the top of the paper tube was a paper propeller. The heat from the lights made the tube rotate, casting coloured light all around the front room, which was full of neighbours and relatives all day long. The blaring TV, Imran's cassette player, which was often on simultaneously, and the rotating disco light, which was always on, made Imran's parlour the most exciting place in the neighbourhood. With Malaysian disco music playing, Imran's five-year-old son and another young lad started to disco dance wildly. 'Tripping! Tripping!' Imran's daughters chorused. 'Look at tripping!' 'Tripping' was the latest Indo-nesian dance craze.

Imran disapproved. He preferred Jim Reeves and Malay love songs. 'Is the tripping in your country too?' he asked.

'Something similar,' I said.

257

When the kids weren't tripping, it was impossible for me to sit there without becoming the centre of attention. 'That old grandmother,' said Imran, pointing out one old lady squatting on the floor and grinning toothlessly, 'comes every day just to look at you.'

As at Ferdy's, I had been assigned my own room, bare save a huge double bed, and Imran, his wife, his mother-in-law and three daughters all slept in a second room. His son and a nephew who was staying slept on the kitchen floor. I was not the first foreigner to be staying at Imran's. A year before, a French engineer had stayed for a week. Imran explained, 'The French, he so tall, he sleep like a sea cucumber!'

Being of normal height, I found the bed very satisfactory, though even if I retired to escape the barrage of people exclaiming at the quality of my skin ('not red and freckled like most foreigners in Ambon') it was hard, unless I was actually sleeping, to be on my own. Imran's son used to creep under the curtain partition just to stare at me. I suggested to Imran that I might spend more time in town, which was a ten-minute walk away. The conversation went like this:

Me: Where are the restaurants in town?

Imran: Why?

Me: Well, I might want to eat . . .

Imran: (glaring)

Me: (realizing we're on tricky ground) or have a coffee.

Imran: (relaxes) Oh, a coffee. Down at the marketplace there are many places you can get coffee. (pause) You see, if you eat food in restaurants people will see you and ask, Why is he doing that? They will think Imran's food is no good, and I'll be ashamed. But coffee is OK.

I escaped to the marketplace to have a coffee. I wasn't too worried about flouting Imran's food ban, but the restaurants I saw did not look so good, and Imran's wife was providing two feasts a day, which, apart from the obligatory *papeeda*, were delicious and filling.

258

As I sat down in the emptiest coffee shop I could find, I was surprised to see Mr Greasy in the corner, reading a book bound in a torn plastic bag. He smiled and waved and came over to talk to me. Perhaps he had washed his long hair that day, but it didn't look greasy at all to me.

He told me of his studies at Al Azhar University, where he had been determined to become a scholar of Muslim law. 'But then I began to see that law was taking me further and further away from the truth of Islam. The truth of Islam is there in the Koran, the world did not need another lawyer explaining that to them.

'There is a kind of thrombosis' (I could tell he was pleased to use this word) 'about modern Islamic thought. In the golden age knowledge was sought as it is in the West now – without dogma and futile preconception. There was no such thing as Islamic physics or Islamic geography – there was simply the truth about the physical world. I was inspired by the example of Ibn Al Haytham to seek knowledge without preconception. But even Al Haytham had his problems with the authorities. Do you know his example?'

I had never heard of Al Haytham.

'He was living in Baghdad when he heard about the flooding of the Nile and offered the Caliph his services. He was a confident scientist and he believed that by making a dam across the Nile he could control its flooding. But when he got to Aswan he found that the problem was far too big for him to deal with. His idea was correct, we now know, but the Eygptians would have to wait for bulldozers and dynamite before it could be effected. Al Haytham now had a problem. He had received money and help from the Caliph and now he had to return and say that he had failed. This meant he risked being executed. He thought and thought about how he could phrase his excuse, but he realized that there is no excuse for failure. He went back and prepared to die, but then he had a genius idea. He did not have to die, only his reputation need die, so he pretended to be greasy—'

'Greasy?'

'Greasy, mad, a lunatic, one who has lost his senses.'

Suddenly it was all making sense.

'So he pretended to be cr-a-zy,' Mr Greasy enunciated more clearly for my benefit, 'for twelve years. Because his idea to dam the Nile was also believed to be crazy, no one suspected him, and as you know, in Islam, the insane must be treated charitably.'

'Brilliant!' I said. Mr Greasy beamed.

'And after twelve years he started to make many more discoveries, such as the exact measure of earth's circumference, the first kind of camera, study of optic – many things.'

'But why twelve years? That seems an awfully long time. Wouldn't, say, four years have been enough?'

'Twelve is a special number. If people say twelve years, then it may mean they study some mystic thing also.'

'So Ibn Haytham was also a mystic?'

'I do not know. But he is an inspiration to all people, all Muslims. There were no limits to where he looked for knowledge, no limits to his thinking. But modern Muslims forget this. Do you know the Prophet said, "Islam arrived as a stranger and will depart as a stranger"?'

'No, I didn't know that.'

I told Mr Greasy about my snake hunt. He replied that the Prophet had said that snakes can sometimes be a kind of jinn, or evil spirit.

Our coffee cups were empty. Mr Greasy repeated his offer for me to visit his house, 'but I am sure you are very busy,' he added. 'I myself am mostly reading.'

When he left, the solicitous café owner made the universal screwy sign by tapping his temple. I had to smile to myself. Mr Greasy had them all fooled, every last one of them.

*

Hearing that I was married, Imran's wife wanted to see a photograph of my wife. Reluctantly I showed them an old passport photo I kept of Samia. The photograph was passed around reverently. They exclaimed at her blond hair and blue eyes, which are, of course, unusual in Egypt. Imran's disfigured mother-in-law held the photograph and sang to herself as she squatted on the floor. 'This is a song to make you have children,' said Imran. 'Though she only had one herself.'

My presence at Imran's gave the low-status Rasey the excuse to drop round almost every day. Imran used these visits as an opportunity to persecute him, smoking all his cigarettes and quoting gleefully from an Islamic fundamentalist text that repeated ad infinitum that Jesus categorically had absolutely no divine status at all. Rasey took it very well, considering he was a keen Christian and smoking was his only luxury. He explained why he had failed to turn up at the school: he had been too tired to walk the four miles from his house to the centre of town. He was too poor to have even a bicycle, and walking backwards and forwards along the beach road wore his frail willpower out. For a while I was gripped by the idea of buying Rasey a bicycle, which Imran confidently asserted would only cost about twenty pounds secondhand. But I knew that the next time Rasey was late it would be because the bicycle had a puncture and he couldn't afford to fix it. And though it was burning hot, four miles wasn't so far. I began to worry if Rasey was eating enough.

One day he dropped by to show Imran his application for an interview in Ambon to gain full-time teacher status. 'My passport to a new life,' he said in a wan voice as he showed me the form.

He invited Imran and me to visit his house later that day. In a lordly way, Imran assented. When Rasey had left, he said, 'It is the first time I visit Mr Rasey's house.'

As we walked along the beach road we passed an after-hours Koranic instruction school. I mentioned that in England, in my school, religious education happened in the normal state school. Imran said, 'If we mix religious education in the school, we have a doomsday.'

Then Imran and I discussed the doomsday ideas of the Hale Bopp suicides, which he had read about in a copy of *Time* magazine he'd seen in Ambon. 'They are crazy, crazy! Why do they believe this?'

I made excuses for lonely people drawn into cults, and how the weird ideas of the cult have to be believed, otherwise the affection of the group is turned off. Imran, who found it impossible to conceive of loneliness, merely said, 'This is the crazy age! Look at the dancing, the tripping, it is crazy!'

'Well, crazy dancing, crazy religion,' I said.

'Even there are crazy Muslims,' Imran agreed.

'Islam came as a stranger and will depart as a stranger,' I repeated with pride.

Imran thought for a moment. 'But only from Pakistan, I think. Our government won't allow such things.'

We rested for a while under a fig tree at the top of a small cliff that overlooked the rocky beach. Imran explained that this was where I should do *berak*, though I had been living for three days in his house without anyone explaining the absence of a loo (I had been using the one at the school). He told me he sometimes came and sat under the tree to do some thinking on his own. Right now he was thinking about building a new house. He had already laid the foundations out next to his existing house. 'If my brother-in-law comes, I will start building,' he said.

I began to sympathize with Rasey as we trailed on and on in the heat to his house. Eventually the road ran out and we reached two rows of what looked like single-storey army barracks. They were dismal concrete with broken windows. A dog frisked in the dust in the street between them and sullen kids eyed us. At one particularly dark-skinned child

Imran chanted (in English, for my amusement), 'Blackie! Blackie!' The boy ran away.

The houses, of which Rasey's was one with unbroken windows, were in fact old army barracks, left over from the time when Buru was a prison island. Though nominal permission was needed to live there, it was effectively free accommodation, though it was so miserable and airless, despite being only about three hundred yards through palm trees from the beach, I would not have ever wanted to live there.

Rasey was incredibly pleased that we had deigned to visit him. He produced the single chair in his house for my benefit and shouted to his wife for '*makan*' – food. The only other furniture visible was a rough table with his English books underneath it. I could tell that he had not believed we would come. Before food he suggested we go for a walk. We passed a home-made basketball hoop – a chair nailed to a tree, with a circular basket shoved into the seat hole. It looked ingenious, but Imran dismissed it with, 'It is a crazy!'

Coming from the palm trees was the high whine of a buzzsaw. We came closer and watched for a while two men cutting perfect planks, using a piece of battery carbon to mark out the logs first. Slowly, slowly the man chainsawed with great care the length of the log, to take off a uniform three-inch plank. On a stump was a triangular file for sharpening the saw. Rasey picked up the file and started to play with it.

I said I would climb a palm tree to get some coconuts. Rasey and Imran expressed horror that I could conceive of such an idea. They said it was too dangerous. But each palm tree had deep footholes cut in its side so I knew it would be easy to climb. In the end they dissuaded me by saying that each tree was owned and they would have to get permission before climbing the tree.

Back at Rasey's house we drank tea and ate biscuits (the

makan) sitting on the step of the house. Rasey was still playing with the metal file and seemed surprised when I remarked on this. Imran stopped a girl in the street and told her to take the file back to the men. I wondered whether Rasey would simply have stolen the file.

We walked back past the power station, which was a noisy collection of big sheds with three diesel generators to provide all the power for Buru. 'You must use up a fair bit with your special light,' I joked.

'But I do not pay,' said Imran. 'You know I am also electrician. One day electricity break' (this happened quite often on Buru) 'so I fix it. After that the meter does not work but electricity come. So it is free!'

Imran also told me about his mother-in-law and the reason for her appalling ugliness. When she had been younger she had been the most beautiful woman in southeast Sulawesi. This was credible since Imran's wife, when she wasn't wearing a face-whitening mud pack, was also a very good-looking woman. The mother-in-law had been so beautiful that she had attracted the attentions of the king of that region and he had decided that she should marry him. But Imran's mother-in-law had already given her promise to another man, a poor fisherman. They decided to run away to Buru together, but when the king found out, he put an *ilmen hitam*, a black-magic curse, on her. On Buru she developed the strange disease that had so disfigured her. Imran grew serious at this point. 'This is not ordinary illness. This is black-magic illness. Face twisted and body arthritic.'

With all this talk about craziness, I wonder about Colonel H.'s own descent into apparent madness. For several years leading up to my father finding him shivering with hypothermia and ready to die, the Colonel had become increasingly eccentric. He had alienated most of the village, either by demanding that his cheques be cashed at any place of business he chose to patronize, or by lawsuits against neighbours that encroached on his land in some way, or simply by being plain weird. He gave up smoking and drinking when he was seventy-five and threw out all his chairs because he felt he was sitting down too much and all his organs were in the wrong place. A few years later he decided that the electricity board were cheating him (don't they cheat everyone, except the Imrans of this world?) and he refused to pay his bill. After it was cut off, he ran his VHF radio with scanner for listening to the police from a dry-cell battery charged by his own wind-powered generator. For lighting he returned to Tilley lights and candles; for heat, log fires, chopping the wood with a Naga headhunting *dao*. Then he came to believe the gas company were defrauding him. He started to cook on a twin burner powered by Calor Gas bottles. Then it was the water board. 'Got my own well. To hell with them all!' the Colonel announced.

He was now living in a state of complete rustic simplicity. I am inclined to believe that the explanation about cheating was just a ruse. He felt he was losing his powers, physically and mentally. Such an idea was unacceptable to the Colonel. He needed to increase control of his life now he could no longer run the honey business. By going backwoods he was at the mercy of no one except God, and any mistake he might make (like falling down the stairs on a dark, cold night). And I think too he remembered those happy days in his life when he had been alone in the jungle with his 'army', building a whole army camp out of nothing, living by his wits, the very opposite of soft so-called civilization.

His house, The Lawn, became a kind of fortress. The Colonel's ferocious half-mad Labrador, Kraken, kept out 'the snoopers', as he called them. Then Kraken died and the Colonel was too upset to get another dog. Normally people fear for old people and how they might be preyed upon by burglars or con men. With the Colonel we feared the opposite, for the potential casual thief or almost innocent

265

rip-off artist who might be foolish enough to pay a visit. 'I've killed men,' said the Colonel, 'but never with my bare hands.' The baseball bat that stood next to the door, a gift from General Vinegar Joe Stilwell, who usually hated Brits, took on a new and ominous significance.

When two people from the social services came round, the Colonel shouted through his kitchen window, 'I've got ten seamstresses all under eleven working here – now bugger off!'

Further eccentricities became evident. The Colonel decided his bed was 'too soft' and converted his huge oak dining table into a sort of sleeping platform. His telephone was cut off ('probably bugged anyway') and his labyrinthine and surprisingly successful share dealing was conducted from the local phone box. In the midst of this chaos he was gleeful about the fortune he made from the privatization of the utility companies he so despised.

He took care to appear sane (after a fashion) to outsiders, but to my uncle and father he started, for the first time, to say things that didn't make any sense. He started to become paranoid: 'Someone broke in the other day and moved everything. Then they moved it all back to the exact same place.' Perhaps there was the slimmest shard of truth in all this. Perhaps someone did break in and steal Saluting Man. By the time the end came, the Colonel was in no condition to say.

I went to visit him at the hospital and found the label on the curtain around his bed read '"Colonel" Twigger'. Two beds down was 'Jesus' Brown. He was now in a world where even the truth was just another symptom of insanity, remembered only in order to humour the inmates. The Colonel was not in his bed.

In found him in the common room. He marched briskly towards me, a very thin, old man, his back still ramrod straight. He glared at me and said (this was the first time I had seen him for about five years), 'What the hell are you grinning for?'

'I'm just happy to see you, Grandad,' I stammered.

He snorted and indicated we should sit down on a sofa. A tall, grey-haired Indian man, apparently in his own world, excused himself and made way for the Colonel. 'Aziz, Pathan. Tough customers, the Pathans.'

An elderly man with a moustache even bigger than the Colonel's came stumbling over. He seemed excited and about to speak. 'Not now, Jimmy,' said the Colonel. The old man looked disappointed but respectfully backed away. 'Jimmy, Eighth Army, first-rate fellow. Killed his wife, rather a sad story.'

We moved to a table and Aziz brought us tea. I began to see what was happening. The Colonel was raising an army! Even here, in the nuthouse, the old instincts, long dormant, were coming into play. Give him time, I thought, and the old bugger will be running the place.

'The tea is doped, of course,' he said, as I took a sip, but I detected the faintest glimmer of humour in his eyes as he spoke. 'They treat me well here. Not a bad billet.'

There was a long and, for me, uncomfortable silence.

'Received your letter about going to Japan.' (This was three years previously.) 'Felt there was something a bit lost about the way you phrased yourself. That sentence about hoping you didn't get caught in an earthquake as Kipling did.' He was at his old tricks, using his encyclopedic knowledge of the evidence to discomfort me.

'I'm not lost,' I said in a meek voice.

'Never ever need to be.' More silence.

Unexpectedly my uncle arrived. He joshed the Colonel good-humouredly, calling him 'a silly old bugger'. The Colonel beamed at the suggestion. 'Know this one?' He

267

tapped my uncle's shoulder and demonstrated a surprisingly deft fist, elbow and back fist attack.

'Done that before?' said my uncle.

'Might have,' snapped the Colonel with a grin.

Just before we left he said, 'Twelve stone, muscle and bone, muscle and bone, I used to be. Now look at me.'

'You're all right,' I said breezily.

'What d'you know?' he said.

'Not a lot,' I tried gamely.

'Less than you think, more than you know,' he added cryptically.

The big ship came to Namlea and anchored about five hundred yards off in the deep channel. Around the customs house and the ferry jetty was a crowd of, I calculated, at least five thousand people. A third of the town had turned out just to welcome the boat. Somehow, Imran and I inveigled our way to the very front. I talked to a fat old soldier who had his 'Tim Tim' (East Timor) and Irian ribbons. A flotilla of outriggers surrounded the huge ship and followed the launch in with the VIP arrivals. It was like a scene from an earlier era. An elderly, distinguished-looking man made a long speech to the big shot from Ambon who arrived with his cortège on the launch. The speech was microphoned and broadcast from speakers in the palm trees. Boys in the outriggers fell about laughing because the speech was in Burunese, which the guest and even half the islanders did not understand. Imran, for example, knew only a few words.

There was a welcoming dance done by a boy covered in hair and swirling a sword. The style of dancing was identical to that I'd seen practised by the Lundaiya in Borneo.

At the last minute Ferdy arrived with several enormous cardboard boxes, his wife, mother-in-law and two daughters. We helped him aboard the launch and waved goodbye. Rasey, though he had said he would be there, was, predictably, not. Imran's wife turned up wearing a headscarf and a very fancy dress. A man asked if I would teach him English. I declined, thinking how, on my arrival such a short time before, I would have welcomed such attention. Imran fired up 'old grandad' and we roared through the streaming crowds back to the school, which turned out to be cancelled for the day as part of the celebration.

Rasey sloped round to Imran's in the afternoon. On the pretext of his uncle knowing about a large snake, he took me round for a visit. In the uncle's garden there was a tall palm tree and Rasey suggested we eat coconuts. Again he begged me not to climb and shinned up himself in fine acrobatic fashion. We drank from the coconuts, though I was not that thirsty and their flavour was too flat and sappy for my liking. Rasey agreed that they were not that good. The uncle, a huge, immobile man, sat in his front room and listened patiently to Rasey's prating. Then he announced he had a headache.

The big snake, it seemed, was a pet, owned by someone he knew, and far from being very big.

(Large pet snakes can be a problem. The King of Thailand had one that swallowed a pet cat that had a silver bell around its neck. Whenever the snake approached after that you could hear the faint tinkling of the bell, lodged in its intestines.)

We left under an apologetic cloud and meandered along the beach road. 'I will take you to meet all my friends,' said Rasey brightly. My heart sank. As we walked on, Rasey brought up the subject of his proposed trip to Ambon and the cost of the exam interview. The exam cost ten pounds, his expenses for the trip another five. 'My uncle could not give me the money,' he explained, shortly after he had explained that his 'uncle' was in fact a very distant relative by marriage. The headache suddenly explained itself, and so did the proposed trip to visit friends. I was to be an extra in Rasey's feeble attempt to scrounge money.

'Do you have debts already?' I asked.

'No,' he said. We walked a bit more. 'Yes,' he conceded.

Fifteen pounds to be rid of Rasey was cheap at the price. I thrust the money into his hand and he tried, to his credit, very hard to refuse, but I forced him.

'But I can never pay you back,' he wailed.

'When you qualify, as I'm sure you will,' I lied, 'pass on the money to another struggling teacher like you used to be.'

He warmed to the thought and grew more cheerful. 'You know,' he said, 'I do not care about money. Not at all. I care nothing for money. I only care about my reputation. That is the important thing, the thing money can't buy. *My reputation.*'

When I got back to the house, Imran was cleaning 'old grandad' in the front room. The disco light was flashing, two children were tripping and the TV was blasting out an old Indian musical movie. The room was swept three times a day so it didn't matter that he was cleaning his bike there.

'Rasey's off to Ambon to do the test,' I said, knowing that it would be very ill advised for my reputation, let alone Rasey's, if I let on where the money had come from.

'I am hope he passes,' said Imran dreamily. 'Rasey is such a poor man.'

'And another thing. You know the greasy man? I met him. He's not greasy at all. Not one bit. I'm an expert in these matters and I can tell you: the greasy man is 100 per cent sane!'

Imran looked surprised at my vehemence, but said nothing, concentrating instead on wiping the oil from his plump fingers.

FOURTEEN

Big Snake

There is a mistaken idea that a python could swallow a human being. This is out of the question, the shoulders being too wide for the snake to attempt such a meal.   *C. J. Ionides*

Mr Lamardie, an illiterate fisherman with a gap-toothed grin and a fool's head of hair, brought news of a big snake. He lived in a shabby hut a few doors down from Imran. Mr Lamardie's hut had a dirt floor and plank walls, though this did not bother him. He grinned and whistled and shouted and lived a good life: up at four to go fishing, back by eight thirty, fish sold by nine, leaving the rest of the day free for gossiping, smoking, wisecracking and lounging. Imran, being a snob, only really tolerated Mr Lamardie because of the news he brought. He was not a young man, he had been beaten around the head by life and looked any age from forty to fifty-five, but he was full of enthusiasm for helping the foreigner catch a snake.

Before becoming a fisherman, Mr Lamardie had been a farmer. He had leased sections of the jungle from the local tribespeople, planted lemons and other fruit trees in these jungle gardens, and sold them in Namlea market. 'Why did you give up?' I asked him.

'Being a farmer is a fool's life,' he said.

Imran added, 'A farmer works all day and makes 150,000 rupiah a month. In ten days a fisherman can make that much. When Lamardie came here, his hut had bamboo walls. Now he has wooden walls. Fishing is a good business.'

271

Mr Lamardie said that he had heard from the people in the jungle where he had farmed that there was a very big snake living there. It lived in a special place and everyone knew about it. This sounded like old news, but Mr Lamardie was adamant. He convinced Imran, who in turn convinced me. It was decided that we should make an expedition into the interior to follow up Mr Lamardie's lead.

In the days before we left, Mr Lamardie took to dropping round and sitting for hours, smoking and watching TV. I did not know Imran was irritated by this. All I detected was a certain increase in Imran's hauteur. One day we were talking about Princess Diana and whether her son would be the next king (I had supplied several crucial pieces of information about the drunken driver of Di's car, and this had raised Imran's status considerably), when Imran told me it was no great thing to be a king; in fact, he himself was a prince in exile.

Imran's father was the king of a small island about six hours by powered dugout from Buru. The island, called Manipa, had resisted every wave of invasion since earliest times. Even now, the only government presence was a light-house on a big rock next to Manipa Island. Imran's father, the current king, had begged Imran to return and take over the throne, but Imran had resisted very strongly.

I got very excited at this point. 'You're a king! Return and rule your people!' At the back of my mind was a plum role for myself as a kind of vizier, an *éminence grise* or some other dodgy and powerful position.

Imran was unmoved by my interest. 'Manipa Island has many . . . difficulties. The King there must be a very strong man, strong in many ways. It is a danger for him. I hide from the people of Manipa when they come looking for me.' Matter-of-factly he added, 'They all want me to be King but I refuse.'

So Imran was a self-exiled prince, but in my mind, from

then on, I thought of him as the exiled King of Manipa Island. In fact his house, with the high-status disco light and big TV, was like the flashy court of exiled royalty. ('Whose is the best picture, mine or Mr Ferdy's?' asked Imran. 'They're the same,' I said. 'I think mine,' said Imran. 'I have bigger antennae than him, twenty-two element, his only fourteen element.')

The expedition to the interior was not carefully planned. I made a long list of things we ought to take and showed it to Imran, but he waved it away and said, 'All is OK there. Houses for us to stay in, equipment and so on.' As an article of faith, Imran packed only a large, blue check handkerchief. Mr Lamardie brought a tattered white plastic bag containing a bunch of tiny bananas. I was torn between wanting to believe Imran and knowing that he was overoptimistic about the resources of the interior. In a waterproof duffel bag I took my mosquito net, Maglite, tape measure, The Tool, some thin nylon rope and the Irish High Toast snuff. And so we set out.

The interior of Buru is mainly swampy forest. In the very centre is Lake Rana, which was very difficult to reach until a logging road was constructed to within twenty miles of the place. As for real roads, there is only one that goes inland. Less than forty miles long, it ends at Unitnam, literally Unit Six, of the old penal colony, which has been transformed into the new villages of the *transmigrasi*, the aided settlement of thousands of Javanese in 'troublesome' areas of Indonesia. Between Unitnam and Unitlima (Unit Five) the road stops going inland and curves round to service the *transmigrasi* areas. Here a track leads into the jungle. If you follow it for three weeks, over mountains and through swamps, you will arrive at Lake Rana. It was in that swampy hinterland that Mr Lamardie's garden was situated. No more than a day's walk separated Unitnam from the jungle village of Wasweedie, the nearest habitation to the garden.

This time there was no expensive chartering of a bus. We sat with the other passengers and bounced through the cultivated rice lands that bordered the interior road. We passed villages with fences made from oil cans hammered flat. People got on and off the bus. If any student got on the bus, Imran questioned them about their teachers, and he always knew one of them. Lamardie fed me tiny bananas and grinned ahead, not speaking, very chuffed at being the expedition guide. When there were no students for a while, Imran began to tell me about his interest in writing a book.

'Do you know *Skingame*?'

'No.'

'I want to write a book like *Skingame* . . . then my ambition can rise like a bird!'

I began to get the picture.

'I see at 12 p.m. in Ambon a blue film. One Negro, one Japanese and one American, small but strong. Maybe they take a special medicine to make them strong!'

'They have extras,' I said. 'Substitutes, stand-ins. They even use stunt-cocks.'

'Stunt-cocks?'

I gestured vaguely with one of Lamardie's tiny bananas. 'You know, an extra one, just for the filming.' Lamardie roared with laughter.

'It's a dirty game!' said Imran, shaking his head.

A little while later Imran asked me how he could be sure of not having any more children. 'Four is enough,' he said.

'You know about condoms?' I said.

'I do not like.' He smiled almost apologetically. 'What about this operation?'

'Vasectomy?'

'Yes, that one. Does it weaken your strength?'

274

'I don't know. I wouldn't do it, though. It can't be reversed.'

'I have hear it weaken you.'

'Probably does.'

'Is there a special medicine to stop children?'

'There is,' I said, 'but it's expensive and dangerous.'

'I need this medicine,' said Imran dreamily.

A few days before, Imran had confronted me about my own lack of children. 'If you have been married two years' (this had been my lying assertion) 'and have no children . . .' He left it hanging in the air, and then continued, 'People on Buru think there is something wrong.'

'I'm not ready for children yet,' I said.

Imran looked at me with blank incomprehension. 'There is a teacher who has been married ten years and she has no children. Her hobby is she have many dolls.'

Ionides wrote: 'Though I was always attracted to women, and never spurned or underrated the pleasures of sex, I looked on marriage as a trap involving a sacrifice of the things I wanted.'

Appoaching Unitnam we could see the old camp buildings set back from the road. Buru had housed ten thousand category-B prisoners from 1969 until the mid-eighties. They were mostly dissenting intellectuals like the composer Subronto Adjouo and the filmmaker Basuki Affendi. Imran told me that all the prisoners had gone home. He was a bit shifty about the whole thing and didn't want to express an opinion. On the subject of the *transmigrasi*, he said cryptically, 'If you like rice it is a good thing. Burunese cannot grow rice. Only Javanese can make good rice.'

'Do you like rice?' I asked.

'Yes.'

'Do you prefer *papeeda*?'

'Of course.'

We ate in a metal hut that served as a restaurant. The owner was Javanese. He told me he had been a prisoner, category B. He was a poet, he said. He was a small, birdlike man, a bundle of man on thin legs, bobbing and hopping about the metal hut with bowls of soup and meat I suspected was poisonous. Imran and Lamardie, especially Lamardie, ate with great gusto. It struck me that poor digestion was a Western city thing. The closer I got to the jungle, the more men wolfed and smacked their lips and demanded more rice. I pecked on resolutely but with little conviction.

Imran told me of a year he had spent in Halmahera, a large island north of Buru. He had gone there on his first teaching assignment, and had looked after himself. 'My favourite food for cooking is eggs, cassava and noodles, so for one year I only eat eggs, cassava and noodles, nothing else.'

'What about vegetables?' I asked, aghast at the thought of his insides after a solid year of eggy noodles.

Imran gave me a look of great scorn and said, in the same manner that Colonel H. used to speak of seatbelts, 'What do I need vegetables for?'

The poet-prisoner-restaurateur served glasses of coffee and whispered his tale of escape from the camps. The guards put excessive salt in the rice and rather than become sick they had escaped. He and twelve other inmates had run into the jungle, there being no fences. As on Devil's Island, it was thought none were needed. The other eleven, he assured us, had all perished in the forest. 'They are city men, intellectuals, writers, artists – men unsuited to the jungle.' Our man had survived by trusting some native Burunese. 'They caught spider's webs,' he said, and I immediately thought of Pa Boah. I asked Imran but he assured me this man had escaped in a place far from Pa Boah's.

Imran said that the man had stayed because of the land

276

given him by the government after the amnesty for all category-B prisoners. I asked the poet and he said, 'I stay in Buru because here I can remind myself often that I am only human after all.'

A truck took us to the end of the road. From now on we had to walk. There were several huts at the side of the track. From one, a man called from his rough veranda, 'Have you medicines? For TB? For diarrhoea?'

'Have you?' asked Imran mechanically.

'No,' I said, but it suddenly struck home that we had left the comforts of urban medical care long behind.

Colonel H. had been in the nursing home for a year before I had a chance to visit him. My father, for the first time in years, was actually enjoying parental visiting. Throughout my teens he had grown increasingly unappreciative of Colonel H.'s crankier turns. For a long while, and for no very good reason, the Colonel got it into his head that my father was a Quaker. He would lace his conversation with references to Quakerism and 'our friends'. In the end my father explained forcefully that he was not, nor ever had been, a Quaker. 'I'm perfectly aware of that,' the Colonel snapped back.

These head games were all part of the Colonel's descent into madness, or what many would call madness. The back-to-nature survivalism was a challenge of the state's right to interfere, to lock him up rather than let him die in his own place and in his own time. Yet I was sure that the Colonel was glad to have been rescued, to be able to extend the final act in a long and eventful life.

'You know,' said my father, 'he's actually quite pleasant now. I think he's suddenly realized that it won't be very nice to be remembered as an appalling old bugger. I only wish he'd been taking those drugs sooner. We might have got on instead of being barely on speaking terms for twenty-five years.'

I wondered if it was the drugs. They certainly made him slower, fatter, forget things he always remembered before. But I think there was more to the benign phase he had now entered in the eighty-ninth year of his life. Something had made him call off the war. He wasn't fighting any more. I wondered how long he would last like that, tough old bird that he was.

Like those Japanese soldiers, still fighting long after the Emperor admitted the Japanese were failing to achieve their war objectives, Colonel H. had never really ceased hostilities. His family, the neighbours, the inhabitants of the small town where he lived, officials he came into contact with – these were the people who suffered from being forced into combat with the Colonel. Somehow that was his function, to act as a sort of toughening-up agent for the world at large. He might have also been a godawful pain in the arse, but probably dough feels that way about yeast. I'm sure there was a mad side to him, but running parallel to it was this dogged programme of trying to remain an autonomous individual in the latter part of the twentieth century.

Independence was what he cared most about in others. Degrees, promotions, top jobs – all that failed to impress him. When he heard I was writing a book he was full of praise and encouragement. He had the same positive belief in a cousin of mine who had started her own saddlery business, a humble enough occupation, but to the Colonel it was one more in the eye for the grey-faced, grey-suited crowds, the 'ordinary people' who waited to be spoonfed by institutions. These people he really despised.

At least a part of my purpose with the Big Snake hunt was to do something he would have approved of. I once remarked on the strength of his hands and compared them to my soft office-worker paws. He gave a wry smile and tapped the side of his head. 'It's what you do with what's up here that counts,' he said.

In a man's world you get advice; this was the world of the Colonel. He knew about life and he cared to pass it on. Unfortunately those closest to him found his methods a little lacking, a little crude, to say the least. He was a nag, a know-all, long in the tooth and mean in the jaw, he spared no one's feelings and had little sympathy for those weaker than himself. Not a nice man really. But nice men don't build army camps out of nothing in the middle of a malarial jungle, nice men are not so good at getting things done. That was what I felt I might learn at one remove from him, how to get it done, finish the job. The snake hunt was a test I had to pass.

There was a rattle of noise and through the bush, along the track, which was still quite wide, came a soldier on a motorbike. He was neat with a small moustache, a corporal, and as soon as he saw me he stopped his bike dead. He wanted my passport straight away. Imran intervened but it seemed of little use. But when the man asked if I had permission to be there, Imran said of course I did. I had permission from the highest authorities. I was glad then of my elaborate visa I'd paid thirty pounds for in Borneo. The soldier turned it around and around and then he gave up, feeling perhaps outgunned by all three of us, and him off the main road too. He folded up my passport and was gone.

'I not afraid of him! I know the rules,' stormed an irate Imran, chastened by having to eat humble pie, even for a few minutes. 'My father was lieutenant in army – I know the rules.'

'I don't think he could read very well,' I said. 'He didn't look at the visa the right way up.'

'You are right, most probably he can only read ABC,' said Imran.

We walked on and the track forked into two narrow paths, overhung by greenery. There was a rattle and an ancient bicycle politely weaved around us and headed up the right-hand fork. The man on the bicycle, who wore shorts and a torn T-shirt, had a murderous-looking spear strapped to his bicycle crossbar. This wasn't a garden tool that happened to look a bit like a spear, this was a genuine, shiny, sharp weapon with angled teeth cut into the blade, all the better to rip your flesh with. We followed the bicyclist up the right fork.

As if to emphasize that we were now in spear country, we met a man and his wife and their dog coming towards us. I was walking out in front but I waited for the others to catch up as I did not want to be the first to meet such a wielder of dangerous equipment. Of course Imran started a conversation with the man, who was very affable. He had one straight-bladed spear and one with a flèche cut into only one side.

As we moved out of earshot, I asked Lamardie what the spears were for.

'Wild boar, or babirusa,' he said, spitting a gob of phlegm on the floor, perhaps to indicate his distaste for such backwardness. 'They are not even Muslims, so they eat pig and even dog!'

We walked for a long while alongside a river and then followed a sandy path between low trees. I regretted not bringing a water bottle as I was mightily thirsty. 'How much further?' I asked Lamardie.

'Less than three hours,' he said.

Another spear-wielder rode by on a bicycle with about eight huge sacks piled so high on the back that you could not see the rider from behind.

'How far to Wasweedie?' asked Imran.

'Ten minutes up there,' said the man and rode off laughing.

'I told you it was less than three hours,' said Lamardie.

*

Wasweedie appeared empty, except for a dog in the dust and some chickens. The village comprised groups of intricately connected sheds around a worn centre of hard mud. There was a felled tree in the centre, half chopped through, work in progress or abandoned.

Lamardie suddenly assumed leadership in the village. He strode with his chest out, swaggered almost, to the headman's hut. A boy with intelligent eyes poked his head past the sack hanging down over the door.

'Get Bapak Adam!' Lamardie ordered in a loud voice. 'And bring something for us to drink!' Then he gobbed into the dust and squinted knowledgeably at the horizon. Imran took off his shoes and sat sideways on the large platform at the end of the headman's veranda. I sat on a stunted home-made chair and stuck my legs a long way out in front of me. I was thirsty and exhausted and regretted having brought my cumbersome duffel bag with me.

A few gawpers appeared from huts and we engaged them in lacklustre conversation. A small stunted weevil of an old man appeared wrapped in a blanket: Bapak Adam. He did not smile. The boy brought young coconuts for us to drink. Lamardie hefted the parang with ease, and gave me the first coconut. I drank greedily for a second or two before the flat, unwelcome taste of coconut juice hit me. Lamardie spat his own juice out and hurled the coconut off the veranda and into the muddy centre. 'Those are rubbish!' he announced with satisfaction. Our hosts looked at us blearily, completely unfazed by this attack on their hospitality.

Lamardie might have been fairly near the bottom of the pecking order in Namlea, but in Wasweedie he was wasting no time in showing who was boss. Not that he eclipsed Imran and me, but he took it upon himself to whip the interior people into shape.

Imran called for a mat and a pillow so that he could recline

281

better on the platform. He ordered the boy, whose name was Rahman, to brush the platform, wipe the rattan mat and place the pillow (pink) for him to lie on. Rahman then showed me a hut where I could leave my bag. He indicated a large double bed in a dark room. I wondered if all three of us would have to sleep in the bed.

Bapak Adam told us that the men of the village were up at the eucalyptus-processing plant. Since the first Portuguese traders arrived, Buru has been known for its eucalyptus oil. It is still processed in exactly the same way as it has been for hundreds of years, using a crude wooden distillation system, which can also be used to distil coconut juice into *sopi*.

The boy Rahman took us to the plant. It was about an hour's walk through varied jungle cut through with deep, muddy streams. The path was well worn and it was only Imran that held us up with his laggardly pace. At one stage we passed through a glade of hundreds of blue butterflies. They were swarming around the sap flowing from a tree. I was reminded of the butterflies I saw similarly in Borneo. In the interior I never saw butterflies except in that particular glade.

You could smell the plant as we came through high swamp grass towards it. A sickly-sweet variation on the familiar smell of eucalyptus. The palm-roofed huts encircled the huge wooden brewing pots which were built into a kind of forge or oven. Around the forge were partitioned-off hut areas full to the brim with eucalyptus leaves. A small girl controlled a horde of kids, just big enough to run with no pants on but too big to be held constantly at their mother's hip. One man working there was thin and naked except for shorts. Another wore a grey boiler suit and no shoes. They let down their head-strapped baskets of leaves and greeted us without enthusiasm.

Imran once more tried his universal native language, the one that had failed so dismally in the classroom when he had pointed out the only real Burunese boy in the class. The men were blank-faced when Imran spoke his favourite words in Burunese-native-speak. Wallace reported there were upwards of twenty dialects on Buru, and I think Imran only had a smattering of one. Lamardie intervened and reminded the men who he was. They remembered all right. Cautiously they became more hospitable, but they did not offer us tea. We sat on the partitions of the leaf boxes. These were planks of wood which could be slid up and removed. There was a loud crack from Lamardie's, and he cursed it for breaking under him. The eucalyptus processors looked on without comment.

The subject of snakes was finally broached. The men became more alive and the women acted fearful. They had lost two chickens to a snake only days before. They knew where it lived. They would take me.

An athletic young chap wearing a singlet and shiny shorts, and sporting a well-groomed but sparse moustache, took us through the swamp which surrounded the village. 'What's your name?' I asked him.

'Stinky,' he replied.

I asked again and the answer was the same. Every time I spoke to him I used his name with the same sort of quivering glee I got as a schoolboy asking a teacher, ever so politely, 'Are you for coffee, sir?'

Stinky wore no shoes. Imran fared badly in his leatherette slip-ons, but did not complain. Lamardie wore see-through plastic sandals, which were usefully equipped with drainholes. My own boots were waterproof, up to a point. Knee-deep in a swamp was past that point, but by then I was past caring – I could see, quite distinctly ahead of me, the snake mound.

Stinky explained that everyone knew about the snake mound. Lamardie heartily agreed – this was what he had heard about when tending his gardens on the other side of the village. With the lack of curiosity that seemed to characterize the Burunese, he had never before been to the eucalyptus-plant area.

Imran sat down on a tree root and waved his hands in a way that conveyed his lack of desire to get close to the snake mound. Lamardie stayed with him and lit up a clove cigarette. Making something of a show of how unafraid I was, I followed the agile Stinky on to the mound. There were three distinct and large holes that had their entrances on the mound. The mound itself was of sandy earth topped with rotting logs and vegetation. It was maybe ten feet high and twenty in diameter. Plenty of room for a big snake underneath. I lent Stinky my torch and he got down by each hole and peered in, anxious to show he was doing a thorough job. After he had peered in for a while, I peered in. The smell was there all right, I convinced myself of that, but not so strong as in the caves, the meaty, musty, urinous smell of snake.

Stinky said that there were three snakes living under the mound. If the chickens were taken a few days ago, they were probably still digesting them right under our feet. I was sure they would want another feed. Pythons are greedy, and even after eating a large meal they can still be tempted with more.

I went and squatted with Imran and Lamardie, who was looking very pleased. Suddenly I felt like a young officer in the First World War, having to take action in a field I knew little about. The men were certainly as reluctant as rankers in the trenches, despite having brought me to the snake mound, but I had learned something on my way. I knew that I had to appear as the expert. I explained to Stinky that we needed some chickens and some rope and forked sticks. He swiftly cut the sticks and Lamardie trimmed their ends carefully. There were several bamboos, which, when rammed through with a heavy stick, made suitable tubes for the snake-catching lassos.

284

After a long while Stinky came back with a short rope. He said the women were reluctant to sell the big chickens until the men came back (other men, it seemed). OK, go and get some small chickens. After another interminable wait, he came back with two small chickens cheeping and squawking and a length of thick string. It was not ideal. 'If this fails,' I said to Stinky as I lashed the chickens' legs together, trying to avoid being pecked, 'we're going to dig that mound out.' Stinky looked pleased at the prospect of that.

Imran and Lamardie both wanted to give me advice on how to set a snake trap. I told them to shut up. The Imran type in England would have protested. Instead Imran told Lamardie to shut up, making a slight gesture of resignation as if it was time to let me have my say now.

The chickens' legs were tied and taped together. They tried to stand up, but fell over. It almost got to me, this cruel sacrifice of young chickenhood; almost, but not quite. My hands were trembling – the snake fever was upon me.

I knew the symptoms. The night before I had had another dream of snakes. It was blurred and indistinct but I awoke knowing that I had to kill, kill them all. I stared up at the palm thatch just letting in a few chinks of early morning light. The dream had vanished but the resolution was there, the steam-heated obsession of all these months – I had to get the snake.

It wasn't the money any more. I knew now that bagging a thirty-footer would be more luck than anything else. The hunt had ceased to be some coldly calculated search guaranteed to bring in a lottery winner's earnings with better odds. It had become a necessary part of me, something I couldn't funk. How could I return to England and tell Colonel H., 'Oh, and by the way, I didn't get anywhere near to catching Big Snake.' I knew I couldn't. My resolve had hardened. This was my proving ground.

*

We watched the chickens from a distance. They squeaked and pecked at each other and eventually settled down. I had tied them to a small tree next to one of the entrances. We would return in the early morning to see if the bait had been taken.

'These people don't eat rice. If we want rice, we should buy it,' said Imran. Though this seemed to contradict his earlier protestations of preferring *papeeda*, I guessed he believed he was doing me a favour. We sent Rahman on a huge dilapidated bicycle to the village at the end of the track to buy rice, sugar, coffee and mosquito coils, if he could get them.

Stinky took us to the river to wash. It was almost dark and the river was wide. A sentence of Hemingway's came to me for about the fiftieth time: 'Every tree root touched with snake fear in the dark.' I used to test myself with that sentence. Sometimes I felt it was true, and other times it most definitely wasn't. This time my imagination took hold. I saw a big thick python in a black log stuck on a sand bar mid-stream. Other snakes rustled away, just too quickly for me to see, as we walked, damp-haired and attended by mosquitoes, back to the village.

Bapak Adam invited us to dinner in his hut. Inside it was pitch dark except for the smoky yellow light cast by the petrol lamps on the table. Made from oily old tin, the lamps cast beguiling shadows over our faces. Bapak Adam had put on a fleece-lined denim jacket with jangly buckles, a strangely juvenile item of clothing for such a wrinkled old man. When the food came, he ate like a horse. He was even more of a face-filler than Lamardie and Imran. There was something brutish and primitive about life in Wasweedie. Many of the smaller kids had bloated stomachs. They hung around and stared as we went about our business. Rahman was, in contrast, bright and efficient. He went to school in Unitnam, staying for a week at a time with relatives. He wanted to join

286

the army and become a soldier. Bapak Adam ignored every-one as he ate. I had read that the women got to eat only the men's leftovers. Imran had laughed when I told him. 'Do you think they get fat on what we leave? They are very clever, women eat all the time!' Certainly no one was going to get fat on Bapak Adam's leftovers. He wiped his face and belched heavily after his third or fourth bowl of rice. Then he squinted at Imran and said, 'Do you come from Ambon?' Imran was taken aback and protested his Buru credentials by explaining how he lived in Namlea. Bapak Adam was not interested.

We were still sitting round the table when the talk turned to snakes. As well as Bapak Adam, Lamardie and Imran, there was Rahman's father Juji and Rahman himself hovering in the shadows. There was something supremely competent about the way Juji carried himself. He was neither a boastful man nor a shy man, he was a man at ease in the world where he found himself. He had caught and killed many snakes, and though he could not understand why anyone would want a live snake, he agreed to help. I outlined my usual story of high rewards for anyone capturing a snake or, as the high-street banks say, providing information that leads to a capture.

At this point Bapak Adam rolled up his trouser leg to reveal a nasty skein of white scar tissue around his knee. 'That is a python,' he said. Then he mimed the huge size of the python (always width, never length) and also the huge size his knee had swollen to when the bite had become infected. Looking at the long scar I was reminded of some-thing Ernie the zoo curator had said: 'After two snakes have been in a fight they look as if they've been at each other with razors.'

'But this bite saved my life,' said Bapak Adam, his coal-like eyes glinting. 'This is during the war. The Japanese come and take men to build a gun fort in Namlea. They take my brothers. They stole our women. They beat you until your head bleeds. If there is no blood they beat some more.

'But I have snakebite and swollen leg. They think that I am dying. They leave me with the old people in the village. Then I thought that I was dying, but when the Japanese left, I was better soon. But two of my brothers never came back from Namlea.

'From then on I have power over the snake, all the snakes in the forest.'

'How do you have power?' I asked.

'Black magic,' Imran hissed in English.

'If I throw a stone,' said Bapak Adam, 'a special stone which I have first blown upon, over the head of a snake, it must turn back.' Everyone nodded. Bapak Adam looked at me so severely I nodded too. But I looked at old toothless Bapak Adam in his denim jacket and thought, Does he really believe he has power over snakes with a special stone?

Imran, as if reading my mind, said, 'It will not work for you, because you do not believe. That is right. It could be dangerous if you believe.'

'It could be dangerous if I don't believe, too, judging by that scar,' I said.

In order to boost our standing with the villagers, Imran explained at length about the magic powers of snuff. I had shown him the container before, but never the contents. This time I took out the snuff and showed the dust around, explaining how lethal it was to a snake. Bapak Adam agreed, putting in that snakes always flee from tobacco smoke. 'One pinch of this,' I said, 'will mean instant death to a ten-metre snake.' There was a hushed silence as I took a pinch of snuff ever so carefully out of the container and placed it on the back of my hand. The light flickered over their fearful faces as they drew back from the proffered poison. I leaned forward as if inspecting the snuff. Then with a mighty sniff I snorted it right up my nose.

There were general sounds of dismay and disbelief. After a second I fell forwards as if unconscious at the table. More cries of dismay, outrage, fear.

Then I sat up and explained that it was fatal only to snakes. There were polite titters, but not the huge laugh I expected. But I still felt absurdly pleased with myself for outmagicking the black magicians.

Juji spoke of a giant snake that lived over the mountains. It was, I gathered, something of Tolkienlike proportions. It would take two days to walk to the lake where the snake lived.

'What about the snake in the mound?' I said, trying to focus on what we had to hand rather than what was over the mountains.

'This could be a very big snake too,' said Juji, 'maybe seven or eight metres. But the snake in the lake is fifteen metres long.'

'No way! I mean, well, are you sure?'

I saw the faces of Juji, Bapak Adam and the others set dead serious in the flickering yellow light. They believed there was a snake fifty feet long. I tried to believe too, but it was no good. I just knew there were no snakes that long. But they weren't kidding me; they had the same certainty I put on when relating the startling results of some scientific study – '15 per cent of men think about killing their wives at least twice a day.' 'No way!' comes the chorus, usually at a dinner party or round a pub table. 'It's absolutely true!' I say with the same vehemence as Juji and Bapak Adam. I mean, 'I read it so it must be true'; they mean, 'I heard it so it must be true.' But it isn't necessarily true in either case.

'Is there any chance the snake in the mound will be nine metres long?' I asked.

'Maybe,' said Juji. Then Lamardie said something that spoke to me of another age. He asked politely if I might relate any of the wonderful things I had seen on my travels while searching for the snake. Bapak Adam nodded vigorously and left the table. He did not return. Being old in Wasweedie meant simply never having to explain yourself.

I felt like a medieval traveller, perhaps returned from the Crusades, and I really wanted to deliver, to give Lamardie a whole host of good stories. But the only thing that came to mind was Raja Ula and his scorpion show. 'He sits in a glass room with five thousand scorpions and is bitten nine times a day.' Lamardie nodded; indeed that was a wonderful thing. I knew he wanted more, but all my other stories needed too long set-ups, nuances, bathos instead of solid amazement. The medieval opportunity faded away.

Imran yawned. 'I shall take this bed here with the boy,' he announced. 'You should have the large bed in the other hut.'

'With Mr Lamardie?'

'I think it is the larger bed.'

Lamardie grinned. He seemed a little too keen to spend the night with me. Imran's bed, I noticed, had a mosquito net all round it, and the boy, the boy was very small.

The hut was dark and surprisingly chill. I had not learned my lesson from Borneo. Never mind the coastal temperatures; the jungle is cold at night. All jungles, even those two degrees south of the equator, like the one I was in now. We made going-to-bed gestures but took only our shoes off as we needed every stitch of clothing we had on. With a certain stiffness, Lamardie and I arranged ourselves on the large bed. There was a bolster which we put chastely between us. There were no covers. I put my feet in the duffel bag and used the mosquito net as a blanket. Lamardie started to snore, but I knew he would wake soon from the bitter cold. My last thoughts were of Imran, probably forcing the boy to keep him warm.

I awoke but it was still dark. Lamardie was shivering next to me. He had pathetically tried to appropriate some of the mosquito net to keep warm. I viciously recovered the net.

'It's cold,' he muttered.

'At least there aren't any mosquitoes,' I said.

I awoke and it was still dark. Lamardie was sitting up in bed and swatting the air. 'There are mosquitoes,' he said.

It was cold and it was still dark. Lamardie was snoring loudly. I pushed the bolster higher to block out the noise. I tried to visualize heat flowing to the surface of my skin. It is something that Tibetan monks practise, and it was something I would have to practise too, because it didn't work without practice. At least now I'd verified that.

As dawn came up I reminded myself that I had to get the snake soon. Time and money were running out. Despite the absurd cheapness of living on Buru, I was still spending a lot on cigarette bribes and general down payments on good will. All my faffing around had been just a preliminary, a warm up. Now I had to make as if I was serious if I was going to catch the snake. The snake knew it too. We were conjoined. That was the black magic for you. I unwrapped the snake stone – it felt warm.

'Hey, I slept with the foreigner!' Lamardie crowed the next morning. Imran ignored him. I was glad to see he, too, was rubbing his arms in an attempt to get warm. We sat and shivered and drank coffee. Then Imran and Lamardie went off to do a shit but I couldn't face it so I sat and shivered some more.

Bapak Adam's wife wanted to catch a glimpse of the foreigner. On a pretence of showing me how they made sago cakes, one of the womenfolk took me to the kitchen at the back. I passed through a darkened passage, past a kind of bunk, like something on a ship. A very old woman's face glimmered out of the darkness. She was bedridden, her eyes adjusted to the gloom. 'I've seen the foreigner,' she whispered as I passed by.

In the end there was no putting off the fact that we had to

make our way to the trap. Mentally I prepared myself for a big fight with an angry snake. I willed the snake to be there. It was time to see where I fitted in with Ionides' 'four stages of the hunter'.

In the beginning he's nervous and apprehensive, even overcareful. Then he learns that in normal conditions, with the wind right, very great liberties can be taken. He takes them, with impunity, and tends to get rather reckless. That's the second stage. Then he either gets a packet by getting a mauling or a narrow escape from one, and learns to be intelligently careful. By now he's assessed the animal at its proper value, and acts accordingly. The fourth and last stage is when he's getting old, and thinks his reactions are still as quick as they were ten years before, which they are not. That's how a lot of old hunters get killed.

I was so nervous I was obviously still at the first stage.

As we approached the mound, I motioned to the others to go quietly. We didn't want to scare the snake into the common flight reaction of throwing up mid-meal and clearing off at high speed. Closer and closer we stalked. There was no sound of chicken cheeping . . . but there they were, sitting side by side on the leaf litter, not a bit perturbed. The big hunt was shaping up like my Tibetan self-heating technique – plenty of theory but obviously more practice needed.

We retired to the eucalyptus plant to make further plans. Imran tried out some more words of his universal native language, which met with the same blank incomprehension until he mentioned the word '*poppo*'. Everyone rolled around laughing. 'It means "short",' Imran protested.

The women especially found it funny. They held their sides and bent double in hilarity. Even the polite Rahman was grinning fit to burst. Eventually he was able to explain, between fits of giggles, '*Poppo* means "women's tools".' I suspected it meant more than that. Imran grinned as if he'd meant to say it, and, banking on his new humorous role, managed to blag a cassava, which he placed in the furnace part of the plant. When he tried to get it out, he couldn't. It was lost in the furnace. I laughed without mercy. We were all beginning to get a bit on each other's nerves.

Rahman came to the rescue and dug Imran's cassava out of the flaming inferno. It was charred as hell on the outside but he made a big show of enjoying the inside. I declined any cassava.

Stinky turned up with some news. A big snake had attacked a wild boar caught in a deer trap. The snake had killed the boar and almost completely eaten it. As far as Stinky knew the snake was still *in situ* with its jaws around the tethered porker.

We went back to Wasweedie – over streams, past the butterfly glade, along the path through head-high grass, a route I was becoming a little bit too familiar with. In Wasweedie we waited until Juji arrived with more news. Bapak Adam appeared, grunted and nodded his head and threw a deft kick at the dog, which whimpered and curled up further along in the dust.

Juji turned up and said that the big snake had swallowed the pig and then, feeling the rope securing the trap, had thrown the whole thing up and left. The pig, he said, was covered in mucus and blood, 'as if it had just been born!' Did we want to see?

I wanted the snake, not the born-again pig. The mound seemed like our best bet. Stinky agreed to help. We assembled a spade, a parang and a fire-blackened spear, which Juji said we could also use for digging.

Before we got to the mound Imran had given the parang to Rahman. I had the spade, which was long and had no crosspiece on the handle, and Stinky had the spear. Lamardie was busy untying the last of the nylon string from the tree.

He said he could use it to make fishing lures. The chickens had been returned, no money back, more good will.

First we removed the rotten trees and logs from the mound. I had given up on Lamardie and Imran, who were muttering among themselves. In an extremely feeble way Imran had started making overtures to Lamardie in an attempt to gang up on me. To Lamardie's credit he either didn't notice or didn't care. After an extremely sweaty session of foliage clearing he said he would go to his old garden and get some 'young coconuts' for us to drink. I think he was genuinely embarrassed to see the foreigner labouring like a pig. Imran had no such qualms. Both he and Lamardie explained they were too frightened to help.

We broke through the leaf mould and into the sandy ground below. It was easy shovelling but there were plenty of roots. Stinky speared with great gusto, Rahman chopped at roots and I shovelled until the blisters on my hands popped and leaked water between my fingers. My shirt stuck to every part of my back.

Imran shouted encouragement from time to time, but this dried up as it was obvious we were totally ignoring him.

In a sudden move backwards Stinky dropped to his ankles, bringing the spear one-handed to the enlarged hole we had been working on.

I saw Big Snake.

It was the weirdest feeling. It was as if I'd been fishing for three months and only now discovered that yes, fish really did exist.

Big Snake disappeared.

'It's there,' I said in a hushed tone.

Stinky nodded.

'How big?'

'Five metre?' he said.

I knew he was being kind to me. From my brief glimpse

of Big Snake's head I guessed him to be less than thirteen feet. It was a young snake, perhaps only a year and a half old, and the head was as small and neat as a computer mouse. But we had to get him, or her. The villagers would not forgive us if we just let such an unwelcome animal get away without a fight.

We dug more, sweated more, flies and mosquitoes circling unheeded. I caught a flickering glimpse of the sun far off above the trees. I was happy here, covered in sweat and earth, digging into the ground, really getting involved, doing something that felt real at last.

I saw the head again, the flicking tongue; were those the labial pits? Could it sense us? Inside the snake's reptilian brain I felt the world shaking. Vague moving images and a familiar smell it knew to avoid. The snake was intelligent, it just chose not to show its intelligence, preferring a solitary life, coming together briefly for mating, then away again, always at night, searching the trail, hunting.

The snake shrank backwards, using a concertina movement to pull away, deeper into the dark security of the mound. The lateral wave movement could not be used here. It was cool in the mound and the snake was not fully alert, but the ancient chemicals of survival were pumping into its brain. It pulled itself deeper and deeper and in the lowest cavern of the mound folded itself into a protective bundle of heavy coils, a last defence against attack.

We dug and chopped and dug and chopped and after another hour it became clear why the snakes had chosen this as their permanent home. The area was entangled with iron-hard tree roots. I remembered an account of Ionides digging a snake out, when in the end he had been defeated by tree roots. We downed tools to sit and think about it.

'You need dynamite,' said Imran.

Stinky went back to the eucalyptus plant and returned with

some water, which I drank without thinking. We poked around with the tools in a half-hearted way. The roots were everywhere and had already blunted the parang.

Big Snake's won again, I thought as we traipsed back to Wasweedie, ostensibly to get some lunch, but really to give up. Juji commiserated, but agreed to take some money as an advance to catching a snake for us. He seemed confident he could do it and asked me to stay on in the village. I couldn't face holing up in Wasweedie on my own. It would be just as effective to return to Namlea and wait for news there.

Lamardie turned up with three coconuts and two lemons in his plastic bag. We ate the coconuts, again disappointing, there being too much juice, neither sweet enough to over-come the coconut taste, nor coconutty enough to overcome its flat, watery flavour. Lamardie solicitously made me a scoop out of a sliver of coconut shell so I could eat up the soft flesh. Imran demanded one of the lemons. He quickly sucked it dry and flung it away into the forest.

Everyone agreed it was time to go home. The word had been put out, that was the main thing. We would simply have to wait or leave.

Going home, I wondered whether the whole trip had been cooked up by Lamardie so that he could visit his garden in the forest. Then I imagined him returning home to his wife and her asking what he had to show for his three days away. One lemon. Somehow I feel this means more than I intend, but factually it's true: we left the forest exactly one lemon richer.

FIFTEEN

The Island of Ghosts

I had spasms of sweating fear; it kept coming over
me in waves. And then of course there were the
nightmares. Very bad they were. Oh, shocking.
C. J. Ionides, long after being mauled by
an enraged cow elephant in Tanzania

Lamardie, much to Imran's chagrin, had become a permanent fixture at his house. His message was simple, and often
repeated: 'I slept with the foreigner.' There were no kinky
overtones to this, indeed Lamardie treated it as a great
honour conferred. He wasn't going to let anyone forget it.
And people were impressed, so Imran couldn't boot him out.
Imran took to chain-smoking Lamardie's cigarettes, but then
I maliciously started giving cigarettes to Lamardie to com-
pensate. Imran couldn't win.

On the way back from Wasweedie we had talked about
black magic. When Imran had satisfied himself that I was
agnostic rather than antagonistic towards the supernatural,
he started to talk about his father's kingdom, Manipa Island.

'It has another name,' he said. 'Pulau Swangi – the Island
of Ghosts.'

'Why's that?'

'Because this is an invisible island. It cannot be seen.'

'What, all the time?'

'Sometimes, in danger times.'

'Can I visit?'

'Yes . . . you can visit. But you must be careful.' Pause.

'Will you give me a letter of introduction to your father?'

'No problem.'

I would be a guest of the King. No problem. But Imran's decided reluctance to visit his home country struck me as odd. 'They might want me to stay,' he said cryptically. His wife had been there only once. She didn't like it. 'Everyone stay in their house on Pulau Swangi. No one walks around.'

Imran told me about his father's powers. 'When I went to Halmahera he gave me a special charm to protect me. He had such a charm himself during the *konfrontasi* and on Tim Tim. He was never hit by a bullet.'

'What was the danger on Halmahera?'

'Other young men. They get jealous easy there. If you talk to a woman they put a magic on you.'

'What was your protection?'

'A special piece of ginger, a see-through stone and some writing. It is a good protection.'

'But how can an island disappear?'

'To be invisible is not to be noticed. My father can make himself invisible, but he is still there.'

'You saw him . . . make himself invisible?'

Imran looked at me as if he suspected I was making fun of him. 'The small black magic only works if you believe. But the big magic works on everyone.'

I was spending my days hanging around Namlea, waiting for news. The word had been spread to all the main areas of the island now. I tried to convince myself that it was just a case of waiting. Looking out over the bay, another clove cigarette dangling from my mouth, watching the sun go down over the calm little waves and further out the bamboo fishing platforms, I felt like a castaway. Waiting. Waiting. I arranged to go out fishing on an outrigger, but it fell through because the fisherman involved suddenly decided to reroof his house. I sat in front of the swirling disco light and watched the little kids tripping. I read Wallace in a desultory

298

fashion. He always had something to stuff when he was waiting, either that or a new beetle to skewer on a pin.

Manipa Island started to worm its way into my imagination, especially after Imran let slip about *gunung kaluhura* and *ula moyung* – the chair of the snake ancestor. On the island, which I gathered was mountainous, at the top of the tallest summit, was a stone chair. 'A rock – it look like chair,' said Imran. This was *gunung kaluhura*. If a man wished to become the chief of all the people, he had to spend a night, or nights, in that chair waiting to be visited by *ula moyung*, the snake ancestor.

'You wait and wait, then you feel the snake coil around you. But it is not a real snake, it is the snake ancestor come to test you. If you cry out you will either die or go mad.' Imran's eyes were shining. 'But a man who meets the snake ancestor will forever be changed; if he survives, he will be king!'

'Did your father do this?'

'Of course, yes.'

'Did you?'

'No, I am frightened!' Imran tried to explain. 'This is not nice place. When I go out to play, my father say, "Please come home if you are hungry."'

'Why?'

'Because in case of some black magic on me, or a poison on me from eating special food. There are no shops on Manipa Island. Chinese merchants come – in one month their shop is finished. No cars, maybe only one or two bicycles. It is bad place for modern things. The government build electricity-generating plant. Oil power. After a few weeks it does not work. They cannot repair. No Portuguese went there, no Dutch went there, no Japanese went there – at these times the island hid itself.'

'If I went, would I be the first foreigner ever to visit?' I asked.

'Apart from government and Chinese, yes.'

My mind was made up. I would visit the Island of Ghosts and face the snake ancestor on my own.

Getting there was another thing. The place was six hours by seagoing dugout from Namlea, or seven hours from the north coast of Ambon. I would have to wait for a boat to turn up and hope there was a place on it.

'There will be place,' said Imran. 'No one want to go to Manipa.'

Imran told me of the magical caves on the island. Caves that opened out to the sea and disappeared right inside the island. No one went into these caves because they were full of ghosts. 'And bats,' said Imran, 'and bat shit – mountains of it.'

He explained that I should not chop indiscriminately at trees with a parang. If the tree was protected, the parang would fly back and cut me. 'Many prohibition areas in Manipa. The tree sometimes guard prohibition area, like mountain or cave. Also the beach.'

'The beach?'

'In the night. Only in the night. If you go down to the beach you will see men dancing with ghosts, like this.' He struck a posture like a Tai Chi master and moved ever so slowly, wrapping his arms around his head. The little kids yelled and clapped for more. Imran ignored them. 'If you see such men, you may become in a trance too. It could be danger, but only if you believe. You must not believe, otherwise it may be danger for you.'

'I won't believe,' I said casually, but I was beginning to stop not believing.

'I will give you a bracelet made from a root from the bottom of the sea. It will protect you,' said Imran, and he went into his bedroom to search through his chest of drawers. 'It is very strong.' More rummaging. 'Oh, I've lost it.'

'Never mind,' I said, though I was thinking, Great, now I have to visit voodoo land without even an amulet.

I went each day down to the harbour to check on boats coming from Manipa. Imran's daughters would run down to the end of the track with me, shouting, 'I am money! I am money!' It took me several days to understand that this meant 'Give me money.'

One day a boat arrived, piloted by a relative of Imran's. 'Though I cannot remember him,' Imran told me, 'I know his father.' A day later it was due to return. That was postponed a day, but eventually even that day arrived. Imran told me to buy batteries to give to his father. His wife asked me to ask my wife to write her a letter via Imran.

Lamardie came to see me off. Under one arm he had a huge bag of pistachio nuts which he picked at with vigour, spitting out the shells. But when I came to leave, he looked like a lost dog there on the quay. 'Be careful!' he shouted, and I saw tears in his eyes.

Imran was less sentimental. He had written out a letter on a page of exercise book for me to give to Pellu, his father. 'Stay with him, then you will be very fine. And watch out for red-eyed man!'

'Why?' The boatman indicated it was time to shove off the beach. I took my shoes and socks off.

'The red-eyed man has the magic! Be careful of him!'

I jumped in the boat and the engine, a fifty-horsepower 'Johnson', fired up. We were off to the Island of Ghosts.

The only other passenger was a fat woman with puffy ankles. Things can't be all that bad, I thought, as she smiled and offered me a piece of star fruit. Then I remembered Imran's warning: accept no food except from his father, and people vouched for by his father. I smiled back, the noise of the outboard drowning out my polite refusal.

The boat headed due east after coming out of the bay. We passed close by one of a series of fishing platforms. They were large bamboo rafts with huts on top. At night fishermen would hang lights from them to attract fish. On the last platform before we swung out into the open sea, I saw a small cat, black and white, sitting on the top of the floating hut. Perhaps it was marooned. It was the first and last cat I saw on Buru, where they are not needed for rodent control – there are more than enough snakes for that job.

The open sea was not rough. The sun shone out of a hot, hazy sky and every now and then a wave would break against the log hull awkwardly, sending welcome spray running down my glasses, cooling my arms and face. The engine droned on. Soon we were almost out of sight of the mainland of Buru, it was just a grey line on the horizon. Knowing the expected pattern of the wind and the waves, the boatman kept right on course. From time to time he smoked cigarettes, shielding them from the wind in his cupped hand. I lay back on a knobbly sack and stared up at the strip of sky just visible from under the brim of my hat. The fat lady munched steadily on her fruit, tossing the stones and skins over the side without looking.

Superstition. I had always had a superstitious strand running through me, but if anyone caught me knocking on wood I'd pretend I was examining the table top for defects. Likewise, I took care to hide any credulity in magic, though as a child my first ambition was to be a magician. I put on magic shows with my sisters as giggling assistants dressed in fairy costumes left over from a village play. There is a picture of me aged seven, overwhelmed by my black cloak, but managing still that look of complacent mystery favoured by magicians.

I came ashore on the empty beach of Manipa. The beach was narrow and long with mangrove trees at the end of the two

302

rocky headlands. Through a wall of palm trees I glimpsed some huts. I walked towards them. There was nothing on the dusty track, not even a chicken. The huts had downward-hinging shutters so it was hard to see if anything was going on. The fat lady gestured towards a construction that looked like a wooden bus stop: a bench inside a roofed structure. Behind the bench and apparently secured by the bench was a door with no handle. I dropped my bag on the bench and waited for someone to turn up or for something to happen.

Nothing did. Perhaps it was my imagination but I felt there were a hundred eyes on me, all peering from the darkness inside the shuttered huts. The stranger had come to town and they were all ignoring him.

After an inordinately long period of time I heard coughing behind the wall I was leaning against. I put my ear against the vertical wooden planking and listened. I was shocked out of this relaxed posture when the door was flung open inwards.

A man stepped out with a long moustache and a blank expression. Wearing a kind of canvas waistcoat over a faded red corduroy shirt, he seemed overdressed for the humid heat of the equator.

'*Permisi*,' I said.

'*Permisi*,' he said.

Having gained his permission, I brought out my letter, but then put it away again. I wanted it to get to the right man. I asked for Pa Pellu, the King, Imran's father. The man indicated I should come from the bright light outside into the dark place behind the door.

This was a dingy waiting room with one plastic chair and two wooden forms. I took the plastic chair. From an even darker room came more noise, and an older man, approaching sixty, appeared: the King himself.

Imran had instructed me in etiquette, though I was somewhat taken aback by His Majesty's rapid appearance. It was hard to square the wooden bus stop with the antechamber of royalty. The correct procedure, said Imran, was to speak of where I had come from and to hand over my letter after this brief preamble. The King nodded and passed the letter before his eyes as if scanning it before handing it to the man in the fancy waistcoat. The King himself was rather casually attired in shell-suit trousers and a fake crocodile Lacoste sports shirt. He had a fine head of grey hair and a puffy, almost feminine face.

I came out with my snake-quest story and got little response. Two boys appeared to sit at the side of the serious King. 'Imran's nephews,' he explained, watching me. It was hard to connect him to Imran's cheery-chappy personality. Maybe the reason he so wished to avoid Manipa was its gloomy way of life. I finished the snake rap, thinking it would be a good time for tea, but there wasn't any. I took out my cigarettes and handed them round. Moustaches took one, but Imran's father touched the front of his chest and smiled a good-natured smile of apology for not smoking.

After a pretty long pause the King started to speak. 'There are snakes on this island but the biggest snakes are on Buru.'

'Yes,' I said.

'It is better to search there.'

'Yes, but I thought you might have some good techniques for catching snakes, special techniques.'

'We kill snakes like this.' He grinned and mimed chopping with a parang. 'Sometimes we light a fire and burn feathers in a sack, we leave this sack and snakes cannot go away.'

'Is that magic?' I said, but he seemed not to understand me.

'Is there somewhere I can stay?' I asked.

'You will stay with me,' said the King. Goody.

I was led through an even darker room and waved a hello at an old woman sitting and teasing at a fibrous piece of wood. Moustaches insisted on carrying my bag. My room was virtually pitch dark, but I was able to open the shutter a fraction to let some light in. I lay on the big sagging bed and fell into a deep, sunburned sleep.

The next day I decided to wander about the island, but when I got to the end of the village and crossed three thick planks over a dry ditch, a boy came running after me to show me the way to the hilltop, which, the night before, over *papeeda* and spinach, I had expressed an interest in visiting. The path ran up through tall, smooth-trunked trees, a kind of eucalyptus, big trees on an island that had never been logged, which, in itself, was a kind of triumph.

The dry path went up and the boy, when out of the village, took to walking backwards up the track, keeping a watchful eye on me. Once he caught his heel in a root and laughed in embarrassment when I caught his eye and smiled. At the top of the hill he waited patiently while I inspected the *gunung kaluhura*, snake chair of the ancestors. It was a large boulder of rock patterned with fossilized coral. It really was chair-shaped, like a sixties sag-bag. I sat in it and looked out to sea and fancied I could see Buru, or perhaps Ambon. I would have to ask. Next to the chair were two *butal*, slivers of wood marked with charcoal. They acted as prayer sticks and indicated places of totemic significance.

'Do snakes come here?' I asked the boy.

He grinned and said, 'Yes.'

At our meal that night I asked his grandfather, the King, the same question. I decided to come clean, though in the past that often hasn't done me much good.

'Yes, the snake of the ancestors comes to that rock,' he said matter-of-factly. 'But you cannot see it.'

'Is this a test for men who want to be strong?'

The King laughed. 'It is a test for boys, not men. For example, a boy who is afraid of the dark might go up there at night . . .'

'But Imran said—'

305

'Imran is still afraid of the dark!'

The King started to move the metal dishes in front of him into a line in the middle of the table. He did not speak for a while.

'People do not understand even simple things. The *batu* you showed me, perhaps it has a magic, perhaps not. Many people, Hindus in the forest, think they have magic *batu*. But if they do not understand the meaning then it is nothing.'

'What about the stone chair?'

'You have already been there. You know what it is like. Are you afraid of the dark too?' He smiled as he said this.

'No.'

'When men go to *gunung kaluhura*, they go in a different way. If you see men on the beach in the evening they are going to *gunung kaluhura*. But you do not have to go to the beach. You can go when you are sleeping.'

'So men dream of the snake ancestor?'

'It is a special kind of dream.'

'Can you teach me?'

The King laughed and shouted something rapidly through the hanging curtain to the kitchen. The women had a good laugh too.

'I am not a guru,' he said. 'Imran is a guru.'

I must have looked crestfallen, because he added, 'If you have a need, then you will have a dream.'

In bed at night I heard the tape recorder playing, using up my gift of batteries, until I fell asleep. I did not dream. In the moments before sleep it occurred to me that perhaps I was doomed to stay on Manipa Island until I dreamed my way off the place. It's stressful forcing yourself to dream, and I can report here, apart from daydreams, it doesn't work.

When I next awoke it was still dark and I was dying to empty my bladder. I lay in bed as long as I could but in the end I headed out to the fenced-off shack with a crushed-coral

306

floor that was the washroom and pisser. Through a gap in the sack I could see the moonlit beach. Relieved now but still waiting, I looked and looked for the men in a trance but saw no one.

The next day I met the red-eyed man. But before that something strange happened at a neighbour's house.

'They've invited you,' the King explained. I went with Moustaches. The King explained he'd join us later. The neighbour, who lived at the far end of the village, was an obsequious man with a bald head. He had hardly got going, moving tea towards us in glasses on the table in his front room. Moustaches reached for his and the glass cracked from the top halfway down, but nothing broke.

Moustaches put the glass down, and fiercely but trembling he told me it was time to leave. The obsequious fellow suddenly came to life with apologies. 'I think it was an accident,' I said, alarmed at this overreaction. We walked fast back through the village, back towards our own safe darkness.

'The cup was poisoned, or had some magic,' Moustaches explained. He was furious. We met the King outside his hut. Moustaches explained the incident in detail, but the King simply nodded, as if to say, I suspected as much.

The red-eyed man came to dinner. He fixed me with his beady red eye, and then I realized he was the red-eyed man. He grinned and offered me a cigarette. I turned it down. Everyone ate in silence. After the meal we drank *sopi* in battered aluminium cups. The subject of my 'magic snuff' and stone came up. The red-eyed man smiled grimly and said, 'Have you a magic kris too?'

I almost said yes, but I recalled Imran's warning. Besides, the kris was back in KL, in my suitcase.

'No.'

The red-eyed man lost interest in me. The talk turned to fishing and the mysteries of the sea. The red-eyed man told me that two hundred metres down off the coast of Manipa there was a layer of fresh water. Dolphins went down there to drink, he said.

Before I went to bed I asked the King about the kris business. 'If a man come to Manipa with a gun or a kris, people think he is here to kill someone.'

Lying on my sagging bed, I was struck by a thought that I knew by its force had to be true. The red-eyed man was the real king of the serpents! He was a modern-day basilisk, capable of killing by a glance. The medieval basilisk, a tiny, mythical red-eyed serpent, could be defended against only by using a mirror, reflecting its evil power back at it. A man on horseback spearing a basilisk could expect the poison of the basilisk to flow like electricity back up the spear, killing man and horse alike.

It was getting to me, being on this gloomy island. I was smoking too much and my stomach was in knots. That morning, before dawn, desperate this time for a crap, I went with my torch to the beach to relieve myself. I squatted behind the rocks and turned off my torch as it was beginning to get light. The sea rushed in almost to my feet and I had to hold up my trouser seat to avoid an embarrassing wetting. Buttoning up, I could see a man by the drawn-up outriggers. He looked like a fisherman, but then I saw he was swaying in the slight breeze, looking out to sea, his arms moving like slow wings, his head rolling.

Before getting into bed I had a sudden mad idea. Maybe the *tamu* merchant had got it the wrong way around. I took out my snake stone and flamed it in the darkness with my lighter. Now the thing really was red hot. The tables were turned. I had called Big Snake.

Back in bed I fell into an uncomfortable half-sleep and started, without willing it, to dream. I was in the stone chair, covered with writhing pythons. Strangely I was still calm. Then I realized I was watching myself in the chair – and the

308

me in the chair had red eyes. When I awoke, I was not in the least bit perturbed. The details of the dream had faded.

I suddenly knew the answer. It was like waking up the day after studying some hard problem. One phrase kept going through my head: 'The snake is inside you. The snake is inside you.' This gnomic statement was like a key for me. It had a meaning that went beyond the value of its words and letters. I valued it especially because it came from a dream. Hadn't Wallace dreamed the theory of evolution whilst fever-ridden in Ternate? In fact, hadn't all his best ideas occurred in dreams?

I knew then why the old chthonic religions had to die. They had ceased being functional. In a more complex world man needed an internally regulated psyche, not one externally patrolled by jealous, dangerous animal gods. He needed conscience, the inner voice. He needed to grow up.

The snake was inside me. I was free to choose. The other snake, Big Snake, was anything I wanted it to be. Desire, ambition, a place in the world. Catching Big Snake proved nothing or everything. Its real meaning was just symbolic. The snake is the messenger. Listen to the message, conscience, and decide. All the things inside me I had been putting off, thinking there was some external solution, or someone just round the corner waiting to deliver the answer on a plate. It wasn't out there at all. It was in here.

On my last day I went alone to the beach after dark. Looking out over the white of the rollers, I knew that the trip ended here and what it all meant I already knew.

There was a dugout going to Ambon, but when I arrived, instead of changing money and taking the nightmare ferry back to Buru, I checked into a three-star hotel, the best in town, and phoned Harun in Malaysia. His voice crackled in bewilderment that I was able to phone him from a place he didn't even know existed (even though I'd told him about it before). 'You better come back,' he said. 'Your dad called from England. I think your grandfather is sick.'

I called home knowing, or half knowing, the truth, and my father confirmed it: the Colonel had died. He had fallen during the night in the bathroom and cracked his head on something hard. He had also had a heart attack. But even at the end the Colonel was putting up a fight: there had to be an autopsy to decide the exact mode of death – was it heart failure or head injury that killed him? This gave me enough time to fly home for the funeral. I checked out and with surprising ease caught a flight to Jakarta, then Kuala Lumpur and on home.

SIXTEEN

Last Will and Testament

I strongly object to being a nuisance after I'm dead. I've been a carnivore all my life, and I'd much rather benefit a few local vultures and jackals than go against nature and have all the nonsense of a conventional burial.   *C. J. Ionides*

Not in his goals but in his transitions man is great.
                                        Ralph Waldo Emerson

The telegram was waiting for me when I arrived in London.

WE HAVEW FOIND A BIG SNAKE WITH EIGHT AND HALF MTRS LONG. WE HAVE CONTACED YOU TWICE BY PHONE BUT DIDN'T MEET YOU. PLEASE CALLING US ON FRIDAY AT FOUR O'CLOCK ON EAST INDIA TIME.

IMRAN PELLU

There was no telephone number to ring and I remembered that it was possible to make international calls from Buru only by going to the telecom centre in Namlea. In any case the four o'clock deadline had passed. The snake, if it was eight and half metres – twenty-eight feet – long, was a world record for a living serpent. It wouldn't win the prize but I was sure a zoo would be interested.

There was no possibility of getting on a plane straight back to Indonesia. Jakarta airport was closed owing to smoke-induced haze. Besides, I had a funeral to attend. In a state of

311

half-paralysed rush I drove down to Oxford, to the cremat-orium with its grassy open-air feel and only a square brick chimney to remind you of its purpose.

Relatives who had not seen each other in years gathered in a glassed-in waiting room with chairs around the walls. People behaved with stiff propriety, talk made lively only by the sight of the Colonel's coffin draped in a Union Jack. So much the symbol of tourist knick-knacks or far-right bully boys, the Union flag, in all its brazen unsubtlety, brought home better the fact of his death, that he had lived and served during a brief blip in history, the gaudy and sancti-monious last days of empire that gave men of all backgrounds the chance to write their will, if not in stars, at least in blood and sweat upon the largest canvas known to man, the countries coloured pinkish red, raw roast beef, on maps no longer made.

The priest, who did not know the Colonel, had been supplied by my uncle with a short description of the Colonel's life and achievements. Perhaps my uncle expected the priest to fillet it for the good bits. Instead he read the lot, a verbatim account in the bluntest terms, listing the man's faults and glories, his moments of madness and splendour, his tireless energy in pursuing a slight, his awkwardness and hectoring lack of sympathy for those that did not match the standards he set himself, which, when he failed to reach them, drove him close to insanity on a few occasions. It was not a pretty speech but there was a wholesome truth about it, a breath of fresh air needed to clear the cloying hidden embarrassment of modern death.

There was one thing the speech missed out: that the Colonel had the ability to inspire others. Nothing to do with Union Jacks, this inspiration was about standing without fear against the imagined good intentions of the crowd. But we liked the fact that we'd been reminded to the very last that he wasn't, actually, a particularly nice man. 'It's what he would have liked,' we all said, as we hastened out of the dimly lit modern chapel and looked quickly and then away at the terrible functionality of the chimney.

After a perfunctory tour of the flowers, everyone tore off to the wake in their cars. A tea on the lawn with beer, wine and sandwiches, the long-lost relatives nodding and smiling and realizing why they did not meet more often.

Ten years before, I had taken my grandfather to the funeral of his cousin in a 2CV with a 'Give Peace a Chance' sticker in the back window. When the Colonel discovered this, he was mortified. 'More like peace at any price,' he said. As we drove back he gave me a short lecture on Alexander the Great, who planted date palms in Afghanistan to feed his troops. 'A date palm will last a hundred years – now there was a man who was planning ahead. Alexander the Great, he knew his onions.'

Back in London I tried to send a telegram to Imran, but it was vastly expensive and served only to let him know I had received his message. Not expecting any result, I dialled, on a complete whim, Ferdinandus's phone number (Imran had no phone). The phone blipped three times and made the noise of the telephonic void, the echoing nothingness of electricity singing down wires. I was about to hang up when it started ringing. Knowing the isolation of Buru, I felt for the first time the full magic of a long-distance call as I spoke to Ferdinandus down the crackly line. Yes, there was a snake. It had been caught by Adam, a nephew of Bapak Adam's. Maybe the old man had cast his stone after all. Improbably, the snake was being kept in a box at Imran's house. 'I will go to get Imran now,' said Ferdinandus.

I pictured him wobbling up to Imran's encampment on his scooter and breaking the news. Half an hour later I called back and spoke to an excited Imran.

'When are you coming?' he asked.

'How long is it?' I asked.

'Seven and a half or eight metres,' he said.

'I cannot come,' I said, almost adding 'because I am getting married'. 'There are no planes flying into Jakarta because of the haze.'

'The villagers are frightened,' said Imran. 'And the snake master is living in my house. There is expense.'

I knew there'd be expense. The key thing was to keep the expense down, including phone calls. I told Imran to take some photos of the snake. 'The villagers are frightened,' he said again. I told him I would send money to his school, hidden in a football magazine, and this cheered him up. 'The snake master caught the snake when it was sleeping. It had eaten many things and was sleeping in the sun.'

It wasn't a prize-winning snake, but if it was the length Imran said, there wasn't a longer snake in captivity. A zoo would buy it. I told Samia that she was about to marry the man who had caught, whose *team* had caught, the longest snake in the world. She pretended to be impressed and then reminded me we were leaving for Cairo the following day.

Cairo. The air, the heat, the noise, a million miles away from the cool, dull calm of the jungle. Eliot was wrong when he said the jungle was 'humped in silence'. This was Conrad's view of the jungle from a ship. From the interior the jungle is a giant woodscape, domestic in everything except its known, and therefore imagined, extent. In short, it's a big wood. Cairo, however, is not just a big city, a bellicose exhaust pipe belching out fumes and people and camel dung and cardamom coffee and the charcoal smell of the *shisha* pipe smokers on every neighbourhood corner. It has, even after the virtual expulsion of the Greeks and Jews in the 1950s, a deeply cosmopolitan centre that makes London at times seem like a suburb.

I tried calling the Wildlife Conservation Society in New York, but from Cairo I found it impossible to get through. I wondered whether a zoo was the right place for a giant python after all. Most survived transportation, but it was unusual for a snake to eat for many months after arriving in a zoo. In one case an albino reticulated python went two years without taking a meal. But further action had to be put off. I had a wedding to attend.

Into this dustball of angry fanatics and solitary Africans, the veiled and the unveiled, blue-black Sudanese and blond Circassians (both descendants of slaves), hooting cars and whistle-blowing soldiers, I sped with Samia and Yusuf the driver to obtain our marriage licence.

We sat like Arab royalty in the car while Yusuf wheedled and bravadoed his way to the front of the licence queue. The building was half open to the air like a place selling train tickets. A blind old woman with a white face like eroded rock and uncovered white hair gave us a blessing through the car window left open a fraction for breathing. I pressed money gratefully into her hand but waved away subsequent beggars. The car park swirled dust as crowds wavered across it in the heat. Yusuf returned for more bribe money and the job was done. We had government authorization; now all that was required was a brief declaration at the Office of Home Affairs, and we could attend the real wedding ceremony, the *zaffr*.

A huge, black Bedouin tent was pitched on the beach at Sharm Al Sheikh in the Sinai peninsula, and a hundred plastic chairs assembled around three sides of a square of long tables. A wooden floor had been laid for dancing and the tent was open at one end to the sea. As night fell and the dancing began, curious holidaymakers, standing side by side in the sand, looked from afar through the sea door of the black marquee.

Zaffr is a ceremonial parade of the bride and her father, with the groom taking over at an early stage. With a full band of tambourinists and a girl dancing with an unsteady seven-branched candelabra on her head, we made slow passage around the swimming pool in the piazza of the luxury hotel. Women ululated, their hands under their noses to hide the unseemly show of tonsils. Small discs of copper, mere slivers, were thrown instead of confetti. One stuck like a lucky golden beauty spot to Samia's white shoulder. Her father beamed stately good humour, as befitting an Egyptian general dressed in English tweeds in a Red Sea diving resort. My own family and friends came out of the crowd in a welcoming caucus. Bald Chris was there, full of a new plan for Internet business success. Zaki, with ponytail and brilliant white teeth, brought a telegram from Harun, announcing he could not come because of the unprecedented collapse of the ringgit.

'Just how bad is it?' I asked Zaki.

'Bad,' he replied. 'All the building has just stopped halfway.' I pictured the skyscraper in progress across from Harun's office, doomed for ever to be just a concrete stump with a spiky head of steel reinforcement bars. Zaki told us he was shot of his English girlfriend and going to Denmark to continue his studies. Antares * Noumion sent his regards, and news of a confluence of stars that coincided with an interdimensional conference at Magick River the following summer.

We feasted on a row of slow-roasting lambs, killed earlier that day in the blood-soaked yard of the cantonment butcher. Piles of saffron rice, calves' livers and kebab were followed by a mountainous display of Egyptian sweetmeats and delicacies, but the rice-puddingy *um-ali*, while good, was not up to Aunt Zaza's standard, everyone agreed. Then the dancing began again.

Stick dancing from Upper Egypt was followed by a whirling dervish who span continuously in one direction for over half an hour. I saw him later drinking an un-Islamic Carlsberg at the bar and not looking a jot dizzy from his rotational devotions. Flag-waving and boot-stomping young men accompanied more women with candelabras like antlered helmets on their heads. At last came the belly dancer, a plump, lascivious entertainer with a belly stocking whose black seam looked like a mane of fur down her back. With narrow, pulsating hips she drew applause for working the crowd with expertise rather than seductive charm. Samia's brother confided that she wasn't half as good as the belly dancer at his wedding. But she wibbled and wobbled and slapped and clapped and sang, and I could not stop smiling from the good humour of it all.

I had escaped being branded with a ring, but Samia wore two to make up for it. I was, at last, firmly married.

The day after the wedding we all set out to climb Mount Sinai. Aunty Mary, at seventy, was the oldest and gamest mountaineer, and refused the cameleers who importuned in broken English from the darkness either side of the mountain path. We started to climb at two in the morning and waited in agonizing cold for the first rays of the sun at the small chapel on the summit. At that hour, and in such surroundings, the sun rising did not seem at all inevitable. It was easy to imagine praying for the sun to rise, begging for its abstract warmth, turning our back for ever on the old chthonic religions of the past. Samia's brother told me that if we saw the green flash of light moments before the sun broken the horizon, our marriage would be blessed. 'It is a rare and valued phenomenon,' he explained.

We waited and waited for the red ball to break from the thin, grey sea of the horizon. And moments before it did, like pale-green sheet lightning, so subtle you might almost miss it, came the unmistakable green flash of light. Like a heliograph from the heavens, the green light signalled its blessing before the sudden, raging glory of the sun.

There were more telegrams awaiting us on our return. The first read:

THE SNAKE HAS BUT AT MY HAUSE IT IS SO BIGGER MTRS LONG HOW IS ABOUT THE SNAKE BAYMENT WE HOBE YOUR COMING SOON.

IMRAN PELLU

The second was in Indonesian and stated that the snake was seven and a half metres long – it was shrinking.

A few days later a letter and some photographs arrived. The snake was still in captivity. Imran wrote:

Dear Roberth!!

How's everything, I hope you are not under the weather and excuse me for my letter comes suddenly. Because of the snake has taken care for three weeks and by this letter we send the picture of the snake. We would like to send the colour picture but it will be come behind, we have spend a lot of our many for feed the snake.

Something is very importanty your coming soon to take the snake according our promise and the snake is still agresive and the colour of the snake is very interesting like batik as your skin of snake. and the snake master still live at my home as you know. all people in my sorronding or my neightbourds are life in worry and fear. and the box we made seems is not so strong so I am very afraid about it.

finally, I and all my family very hope your coming soon. I hope indeed, and before that's all please inform me by phone via ferdinandus phone calling your first gitf is the British football player had accepted by me but the second one not yet.

318

Please remember me to your wife and all of you family in London. waiting for your coming soon in Namlea the short time.

Sincerely yours,
The best friend of you

Imran Pellu

I looked at the photographs but did not show them to Samia. With everyone there, Sharm Al Sheikh had hardly been a real honeymoon. There were days left before Samia had to return to work. Surely a marriage would entitle more leave? Folding the letter from Imran, I looked at my new wife across the breakfast table, and said as casually as I could muster, 'It's spur of the moment, but I've got a great idea for a place where we can spend our honeymoon . . .'

Colonel H's belongings were released from my uncle's care. I received the old six-inch shell case he'd kept his umbrella in and a Naga *dao* he'd used in his final days for chopping wood. The blade was made from the hammered iron of a ploughshare brought by the Christian missionaries of the late nineteeth century. The haft was decorated with red-dyed human hair, silkier to the touch than the later models decorated with horsehair.

My father took only Laughing Buddha. It sits on his desk, forever fat and mirthful. I hope, when my turn comes, to have it sitting on my desk too. Of Saluting Man there was no trace. Chopped for firewood, or sold a long time ago, the man with the red tiger hat no longer exists.